P9-CQX-082

STRATEGY AND THE BUSINESS LANDSCAPE

Pankaj Ghemawat

Prentice Hall

Boston Columbus Indianapolis New York San Francisco Upper Saddle River
Amsterdam Cape Town Dubai London Madrid Milan Munich Paris Montreal Toronto
Delhi Mexico City Sao Paulo Sydney Hong Kong Seoul Singapore Taipei Tokyo

Editorial Director: Sally Yagan
Editor in Chief: Eric Svendsen
Acquisitions Editor: Kim Norbuta
Editorial Project Manager: Claudia
  Fernandes
Director of Marketing: Patrice
  Lumumba Jones
Senior Marketing Assistant:
  Ian Gold
Project Manager: Renata Butera
Creative Art Director: Jayne Conte
Manager, Rights and Permissions:
  Charles Morris
Cover Art: Andrei Linde and
  Dimitri Linde

"Computer simulations of
stochastic processes during the
stage of cosmic inflation soon
after the Big Bang."
Full-Service Project Management:
  Saraswathi Muralidhar,
  GGS Higher Education Resources
Composition: GGS Higher
  Education Resources, A Division
  of PreMedia Global Inc.
Printer/Binder: Edwards
  Brothers
Cover Printer: Lehigh-Phoenix
  Color/Hagerstown
Text Font: 10/12 Palatino

Credits and acknowledgments borrowed from other sources and
reproduced, with permission, in this textbook appear on appropriate page
within text.

10 9 8 7 6 5 4 3 2 1

Prentice Hall
is an imprint of

www.pearsonhighered.com

ISBN 10:   0-13-601555-7
ISBN 13:   978-0-13-601555-0

In Memory of Dr. C. R. Mitra,
Educator Extraordinaire

CONTENTS

PREFACE

The third edition of *Strategy and the Business Landscape* has been thoroughly updated as well as expanded to include a new chapter on global strategy that is based on my last ten years of work on that topic. Most of the chapters have also been revised to include brief discussions of how economic downturns affect strategy. But this edition's similarities with the earlier ones greatly outweigh the differences. In particular, it continues to emphasize rigor, relevance and readability.

In terms of rigor, *Strategy and the Business Landscape* is based on contemporary research in the field of strategy and adopts a value-focused perspective that is consistent with recent work on value addition and appropriation. In addition to deriving some rigor from such microfoundations, this perspective helps tie together the discussions in the different chapters.

In terms of relevance, *Strategy and the Business Landscape* is squarely aimed at practitioners or practitioners-to-be, for whom it has been written as a short introduction to or refresher on strategy. That target readership has influenced decisions about how much detail to go into regarding academic research, and how much to draw on insights from business and consulting.

Readability is enhanced by the maintenance of a unified perspective throughout, richly detailed examples, including some featuring "inside" perspectives, and the fact that, despite the new chapter on global strategy, this book is still shorter than most trade books, let alone strategy textbooks.

The first edition of *Strategy and the Business Landscape* included a set of Harvard Business School cases that were meant to illustrate, deepen, and extend the concepts developed in the text. Given trends in case usage, affording users flexibility in this regard seemed a superior option for the second edition and continues to be so for the third edition. However, a suggested case map is included on the front inside cover of the text for reference.

It would have been impossible to prepare this book without aid and support from a number of different quarters. My most obvious debt is to my coauthors on the individual chapters in this book, Bruno Cassiman, David J. Collis, and Jan W. Rivkin (twice over). None of the three, however, should be presumed to have signed off on the entire end product.

I am also indebted to other current and former colleagues at Harvard Business School and at IESE Business School, Barcelona, for very helpful comments on one or more of the chapters in this book, particularly Bharat Anand, Adam Brandenburger, Estelle Cantillon, Ramon Casadesus-Masanell, Giovanni Gavetti, Tarun Khanna, Cynthia Montgomery, Felix Oberholzer-Gee, Gary Pisano, Joan Ricart I. Costa, Jordan Siegel, John Wells, and Dennis Yao. In addition, consultants at Booz Allen Hamilton, the Boston Consulting Group, Marakon/Trinsum, McKinsey & Company, and the Monitor Group all provided useful inputs.

I am also grateful to a number of reviewers for their guidance in this edition and past editions:

James Belohlav, *DePaul University*

Robert Black, *Houghton College*

Ralph Biggadike, *Columbia University*

Debi Cartwright, *Truman State University*

Thomas Chandy, *Binghamton University*

Robert Cline, *Binghamton University*

Tim Dacin, *Texas A&M University*

Charles Dhanaraj, *Indiana University*

Betty Diener, *Barry University*

James Dittmar, *Geneva College*

Daniel Elfenbein, *Washington University*

Jonathan Elimimian, *Albany State University*

Linda Fried, *University of Colorado–Denver*

Mike Geringer, *California Polytechnic State University San Luis Obispo*

David Gilliss, *San Jose State University*

Constance Helfat, *Dartmouth College*

Marty Hornyak, *University of West Florida*

Gary Judd, *Rensselaer Polytechnic Institute*

Jongwook Kim, *Western Washington University*

Michael Lenox, *Duke University*

Daniel E. Levinthal, *University of Pennsylvania*

Joseph Mahoney, *University of Illinois at Urbana-Champaign*

George Meier, *Robert Morris College*

Donatus Okhomina, *Fayetteville State University*

George Puia, *Indiana State University*

Jim Robison, *Sonoma State University*

John A. Seeger, *Bentley College*

Mark Shanley, *Northwestern University*

Richard Spinello, *Boston College*

John Stevens, *Lehigh University*

Gerardo Ungson, *San Francisco State University*

Gordon Von Stroh, *University of Denver*

Robert Welch, *Lansing Community College*

Duane Windsor, *Rice University*

Todd Zenger, *Washington University*

I also thank the editorial team at Pearson Prentice Hall for their enthusiasm about this textbook, Beulah D'Souza for research assistance, Susana Minguell, for administrative support and Jordi Ollé for help with copyediting.

Finally, a book such as this would have been infeasible without the work of all the scholars that underlies it, as well as all the students and practitioners whom I have interacted with and learned from about these topics in the course of 25 years of teaching and researching strategy. The brevity of this acknowledgment should not detract from how deeply it is felt.

Barcelona
May 2009

ABOUT THE AUTHOR

 Pankaj Ghemawat received his bachelor's degree in Applied Mathematics (and was elected to Phi Beta Kappa) and his Ph.D. in Business Economics from Harvard University. After a stint at McKinsey & Company, he spent 25 years on the full-time faculty at Harvard Business School, where, in 1991, he was appointed the youngest full professor in the school's history. Since 2006, Ghemawat has been the Anselmo Rubiralta Professor of Global Strategy at IESE Business School in Barcelona.

Ghemawat's award-winning book, *Redefining Global Strategy*, was published in 2007 by Harvard Business School Press. His other books include *Commitment* and *Games Businesses Play*. Ghemawat is also one of the world's best-selling writers of teaching cases. He served as the editor of the Business Strategy department of *Management Science* from 2003 to 2009 and on the AACSB's Globalization of Management Education task force.

Ghemawat's recent honors include the McKinsey Award for the best article published in the *Harvard Business Review*, the IESE-Fundacion BBVA Economics for Management Prize, and the Irwin Award for the Educator of the Year from the Business Policy and Strategy Division of the Academy of Management. Ghemawat is a Fellow of the Strategic Management Society and the Academy of International Business.

For more information, including freeware to accompany this book, visit www.ghemawat.org.

CHAPTER 1

The Origins of Strategy

If we wish to increase the yield of grain in a certain field and on analysis it appears that the soil lacks potash, potash may be said to be the strategic (or limiting) factor.

—CHESTER I. BARNARD

The term "strategy" . . . is intended to focus on the interdependence of the adversaries' decisions and on their expectations about each other's behavior.

—THOMAS C. SCHELLING

Strategy can be defined as the determination of the basic long-term goals and objectives of an enterprise, and the adoption of courses of action and the allocation of resources necessary for carrying out those goals.

—ALFRED D. CHANDLER, JR.

This chapter reviews the history of strategic thinking about business through the mid-1970s. The historical perspective maintained throughout this book is attractive for at least three reasons:

- Interest in defining and redefining **strategy** is an ongoing endeavor despite thoughtful attempts over the decades, some of which are cited above.[1] It would therefore be idiosyncratic to begin by tossing yet another definition onto the pile. Examining the history of strategic ideas and practice constitutes a less arbitrary approach to the study of strategy.
- The historical perspective organizes changing conceptions of strategy as envisioned or enacted by the participants in this field—academics, managers, and

consultants—allowing us to identify patterns in what might otherwise seem to be the chaotic churn of ideas. Patterns of this sort are evident in all the chapters of this book: co-evolution with the environment, the development and diffusion of particular strategic paradigms, paradigm shifts, the recycling of earlier ideas, to name a few.

- Most ambitiously, the idea of path-dependence (one of the rallying cries of academic strategists since the mid-1980s) suggests that understanding the history of ideas about strategy is essential to developing a more informed sense of where the field might go in the future.

In this chapter, we briefly discuss the origins of strategic ideas. We begin with some background, including military antecedents, and then move on to discuss the ideas about strategy, especially portfolio planning, that were developed and disseminated by academics and consultants in the 1960s and early 1970s. We conclude by reviewing the dissatisfaction with the state of the field that had developed by the second half of the 1970s. In particular, the underdevelopment of the two basic dimensions of portfolio planning grids—environmental attractiveness and competitive positioning—set the stage for much of the subsequent work on these topics that is discussed in Chapters 2 and 3, respectively, and revisited from the perspectives of corporate and global strategy in Chapters 6 and 7. Chapters 4 and 5 address the other weakness of portfolio planning by emphasizing the dynamic dimension of strategic thinking.

BACKGROUND

"Strategy" is a term that can be traced back to the ancient Greeks, who used the word *strategos,* from which it is derived, to designate a chief magistrate or a military commander-in-chief. Over the next two millennia, refinements of the concept of strategy continued to focus on its military aspects. Carl von Clausewitz's attempted synthesis in the first half of the nineteenth century is an especially notable example: He wrote that whereas "tactics . . . [involve] the use of armed forces in the engagement, strategy [is] the use of engagements for the object of the war."[2] The adaptation of strategic terminology to a business context, however, had to await the Second Industrial Revolution, which began in the second half of the nineteenth century but really took off only in the twentieth century.[3]

The First Industrial Revolution (which spanned the mid-1700s to the mid-1800s) failed to induce much in the way of strategic thinking or behavior. This failure can be attributed to the fact that while the period was marked by intense competition among industrial firms, virtually none of them had the power to influence market outcomes to any significant extent. Most businesses remained small and employed as little fixed capital as possible. The chaotic markets of this era led economists such as Adam Smith to describe market forces as an "invisible hand" that remained largely beyond the control of individual firms. Such firms required little or no strategy in any of the senses described in the quotations at the beginning of this chapter.

The Second Industrial Revolution, which began in the last half of the nineteenth century in the United States, saw the emergence of strategy as a way to shape market forces and affect the competitive environment. In the United States, the construction of key railroads after 1850 made it possible to build mass markets for the first time. Along with improved access to capital and credit, mass markets encouraged large-scale investment to exploit economies of scale in production and economies of scope in distribution. In some capital-intensive industries, Adam Smith's "invisible hand" came to be supplemented by what Alfred D. Chandler, Jr., a famous historian, has termed the "visible hand" of professional managers. By the late nineteenth century, a new type of firm began to emerge, first in the United States and then in Europe: the large, vertically integrated company that invested heavily in manufacturing and marketing and in management hierarchies to coordinate those functions. Over time, the largest companies of this sort began to alter the competitive environment within their industries and even to cross industry boundaries.[4]

The need for explicit strategic thinking was first articulated by high-level managers at these large companies. For example, Alfred P. Sloan, the chief executive of General Motors from 1923 to 1946, devised a successful strategy based on the perceived strengths and weaknesses of his company's critical competitor, the Ford Motor Company, and wrote it up after he retired.[5] And in the 1930s, Chester I. Barnard, a senior executive with New Jersey Bell, argued that managers should pay very close attention to "strategic factors," which depend on "personal or organizational action."[6]

World War II supplied a vital stimulus to strategic thinking in business as well as in the military domain, because it sharpened the problem of allocating scarce resources across the entire economy. New operations research techniques (e.g., linear programming) were devised, which paved the way for the use of quantitative analysis in formal strategic planning. In 1944, John von Neumann and Oskar Morgenstern published their classic work, *The Theory of Games and Economic Behavior*[7], which solved the problem of zero-sum games (many military ones) and framed the issues surrounding non-zero-sum games (most business situations, as discussed further in these terms in Chapter 4). The concept of the **learning curve**, first noted in the military aircraft industry in the 1920s and 1930s as manufacturers realized that direct labor costs decreased by a constant percentage as the cumulative number of aircraft produced doubled, also became an important tool for production-planning efforts in wartime.

Wartime experiences encouraged not only the development of new tools and techniques but also, in the view of some observers, the use of formal strategic thinking to guide management decisions. Peter Drucker, writing about this period, argued that "management is not just passive, adaptive behavior; it means taking action to obtain the desired results come to pass." He noted that economic theory had long treated markets as impersonal forces, beyond the control of individual entrepreneurs and organizations. In the age of large corporations, however, managing "implies responsibility for attempting to shape the economic environment, for planning, initiating, and carrying through changes in that economic environment, for constantly pushing back the limitations of economic circumstances on the enterprise's freedom of action."[8] This insight became the key rationale for business strategy—that is, by consciously using formal planning, a company could exert some positive control over market forces.

These insights into the nature of strategy seemed, however, to lie fallow through the 1950s. In the United States, rationing or outright bans on production during World War II combined with high levels of private savings to create excess demand for many products. The Korean War provided a further boost in demand. Europe and Japan experienced even more severe postwar dislocations, which induced greater governmental control of what Lenin had called the "commanding heights" of an economy, namely its key industries and enterprises. Similar increases in governmental control, as opposed to reliance on market forces, were observed in poorer countries, including many of the new ones that emerged as colonialism unwound itself.[9]

A more direct bridge to the development of strategic concepts for business applications was provided by interservice competition in the U.S. military after World War II. During this period, American military leaders began debating the arrangements that would best protect legitimate competition among the four military services while still maintaining the needed integration of strategic and tactical planning. Many argued that the Army, Navy, Marine Corps, and Air Force would be more efficient if they were unified into a single organization. As the debate raged, Philip Selznick, a sociologist, noted that the Navy Department "emerged as the defender of subtle institutional values and tried many times to formulate the distinctive characteristics of the various services." In essence, "Navy spokesmen attempted to distinguish between the Army as a 'manpower' organization and the Navy as a finely adjusted system of technical, engineering skills—a 'machine-centered' organization. Faced with what it perceived as a mortal threat, the Navy became highly self-conscious about its distinctive competence."[10] The concept of **distinctive competence** would turn out to have great resonance for strategic management, as we will see.

ACADEMIC UNDERPINNINGS

Eminent economists produced some of the earliest academic writings about strategy. For example, John R. Commons, an institutionalist, wrote in his 1934 book about the focus of business firms on strategic or limiting factors in a way that was picked up a few years later—the potash example and all—by Chester I. Barnard (see the first quotation at the beginning of this chapter).[11] Ronald H. Coase, who might be called the first organizational economist, published a provocative article in 1937 that asked why firms exist—an article that continues to be cited seventy-five years later and that garnered its author a Nobel Prize.[12] Joseph Schumpeter, a technologist, discussed in his 1942 book the idea that business strategy encompassed much more than the price setting contemplated in orthodox microeconomics.[13] And a book published in 1959 by Edith Penrose explicitly related the growth of business firms to the resources under their control and the administrative framework used to coordinate their use.[14] Overall, however, economists had much less direct impact on the early evolution of academic thinking about business strategy than did academics located in business schools.

The Second Industrial Revolution had witnessed the founding of many elite business schools in the United States, beginning with the Wharton School in 1881. The Harvard Business School, founded in 1908, was one of the first to promote the idea that managers should be trained to think strategically rather than just act as functional administrators, although strategy itself was not explicitly invoked until the 1960s. In 1912, Harvard introduced a second-year course required in "Business Policy" that was designed to integrate the knowledge gained in functional areas like accounting, operations, and finance. The goal was to give students a broader perspective on the strategic problems faced by corporate executives. A course description from 1917 claimed that "an analysis of any business problem shows not only its relation to other problems in the same group, but also the intimate connection of groups. Few problems in business are purely intradepartmental." Also, the policies of each department were supposed to maintain a "balance in accord with the underlying policies of the business as a whole."[15]

In the early 1950s, two professors of business policy at Harvard, George A. Smith, Jr., and C. Roland Christensen, encouraged students to question whether a firm's strategy matched its competitive environment. In reading cases, students were taught to ask the following question: Does a company's policies "fit together into a program that effectively meets the requirements of the competitive situation?"[16] Students were told to address this problem by asking, "How is the whole industry doing? Is it growing and expanding? Is it static? Is it declining?" Then, having "sized up" the competitive environment, the student was to ask still more questions: "On what basis must any one company compete with the others in this particular industry? At what kinds of things does it have to be especially competent, in order to compete?"[17]

In the late 1950s, another Harvard business policy professor, Kenneth R. Andrews, expanded upon this thinking by arguing that "every business organization, every subunit of organization, and even every individual [ought to] have a clearly defined set of purposes or goals which keeps it moving in a *deliberately chosen direction* and prevents its drifting in undesired directions" (emphasis added). Like Alfred P. Sloan at General Motors, Andrews thought that "the primary function of the general manager, over time, is supervision of the continuous process of determining the nature of the enterprise and setting, revising, and attempting to achieve its goals."[18] His conclusions were motivated by an industry note and company cases that Andrews had prepared on Swiss watchmakers, which uncovered significant differences in performance associated with different strategies for competing in that industry.[19] This format of combining industry notes with company cases soon became the norm in Harvard's Business Policy courses.[20]

In the 1960s, classroom discussions in business schools began to focus on matching a company's "strengths" and "weaknesses"—its distinctive competence—with the "opportunities" and "threats" (or risks) that it faced in the marketplace. This framework, which came to be referred to by the acronym **SWOT**, represented a major step forward in explicitly bringing competitive thinking to bear on questions of strategy. Kenneth R. Andrews combined these elements in a way that emphasized that competencies or resources had to match environmental needs to have value (see Exhibit 1.1).[21]

In 1963, a business policy conference was held at Harvard that helped diffuse the SWOT concept in both academia and management practice. The conference was well attended, but the ensuing popularity of SWOT—which is still used by many firms in the twenty-first century—did not bring closure to the problem of actually defining a firm's distinctive competence. To solve this problem, strategists had to decide which aspects of the firm were "enduring and unchanging over relatively long periods of time" and which were "necessarily more responsive to changes in the marketplace and the pressures of other environmental forces." This distinction was crucial, because "the *strategic* decision is concerned with the long-term development of the enterprise" (emphasis added).[22] When strategy choices were analyzed from a long-range perspective, the idea of "distinctive competence" took on added importance because most long-run investments involved greater risks. Thus, if the opportunities a firm was pursuing appeared "to outrun [its] present distinctive competence," then the strategist had to consider a firm's "willingness to gamble that the latter can be built up to the required level."[23]

EXHIBIT 1.1   Andrew's Strategy Framework.

The debate over a firm's "willingness to gamble" on its distinctive competence in its pursuit of an opportunity continued throughout the 1960s, fueled by a booming stock market and corporate strategies that were heavily geared toward growth and diversification. In a classic 1960 article that anticipated this debate, titled "Marketing Myopia," Theodore Levitt had been sharply critical of any firm that focused too narrowly on delivering a specific product, presumably exploiting its distinctive competence, rather than consciously serving the customer. Levitt argued that when companies fail, "it usually means that the product fails to adapt to the constantly changing patterns of consumer needs and tastes, to new and modified marketing institutions and practices, or to product developments in complementary industries."[24]

Another leading strategist, H. Igor Ansoff, disagreed with this position arguing that Levitt asked companies to take unnecessary risks by investing in new products that might not match the firm's distinctive competence. Ansoff suggested that a company should first ask whether a new product had a "common thread" with its existing products. He defined the common thread as a firm's "mission"—its commitment to

EXHIBIT 1.2   Ansoff's Product/Mission Matrix.

	Present Product	New Product
Present Mission	Market Penetration	Product Development
New Mission	Market Development	Diversification

exploit an existing need in the market as a whole.[25] According to Ansoff, "sometimes the customer is erroneously identified as the common thread of a firm's business. In reality a given type of customer will frequently have a range of unrelated product missions or needs."[26] To enable a firm to maintain its strategic focus, Ansoff suggested four categories for defining the common thread in its business/corporate strategy, as depicted in Exhibit 1.2.[27] Ansoff and others also worked to translate the logic built into the SWOT framework into complex flowcharts of concrete questions that needed to be answered in the development of strategies (see Exhibit 1.2).[28]

In the 1960s, diversification and technological changes increased the complexity of the strategic situations that many companies faced and their need for more sophisticated measures that could be used to evaluate and compare many different types of businesses. Because academics at business schools remained strongly wedded to the idea that strategies could be analyzed only on a case-by-case basis that accounted for the unique characteristics of every business, corporations turned elsewhere to satisfy their craving for standardized approaches to strategy making.[29] According to a study conducted by the Stanford Research Institute, most large U.S. companies had set up formal planning departments by 1963.[30]

General Electric (GE) served as a leader in developing planning techniques. It used business school faculty quite extensively in its executive education programs but also developed an elaborate computer-based "Profitability Optimization Model" (PROM) on its own that appeared to explain a significant fraction of the variation in the return on investment afforded by its various businesses.[31] Over time, GE, like many other companies, also sought the help of consulting firms. Although consultants made multifaceted contributions to business (e.g., to planning, forecasting, logistics, and long-range research and development), the next section focuses on their impact on mainstream strategic thinking.

THE RISE OF STRATEGY CONSULTANTS

The 1960s and early 1970s witnessed the rise of a number of strategy consulting practices. In particular, the Boston Consulting Group (BCG), founded in 1963, had a major impact on the field by applying quantitative research to problems of business and corporate strategy. BCG's founder, Bruce D. Henderson, believed that a consultant's job was to find "meaningful quantitative relationships" between a company and its chosen markets.[32] In his words, "good strategy must be based primarily on logic, not . . . on experience derived from intuition."[33] Indeed, Henderson was convinced that economic theory would eventually lead to the development of a set of universal rules for strategy. As he explained, "in most firms strategy tends to be intuitive and based upon traditional patterns of behavior which have been successful in the past." In contrast, "in growth industries or in a changing environment, this kind of strategy is rarely adequate."[34]

In order to help executives make effective strategic decisions, BCG drew on the existing knowledge base in academia: one of its first employees, Seymour Tilles, was formerly a lecturer in Harvard's Business Policy course. BCG also struck off in a new direction that Bruce D. Henderson described as "the business of selling powerful oversimplifications."[35] In fact, BCG came to be known as a "strategy boutique"— early in its history, its business was largely based on a single concept: the experience curve (discussed in the following text). Using a single concept proved valuable because "in nearly all problem solving there is a universe of alternative choices, most of which must be discarded without more than cursory attention." Hence, some "frame of reference is needed to screen the . . . relevance of data, methodology, and implicit value judgments" involved in any strategy decision. Given the complexities of decision making, the most useful "frame of reference is the concept. Conceptual thinking is the skeleton or the framework on which all other choices are sorted out."[36]

BCG and the Experience Curve

BCG first developed its version of the learning curve—what it labeled the **experience curve**—in 1965–1966. According to Bruce D. Henderson, "it was developed to try to explain price and competitive behavior in the extremely fast growing segments" of industries for clients such as Texas Instruments and Black and Decker.[37] As BCG consultants studied these industries, they naturally asked, "[why does] one competitor [outperform] another (assuming comparable management skills and resources)? Are there basic rules for success? There, indeed, appear to be rules for success, and they relate to the impact of accumulated experience on competitors' costs, industry prices and the interrelation between the two."[38]

BCG's standard claim for the experience curve was that, for each doubling of cumulated output, *total* costs would decline roughly 20 percent because of economies of scale, organizational learning, and technological innovation. Exhibit 1.3 illustrates an 84 percent experience effect, implying a 16 percent cost reduction associated with each doubling of experience, for Ford's Model T. The strategic implications, according to BCG, were that "the producer ... who has made the most units should have the lowest costs and the highest profits."[39] Bruce D. Henderson claimed that with the experience curve, "the stability of competitive relationships should be predictable, the value of market share change should be calculable, [and] the effects of growth rate should [also] be calculable (see Exhibit 1.3)."[40]

From the Experience Curve to Portfolio Planning

By the early 1970s, the experience curve had led to another "powerful oversimplification" by BCG: the so-called growth-share matrix, which represented the first use of **portfolio planning**. The relative potential of a diversified company's portfolio of

EXHIBIT 1.3   Experience Curve for Ford's Model T, 1910–1926.

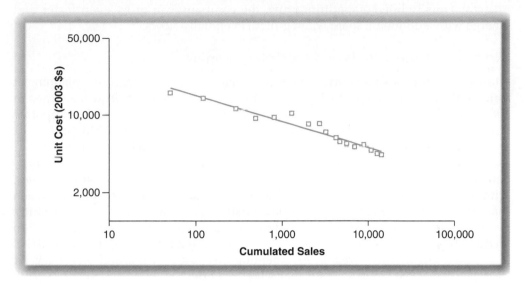

business units as areas for investment was compared by plotting them on the grid shown in Exhibit 1.4.[41]

BCG's basic strategy recommendation was to maintain a balance between "cash cows" (that is, mature businesses) and "stars" while allocating some resources to fund "question marks" (that is, potential stars). "Dogs" were to be sold off. Using more sophisticated language, a BCG vice president explained that "since the producer with the largest stable market share eventually has the lowest costs and greatest profits, it becomes vital to have a dominant market share in as many products as possible. However, market share in slowly growing products can be gained only by reducing the share of competitors who are likely to fight back." In a rapidly growing

EXHIBIT 1.4   BCG's Growth-Share Matrix.

product market, in contrast, "a company can gain share by securing most of the growth. Thus, while competitors grow, the company can grow even faster and emerge with a dominant share when growth eventually slows."[42]

Strategic Business Units and Portfolio Planning

Numerous other consulting firms developed their own grids for portfolio planning at roughly the same time as BCG. McKinsey & Company's effort, for instance, began in 1968 when Fred Borch, the CEO of GE, asked McKinsey to examine GE's corporate structure. At the time, GE consisted of 200 profit centers and 145 departments arranged around ten groups. The boundaries for these units had been defined according to theories of financial control, which the McKinsey consultants judged to be inadequate. They argued instead that the firm should be organized on more strategic lines, with greater concern for external conditions and a more future-oriented approach than was possible using measures of past financial performance. McKinsey's study recommended a formal strategic planning system that would divide the company into "natural business units," which Borch later renamed **strategic business units (SBUs)**.

After spending two years implementing this advice, GE asked McKinsey for help evaluating the strategic plans that were being devised by the company's many SBUs. GE had already considered using the BCG growth-share matrix to decide the fate of its SBUs, but its top management had then decided that they could not set priorities on the basis of just two performance measures. After studying the problem, a McKinsey team produced what came to be known as the GE/McKinsey nine-block matrix (see Exhibit 1.5).[43] The nine-block matrix used approximately one dozen measures to screen for industry attractiveness and another dozen to screen for competitive position, although the weights attached to the measures were not specified.[44]

Another, more quantitative approach to portfolio planning was developed at roughly the same time under the aegis of the "Profit Impact of Market Strategies" (PIMS) program. PIMS was the multicompany successor to the PROM program that GE had started a decade earlier. By the mid-1970s, PIMS contained data on 620 SBUs drawn from fifty-seven diversified corporations.[45] These data were originally used to explore the determinants of returns on investment by regressing historical returns on several dozen variables, including market share, product quality, investment intensity, and marketing and R&D expenditures. The regressions established what were supposed to be benchmarks for the potential performance of SBUs with particular characteristics against which their actual performance might be compared.

In all these applications, segmenting diversified corporations into SBUs came to be recognized as an important precursor to analyzing economic performance.[46] This step forced "deaveraging" of cost and performance numbers that had previously been calculated at more aggregated levels. In addition, it was thought that with such approaches, "strategic thinking was appropriately pushed 'down the line' to managers closer to the particular industry and its competitive conditions."[47]

In the 1970s, virtually every major consulting firm used some sort of portfolio planning—either a variant on the two matrices already discussed or its own internally developed program (e.g., Arthur D. Little's 24-box life-cycle matrix)—to generate strategy recommendations. Portfolio analyses became especially popular after the oil crisis of 1973 forced many large corporations to rethink, if not discard, their existing

EXHIBIT 1.5 The Industry Attractiveness–Business Strength Matrix.

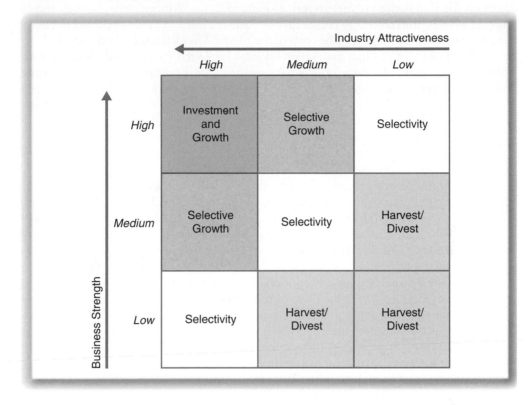

long-range plans. A McKinsey consultant noted that with "the sudden quadrupling of energy costs [due to the OPEC embargo], followed by a recession and rumors of impending capital crisis, [the job of] setting long-term growth and diversification objectives was suddenly an exercise in irrelevance." Strategic planning was now supposed to involve "sorting out winners and losers, setting priorities, and husbanding capital." In a climate where "product and geographic markets were depressed and capital was presumed to be short,"[48] portfolio planning gave executives a ready excuse to get rid of underperforming business units while directing more funds to the "stars." By 1979, a survey of the *Fortune 500* industrial companies concluded that 45 percent of those firms had introduced portfolio planning techniques of some sort.[49]

PROBLEMS AND PROMISE

Somewhat ironically, the very macroeconomic conditions that (initially) increased the popularity of portfolio planning also inspired questions about the experience curve. The high inflation and excess capacity (due to downturns in demand) induced by the oil shocks of 1973 and 1979 disrupted historical experience curves in many industries, suggesting that Bruce D. Henderson had oversold the concept in a 1974 pamphlet entitled *Why Costs Go Down Forever*. Another problem with the experience curve was pinpointed by a classic 1974 article by William J. Abernathy and Kenneth Wayne, which argued that "the consequence of intensively pursuing a cost-minimization strategy [for example, one based on the experience curve] is a reduced ability to make innovative changes and to respond to those introduced by competitors."[50] Abernathy and Wayne pointed to Henry Ford's obsession with reducing the costs of the Model T, which left his company vulnerable to the strategy of product innovation initiated by Alfred P. Sloan at General Motors. The experience curve also drew criticism for treating cost reductions as automatic rather than something to be managed, for assuming that most experience could be kept proprietary, for mixing up different sources of cost reduction with very different strategic implications (e.g., learning versus scale versus vertical integration), and for leading to stalemates as multiple competitors pursued the same experience-based strategy.[51]

In the late 1970s, portfolio planning came under attack as well. One problem was that the strategic recommendations for an SBU were often inordinately sensitive to the specific portfolio planning technique employed. For instance, when an academic study applied four different portfolio techniques to a group of 15 SBUs owned by the same *Fortune 500* corporation, it found that only one out of the 15 SBUs fell in the same area of each of the four matrices and only five of the SBUs were classified similarly in three of the four matrices.[52] This level of agreement was only slightly higher than would have been expected if the 15 SBUs had been classified randomly four separate times!

Second and more seriously, even if one could figure out the "right" technique to employ, the mechanical determination of resource-allocation patterns on the basis of historical data was inherently problematic, as was the implicit assumption that financial capital was *the* scarce resource on which top management had to focus. Some consultants readily acknowledged these problems. In 1979, Fred Gluck, the head of McKinsey's strategic management practice, ventured the opinion that "the heavy dependence on 'packaged' techniques [has] frequently resulted in nothing more than a tightening up, or fine tuning, of current initiatives within the traditionally configured businesses." Even worse, technique-based strategies "rarely beat existing competition" and often leave businesses "vulnerable to unexpected thrusts from companies not previously considered competitors."[53] Gluck and his colleagues sought to loosen some of the constraints imposed by mechanistic approaches by proposing that successful companies' strategies progress through four phases (depicted in Exhibit 1.6) that involve

EXHIBIT 1.6   Four Phases of Strategy.

EXHIBIT 1.7   Two Determinants of Profitability.

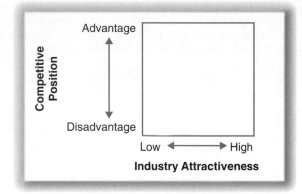

grappling with increasing levels of dynamism, multidimensionality, and uncertainty and therefore become less amenable to routine quantitative analysis.[54]

An even more stinging attack on the analytical techniques popularized by strategy consultants was offered by two Harvard Business School professors, Robert H. Hayes and William J. Abernathy, in 1980. They argued that "these new principles [of management], despite their sophistication and widespread usefulness, encourage a preference for (1) analytic detachment rather than the insight that comes from 'hands on experience' and (2) short-term cost reduction rather than long-term development of technological competitiveness."[55] Hayes and Abernathy particularly criticized portfolio planning as a tool that led managers to focus on minimizing financial risks rather than investing in new opportunities that required a long-term commitment of resources.[56]

These criticisms notwithstanding, portfolio planning had a lasting influence on subsequent work on business strategy because it focused attention on the need for more careful analysis of the two basic dimensions of the portfolio planning grid shown in Exhibit 1.7: industry attractiveness and competitive position. Although these two dimensions had been identified earlier—in the General Survey Outline developed by McKinsey & Company for the internal use of its consultants in 1952, for example— portfolio planning underscored their usefulness in analyzing the effects of competition on business performance. Specifically, a business's performance could be thought of as the sum of the average profitability of the industry in which it operated plus its competitive advantage (or minus its competitive disadvantage) relative to the average competitor within that industry. Subsequent work aimed to dig deeper into the determinants of industry attractiveness and competitive position and is discussed in Chapters 2 and 3 respectively. But the attractions of an explicitly competitive perspective, involving direct comparisons with reference competitors, had already overcome traditional hesitations based on the uniqueness of companies and the implied difficulties of comparing them.

Summary

This chapter reviewed the history of strategic thinking about business through the mid-1970s. The early history of business-strategic thinking was affected in many ways by military concepts and considerations. Sociology, with its construct of distinctive competence, seems to have been the academic field that most influenced early elaborations of the concept of strategy in business, mostly by professors at business schools.[57] Consulting firms disseminated academic insights and developed sets of tools to help top managers (even of very highly diversified companies) monitor the strategies of the business units under them. Although disillusionment with specific tools was quick to set in, this line of work nevertheless framed the agenda for future research and development in the field of strategy.

Glossary

distinctive competence	portfolio planning	strategy
experience curve	strategic business units	SWOT
learning curve	(SBUs)	

Notes

1. Consult, for instance, the two McKinsey Award winners from the 1996 volume of the *Harvard Business Review:* "Strategy as Revolution" by Gary Hamel and "What Is Strategy?" by Michael E. Porter.

2. Carl von Clausewitz, *On War,* trans. and ed. Michael Eliot Howard and Peter Paret (1976; reprint, Princeton, N.J.: Princeton University Press, 1984), p. 128.

3. For a depiction of business history in terms of these industrial revolutions and a third one, see Thomas K. McCraw, ed., *Creating Modern Capitalism: How Entrepreneurs, Companies, and Countries Triumphed in Three Industrial Revolutions* (Cambridge, Mass.: Harvard University Press, 1997). For an extended account of the evolution of business strategies through to the end of the twentieth century, see Pankaj Ghemawat, "Competition and Business Strategy in Historical Perspective," *Business History Review,* 76 (Spring 2002): 37–74.

4. Alfred D. Chandler, Jr., *Strategy and Structure: Chapters in the History of the Industrial Enterprise* (Cambridge, Mass.: MIT Press, 1962) and *Scale and Scope: The Dynamics of Industrial Capitalism* (Cambridge, Mass.: Belknap Press of Harvard University Press, 1990).

5. Alfred P. Sloan, *My Years with General Motors* (New York: Doubleday, 1963).

6. Chester I. Barnard, *The Functions of the Executive* (1938; reprint, Cambridge, Mass.: Harvard University Press, 1968), pp. 204–205.

7. John von Neumann and Oskar Morgenstern, *The Theory og Games and Economic Behavior* (Princeton, N.J.: Princeton University Press, 1944).

8. Peter Drucker, *The Practice of Management* (New York: Harper, 1954), p. 11.

9. Daniel Yergin and Joseph Stanislaw, *The Commanding Heights: The Battle between Government and the Marketplace That Is Remaking the Modern World* (New York: Simon & Schuster, 1998).

10. Philip Selznick, *Leadership in Administration: A Sociological Interpretation* (New York: Harper & Row, 1957), pp. 49–50.

11. John R. Commons, *Institutional Economics: Its Place in Political Economy* (New York: Macmillan Co., 1934); Barnard, *Functions of the Executive.*

12. Ronald H. Coase, "The Nature of the Firm," *Economica* 4, no. 16 (1937): 386–405. Reprinted in George Joseph Stigler and Kenneth E. Boulding, eds., *Readings in Price Theory* (Chicago: Richard D. Irwin, 1952). In addition to Coase's article, which influenced thinking about both strategy and organizations, a number of other authors made pioneering contributions to organizational theory that cannot be fully recognized here: Henri Fayol on administrative theory, Elton Mayo and Melville Dalton on human relations, and Herbert Simon and James March on information processing, to cite just a few.

13. Joseph Schumpeter, *Capitalism, Socialism, and Democracy* (New York: Harper, 1942).

14. Edith Penrose, *The Theory of the Growth of the Firm* (Oxford: Basil Blackwell, 1959).

15. Official Register of Harvard University, March 29, 1917, pp. 42–43.

16. George A. Smith, Jr., and C. Roland Christensen, *Suggestions to Instructors on Policy*

Formulation (Chicago: Richard D. Irwin, 1951), pp. 3–4.

17. George A. Smith, Jr., *Policy Formulation and Administration: A Casebook of Top-Management Problems in Business* (Chicago: Richard D. Irwin, 1951), p. 14.

18. Kenneth R. Andrews, *The Concept of Corporate Strategy* (Homewood, Ill.: Richard D. Irwin, 1971), p. 23.

19. See Edmund Learned, C. Roland Christensen, and Kenneth R. Andrews, *Problems of General Management; Business Policy: A Series Casebook* (Homewood, Ill.: Richard D. Irwin, 1961), pt. I.

20. Interview with Kenneth R. Andrews, April 2, 1997.

21. Kenneth R. Andrews, *The Concept of Corporate Strategy*, rev. ed. (Homewood, Ill.: Richard D. Irwin, 1980), p. 69.

22. Ibid. (1971 ed.), p. 29.

23. Ibid., p. 100.

24. Theodore Levitt, "Marketing Myopia," *Harvard Business Review* 53, no. 5 (1975): 45–56.

25. H. Igor Ansoff, *Corporate Strategy: An Analytic Approach to Business Policy for Growth and Expansion* (New York: McGraw-Hill, 1965), pp. 106–109.

26. Ibid., pp. 105–108.

27. Exhibit 1.2 is based on Henry Mintzberg's adaptation of Ansoff's matrix. Henry Mintzberg, "Generic Strategies," in *Advances in Strategic Management* (Greenwich, Conn.: JAI Press, 1988), p. 2. For the original, see Ansoff, *Corporate Strategy*, p. 128.

28. Michael E. Porter, "Industrial Organization and the Evolution of Concepts for Strategic Planning," in *Corporate Strategy: The Integration of Corporate Planning Models and Economics*, ed. Thomas H. Naylor (New York: North-Holland, 1982), p. 184.

29. Adam M. Brandenburger, Michael E. Porter, and Nicolaj Siggelkow, "Competition and Strategy: The Emergence of a Field" (paper presented at the McArthur Symposium, Harvard Business School, October 9, 1996), pp. 3–4.

30. Stanford Research Institute, *Planning in Business*, Menlo Park, Calif., 1963.

31. Sidney E. Schoeffler, Robert D. Buzzell, and Donald F. Heany, "Impact of Strategic Planning on Profit Performance," *Harvard Business Review* 52, no. 2 (1974): 137–145.

32. Interview with Seymour Tilles, October 24, 1996. Tilles credits Henderson for recognizing the competitiveness of Japanese industry at a time, in the late 1960s, when few Americans believed that Japan or any other country could compete successfully against American industry.

33. Bruce D. Henderson, *The Logic of Business Strategy* (Cambridge, Mass.: Ballinger, 1984), p. 10.

34. Bruce D. Henderson, *Henderson on Corporate Strategy* (Cambridge, Mass.: Abt Books, 1979), pp. 6–7.

35. Interview with Seymour Tilles, October 24, 1996.

36. Henderson, *Henderson on Corporate Strategy*, p. 41.

37. Bruce D. Henderson explained that unlike earlier versions of the learning curve, BCG's experience curve "encompasses all costs (including capital, administrative, research, and marketing) and traces them through technological displacement and product evolution. It is also based on cash flow rates, not accounting allocation." Bruce D. Henderson, preface to Boston Consulting Group, *Perspectives on Experience* (1968; reprint, Boston: BCG, 1972).

38. Ibid., p. 7.

39. Patrick Conley, *Experience Curves as a Planning Tool*, BCG Pamphlet (1970), p. 15.

40. Henderson, preface to *Perspectives on Experience*.

41. See George Stalk and Thomas M. Hout, *Competing against Time: How Time-Based Competition Is Reshaping Global Markets* (New York: Free Press, 1990), p. 12.

42. Conley, *Experience Curves as a Planning Tool*, pp. 10–11.

43. Arnoldo C. Hax and Nicolas S. Majluf, *Strategic Management: An Integrative Perspective* (Englewood Cliffs, N.J.: Prentice Hall, 1984), p. 156.

44. Interview with Mike Allen, April 4, 1997.

45. Schoeffler, Buzzell and Heany, "Impact of Strategic Planning on Profit Performance." *Harvard Business Review* 52, no. 2 (1974): 137–145.

46. Walter Kiechel, "Corporate Strategies under Fire," *Fortune*, December 27, 1982.

47. Frederick W. Gluck and Stephen P. Kaufman, "Using the Strategic Planning Framework," McKinsey internal document in *Readings in Strategy* (1979), pp. 3–4.

48. J. Quincy Hunsicker, "Strategic Planning: A Chinese Dinner?" (McKinsey staff paper, December 1978), p. 3.

49. Philippe Haspeslagh, "Portfolio Planning: Uses and Limits," *Harvard Business Review* 60, no. 1 (1982): 58–73.

50. William J. Abernathy and Kenneth Wayne, "Limits of the Learning Curve," *Harvard Business Review* 52, no. 5 (1974): 109–119.

51. Pankaj Ghemawat, "Building Strategy on the Experience Curve," *Harvard Business Review* 63, no. 2 (1985): 143–149.

52. Yoram Wind, Vijay Mahajan, and Donald J. Swire, "An Empirical-Comparison of Standardized Portfolio Models," *Journal of Marketing* 47, no. 2 (1983): 89–99. The statistical analysis of Wind et al.'s results is based on an unpublished draft by Pankaj Ghemawat.

53. Gluck and Kaufman, "Using the Strategic Planning Framework," pp. 5–6.

54. Adapted from Frederick W. Gluck, Stephen P. Kaufman, and A. Steven Walleck, "The Evolution of Strategic Management," McKinsey staff paper (October 1978), p. 4. Reproduced in modified form in the same authors' "Strategic Management for Competitive Advantage," *Harvard Business Review* 58, no. 4 (1980): 154–161.

55. Robert H. Hayes and William J. Abernathy, "Managing Our Way to Economic Decline," *Harvard Business Review* 58, no. 4 (1980): 67–77.

56. Ibid., p. 71.

57. The doctrine of distinctive competence was recycled, with great success, in the 1990s. See the discussion of core competence in Chapter 6.

CHAPTER

Mapping the Business Landscape

Pankaj Ghemawat and David Collis[1]

*When an industry with a reputation for difficult economics
meets a manager with a reputation for excellence, it is
usually the industry that keeps its reputation intact.*

—WARREN BUFFET

Warren Buffet may have overstated the case. Nevertheless, there is considerable evidence to support the idea—explicit in the techniques for portfolio analysis discussed in Chapter 1—that the industry in which a business operates has a strong influence on its economic performance. Statistical analyses show that 10–20 percent of the variation in businesses' accounting profitability reflects the industries in which they operate.[2] The key implication for managers—that the industry environment matters—is illustrated in Exhibit 2.1, which summarizes the extent to which average profitability has differed across broad industry groups over nearly two decades.[3] Note that the vertical axis subtracts out the estimated costs of (equity) capital from reported profitability (return on equity) so as to focus on economic profitability instead of accounting profitability. And the horizontal axis, which maps the size of each industry group in terms of the amount of equity capital invested in it, links measures of economic profitability to total economic value created or destroyed.

In addition, Exhibit 2.1 suggests a way of visualizing the profit potential afforded by a business environment—by mapping it into a landscape in which the vertical dimension captures the level of economic profitability (or unprofitability).[4] A two-dimensional landscape, such as the one shown in Exhibit 2.1, permits inclusion of just one dimension of choice—in this case, which industry to compete in. A three-dimensional landscape, such as the one in Exhibit 2.2, allows for two dimensions of

EXHIBIT 2.1   Average Economic Profits of U.S. Industry Groups (1989–2006).
Source: Marakon/Trinsum

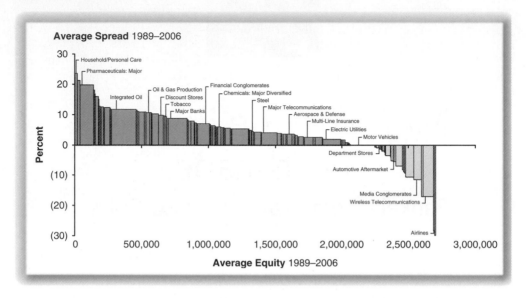

choice—for example, where to compete along one dimension and how to compete along the other. Most businesses are best envisioned as operating in a high-dimension space of choices, with each location in this space representing a different strategy—that is, a different set of choices about what to do and how to do it. A **business landscape** maps each strategy's elevation according to its economic profitability. The central challenge of strategy is to guide a business to a relatively high point on this landscape.

EXHIBIT 2.2   A Three-Dimensional Business Landscape.

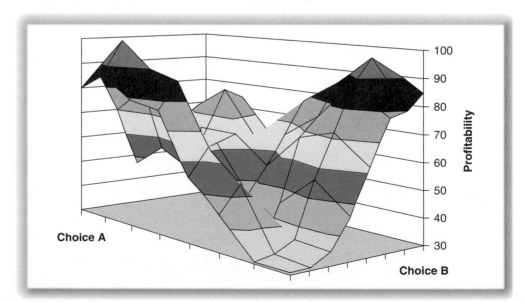

The chapters that follow will elaborate further on the landscape metaphor. In the context of this chapter, it can be used to highlight the fact that the profitability of direct competitors tends to have a common industry-specific component. Because of this industry-specific component, the average height above (or below) the zero-margin line—the average economic margin—will vary systematically across different industries. Clearly, businesses in some industry groups (e.g., pharmaceuticals) have generally operated on profit plateaus, whereas businesses in others (e.g., airlines) have mostly remained stuck in deep troughs.

Managers' first-hand experience of such differences in average profitability across industries largely explains why many tend to take Warren Buffet seriously, despite his somewhat constraining view of what they can achieve. But managers need to do more than recognize how profitable particular industry arenas have proved in the past. They also need to understand the reasons behind such effects in order to decide where and how their firms will compete, to assess the implications of major changes in the relevant parts of the business landscape, and to adapt to or, better yet, shape the business landscape.

Such ambitions combine with the complexities of the real world to place a sizable premium on finding simple, yet structured ways of thinking about business landscapes. This chapter begins by describing three successively more general structures that have been proposed as solutions to this problem: the **supply-demand analysis** of individual markets, the **"five forces" framework** for industry analysis developed by Michael E. Porter, and the **value net** devised by Adam M. Brandenburger and Barry J. Nalebuff.[5] We then examine the actual process of mapping a business landscape in detail.

The concept of the business landscape is deliberately meant to be broader than the usual conception of an "industry." Although this chapter focuses on so-called industry-level effects on performance, we want to explore such effects within a broader set of relationships than the ones that have come to be associated with traditional industry analysis.

SUPPLY-DEMAND ANALYSIS

Supply and demand are the grandparents of all attempts at landscape analysis. The idea that the interplay of supply and demand determines a natural price goes back—at least in Western culture—to the scholastic professors (mostly clerics) of the Middle Ages.[6] Although many of the elements of supply-demand analysis were formalized by the scholastics and their successors, Alfred Marshall (in the late nineteenth century) was the first to combine them into the conventional supply-demand diagram depicted in Exhibit 2.3.

The development of the "Marshallian scissors" was motivated by the continuing debate about whether "value" was governed by supply-side costs or demand-side willingness to pay. This debate seemed no more reasonable to Marshall than disputes about whether the lower (or the upper) blade of a pair of scissors is the one that actually cuts paper. He suggested that price would instead be determined by the "equilibrium" point at which the **demand curve** for a particular product, summed across its buyers in decreasing order of their willingness to pay, intersected with its **supply curve**, summed across its suppliers in increasing order of their costs of production.[7]

The downward-sloping demand curve that underpins this line of analysis was treated as self-evident by Marshall, who also introduced the notion of the

EXHIBIT 2.3   Supply-Demand Analysis.

price-elasticity of demand. Demand is said to be relatively price-elastic if changes in price induce relatively large changes in the aggregate quantity demand (i.e., if the demand curve is close to horizontal); it is deemed relatively price-inelastic if the reverse is true (i.e., if the demand curve is close to vertical). On the supply side, Marshall argued that upward-sloping supply curves tend to become flatter—or even become horizontal—as the period lengthens. He had trouble, however, with his attempts to analyze supply curves that slope downward rather than upward (i.e., display increasing returns to scale). Additionally, his analysis assumed that individual buyers and sellers would be small in relation to the size of the overall market and homogenous in the sense that a given buyer would have the same willingness to pay for the product of each supplier, and a given supplier would face the same costs in supplying its product to each buyer.

Supply-demand analysis was incorporated relatively quickly into economics and marketing courses at business schools. It seems to have had less impact on the teaching and practice of business strategy until the recessions of the 1970s and early 1980s, when downward shifts in demand curves reinforced the importance of developing a more thorough understanding of supply curves or, more precisely, cost curves that could help determine where prices would settle down.

For an example of this sort of analysis, consider Exhibit 2.4, which traces the cost curve for hospitals in the Greater Boston area in the early 1990s, as developed by Bain and Company, a consulting firm. This simple piece of analysis helped sensitize the high-cost Harvard Medical Center (HMC) teaching hospitals to the dire implications of the expected decrease in hospital utilization rates in Massachusetts from 80 percent to 40–60 percent by the late 1990s, as "hospital bed days" per person declined from 1.2 per year toward the national average of 0.6 per year.[8] Note that with 40–60 percent utilization, the HMC hospitals were all stuck farther out on the cost curve than its point of intersection with demand.

This example also illustrates the limitations of Marshallian supply-demand analysis. First, it is unrealistic to treat the hospitals in the local market as individually small and lacking market power. In fact, the two largest teaching hospitals affiliated with the HMC, Massachusetts General Hospital and Brigham and Women's Hospital, decided to

EXHIBIT 2.4   Supply Curve for Boston Hospitals.
Source: Gary Pisano, Partners HealthCare System, Inc. (A), ICCH No. 696-062. © Copyright 2007 Partners HealthCare System, Inc.

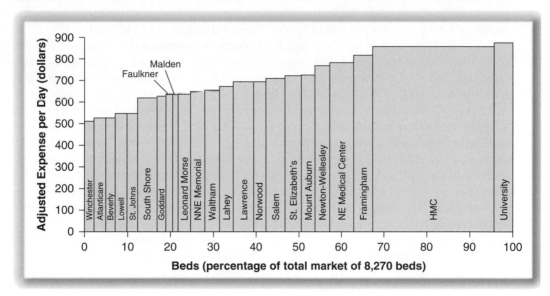

join forces in the aftermath of Bain's study to attain a combined market share of 21 percent and improve their "clout." Second, the example also violates the assumption of homogeneity. Patients' needs differ, as do hospitals' relative effectiveness in fulfilling those needs, to an extent that can only partially be controlled for by adjusting hospitals' costs on the basis of their case mix. It would therefore be useful to generalize the specializing assumptions associated with supply-demand analysis in this case and many others. The attempt to do so that has met with the greatest success in the business community is considered next in its own historical context.

THE "FIVE FORCES" FRAMEWORK

The large-numbers assumption built into conventional supply-demand analysis had already been relaxed more than half a century before Marshall offered his synthesis. In 1838, Antoine A. Cournot provided the first analytical characterizations of equilibrium prices under monopoly and with duopolists (two sellers) independently deciding how much to produce.[9] The homogeneity assumption was relaxed in two books published in 1933, one by Edward Chamberlin and the other by Joan Robinson, on monopolistic competition—that is, situations in which the individual firm monopolized its own products but confronted a large number of competitors, similarly situated, that offered substitute products.[10] From a business-strategic perspective, however, these attempts to posit a large number of firms with different products that otherwise resembled one another offered limited benefits: they missed the subtleties of **oligopolistic competition** (i.e., competition among the few).

A more important role was reserved for other economists in what came to be called the Harvard School, whose proponents argued that the structure of some industries might permit incumbent firms to earn positive economic profits over long periods of time.[11] Edward S. Mason, a member of the Harvard Economics Department, suggested that an industry's structure would determine the conduct of buyers and sellers—their choices of key decision variables—and, by implication, the industry's performance in terms of profitability, efficiency, and innovation.[12]

Joe S. Bain, also of the Harvard Economics Department (but unrelated to the consulting firm of the same name), sought to uncover relationships between industry structure and performance through empirical work focused on a limited number of structural variables. Two studies that he published in the 1950s were particularly notable. The first study found that manufacturing industries in which the eight largest competitors accounted for more than 70 percent of sales were nearly twice as profitable as industries with eight-firm concentration ratios less than 70 percent.[13] The second study explained how, in certain industries, "established sellers can persistently raise their prices above a competitive level without attracting new firms to enter the industry."[14] Bain identified three basic types of **entry barriers**: (1) an absolute cost advantage for an established firm (an enforceable process patent, for instance); (2) a significant degree of product differentiation; and (3) economies of scale.

Bain's insights enabled the rapid growth of a new subfield of economics, known as **industrial organization (IO)**, that explored the structural reasons why some industries were more profitable than others. By the mid-1970s, IO economists had carried out several hundred inter-industry empirical studies. Although the relationships between structural variables and performance proved more complicated than earlier work had suggested,[15] these studies confirmed that some industries have inherently higher long-run profitability, or "attractiveness," than others.

IO's immediate impact on business strategy was limited by the focus of Bain and his successors on public rather than private policy and by their emphasis on using a short list of structural variables to explain industry profitability in a way that slighted business strategy. Both problems were addressed by Michael E. Porter, who had worked with another IO economist at Harvard, Richard E. Caves, to study industry structure and business strategy. In 1974, Porter prepared a "Note on the Structural Analysis of Industries" that represented his first attempt to turn IO on its head by focusing on the business policy objective of profit maximization rather than the public policy objective of minimizing "excess" profits.[16] In 1980, he published *Competitive Strategy*, a book that owed much of its success to his "five forces" framework. This framework, which is reproduced in Exhibit 2.5, sought to relate the average profitability of the participants in an industry to five competitive forces.

Porter's framework for industry analysis generalized the supply-demand analysis of individual markets in several respects. First, it relaxed the assumptions of both large numbers and homogeneity—that is, of a large number of representative competitors. Second, along the vertical dimension, it shifted attention from two-stage vertical chains, each consisting of a supplier and a buyer, to three-stage chains made up of suppliers, rivals, and buyers. Third, along the horizontal dimension, it accounted for potential entrants and substitutes as well as direct rivals. These generalizations did, however, force Porter to reach beyond scientific evidence into the realm of common sense. Indeed, a survey of empirical IO more than a decade after Porter first developed his framework revealed that of all the influences that Porter flagged, only a few—the ones in boldface in Exhibit 2.5—commanded strong empirical support.[17]

EXHIBIT 2.5   The "Five Forces" Framework for Industry Analysis.

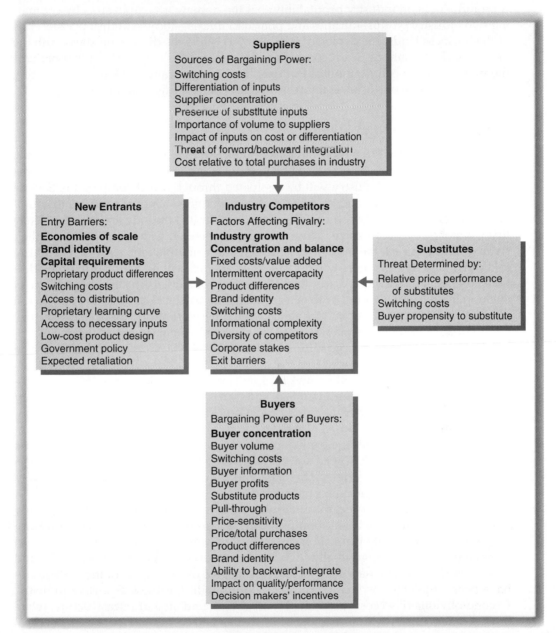

Despite such problems, the "five forces" framework's focus on business concerns rather than public policy, its emphasis on **extended competition** for value rather than just competition among existing rivals, and its (relative) ease of application inspired numerous companies as well as business schools to adopt its use. A survey by Bain (the consulting firm) suggested a 25 percent usage rate in 1993.[18] Given the clear impact of this framework, we will discuss it in detail. We will also illustrate the structural influences on industry profitability that the framework emphasizes by comparing two industry groups—airlines and pharmaceuticals—located at the opposite ends of the business landscape depicted in Exhibit 2.1. While the discussion starts with the degree of **rivalry** among direct competitors in an industry, keep in mind that perhaps the most valuable contribution of Porter's "five forces" framework is its suggestion that rivalry is only one of several forces that determine industry attractiveness.

Force 1: The Degree of Rivalry

The degree of rivalry is the most obvious of the "five forces" in an industry—and the one on which strategists have focused historically. It influences the extent to which the value captured by an industry will be dissipated through direct competition. Several types of structural determinants of rivalry can be identified. One set concerns the number and relative size of competitors. The more concentrated the industry, the more likely that competitors will recognize their mutual interdependence and so will restrain their rivalry. If, in contrast, the industry includes many small players, each will be apt to think that its effect on others will go unnoticed and so may be tempted to grab additional market share, thereby disrupting the market. For similar reasons, the presence of one dominant competitor rather than a set of equally balanced competitors may lessen rivalry: the dominant player may be able to set industry prices and discipline defectors, while equally sized players may try to outdo one another to gain an advantage.

A good example of these influences is seen in the U.S. airline industry, which was much more profitable prior to deregulation in 1978. Deregulation allowed many new airlines to enter profitable routes leading to price reductions and declining margins.[19] Given the lack of a dominant firm, attempts by a single carrier to raise fares or alter fare structures are often rescinded if not quickly matched by all major competitors. To illustrate, in early 1990s, American Airlines introduced 'value pricing' (a simplified fare structure) with the explicit intent of providing 'price leadership.'[20] For a short time, competitors followed suit and the share prices of all major airlines rose, but the initiative quickly fell apart as some other carriers, starting with TWA, engaged in aggressive price discounting.[21]

A second set of structural attributes that influence rivalry is more closely related to the industry's basic conditions. In capital-intensive industries, for example, the level of capacity utilization directly influences firms' incentive to engage in price competition. More generally, high fixed costs, excess capacity, slow growth, and lack of product differentiation all increase the degree of rivalry. All of these attributes have been implicated as factors in the low profitability of the U.S. airline industry. Beyond obvious fixed costs associated with aircraft and airport infrastructure, when one considers the individual flight or seat, virtually all costs are fixed. Highly cyclical demand for air travel has often resulted in overcapacity during downturns, leading to steep losses. And despite tremendous creative energies devoted by passionate managers, there is basically no product or service differentiation outside of long-haul premium services for which passengers are willing to pay higher fares.

The pharmaceutical industry presents a very different sort of picture. Fixed manufacturing costs are limited as a percentage of sales or value added. In fact, gross margins range above 90 percent for some blockbuster drugs. Demand has grown at double-digit rates, and differences among products, brand identity, and switching costs—discussed at greater length in the section "Force 4: Buyer Power"—have created insulation among competitors that is reinforced by patent protection.

Finally, the degree of rivalry also has behavioral determinants. If competitors are diverse, face high exit barriers, or attach high strategic value to their positions in an industry, they are more likely to compete aggressively. In the airline industry, for instance, low-cost carriers operating point-to-point service with standardized fleets, high aircraft utilization, and limited amenities have added diversity and complicated efforts by large hub-and-spoke operators to establish pricing discipline. Exit barriers are high because when an airline does shut down or scale back, its underlying capacity usually does not go away. Instead, the planes are parked in the desert, waiting for another airline to bring them back into service. In addition, exit barriers are compounded by U.S. bankruptcy laws: all major network carriers except one have filed for bankruptcy since 2001, but none has been liquidated. Airline industry performance has also been depressed by firms pursuing nonmarket objectives, such as government-owned flag carriers outside the United States and flamboyant executives building operations more reflective of their own hubris than true market demand. In pharmaceuticals, in contrast, both U.S. and non-U.S. firms have been able to effectively coordinate lobbying and other market-enhancement activities in the lucrative U.S. market under the auspices of the Pharmaceutical Research and Manufacturers of America association. Note that these pressures applied even before rivalry was exacerbated by the downturn in the United States and world economies.

Force 2: The Threat of Entry

Average industry profitability is influenced by potential as well as existing competitors. The key concept in analyzing the threat of entry are entry barriers, which prevent an influx of firms into an industry whenever profits, adjusted for the cost of capital, rise above zero. Entry barriers exist whenever it is difficult or not economically feasible for an outsider to replicate the incumbents' positions. Entry barriers usually rest on irreversible resource commitments, as discussed next and elaborated in Chapter 5.

Exhibit 2.5 illustrates the diverse forms that entry barriers can take. Some barriers reflect intrinsic physical or legal obstacles to entry. The most common forms of entry barriers, however, are usually the scale and the investment required to enter an industry as an efficient competitor. For example, when incumbent firms have well-established brand names and clearly differentiated products, a potential entrant may find it uneconomical to undertake the marketing campaign necessary to introduce its own products effectively. The magnitude of the required expenditures may be only part of the entrant's problem in such a situation: it may take years for the firm to build a reputation for product quality, no matter how large its initial advertising campaign. Also, entry barriers are not purely exogenous: they can be contrived along these dimensions and many others. Credible threats of retaliation by incumbents represent perhaps the clearest example.

To illustrate the difference that entry barriers can make, consider two very different **strategic groups**—as in groups of firms following very different business strategies—within the pharmaceutical industry: research-based pharmaceutical companies versus manufacturers of generic pharmaceuticals. Research-based companies have historically been far more profitable, largely because they are protected by higher entry barriers. These barriers, some of which are discussed in more detail in Chapter 5, include patent protection; a new-drug development process that costs hundreds of millions of dollars and stretches over more than a decade: carefully cultivated brand identities backed, in some cases, by substantial advertising campaigns: and large sales forces that call on individual doctors. In contrast, the generic drug segment of the industry is characterized by a lack of product patents, much smaller requirements of capital and time for product development, weak to nonexistent brand identities, and distribution efforts that focus on serving large accounts that purchase in bulk at low prices. As a result, the average profitability of generic companies has been much lower although, in keeping with the discussion in the previous section of the effects of competitive diversity, that has also begun to put substantial pressure on the profitability of research-based pharmaceutical companies.

Barriers to entry in the airline industry, in contrast, are generally low with the exception of the hub-and-spoke operations relied on by most of the major airlines, which tend to be difficult if not impossible for entrants to replicate. But point-to-point entry has been much easier, which is why nearly 200 airlines have entered the U.S. market since deregulation. Leisure travelers, in particular, have facilitated entry because they will readily fly a small new airline offering low fares, confident that government oversight has ensured its safety. Boeing and Airbus help by offering services specifically tailored to helping new airlines set up operations and become new airplane customers. Airplanes can be leased to reduce up front capital requirements. And labor costs actually serve as a gateway rather than a barrier to entry since the employees of new airlines start out with no seniority, implying significant cost savings versus established carriers.

Force 3: The Threat of Substitutes

The threat that **substitutes** pose to an industry's profitability depends on the relative price-to-performance ratios of the different types of products or services to which customers can turn to satisfy the same basic need.[22] The threat of substitution is also affected by switching costs—that is, the costs in areas such as retraining, retooling, or redesign that are incurred when a customer switches to a different type of product or service. In many cases, the substitution process follows an S-shaped curve. It starts slowly as a few trendsetters risk experimenting with the substitute, picks up steam if other customers follow suit, and finally levels off when nearly all of the cost-effective substitution possibilities have been exhausted.

While there are no effective substitutes for airlines for many long-haul travelers, substitutes such as automobiles, high-speed rail, and low-cost buses do exert substantial pressure for short-distance travel. Pressure is also exerted by fractional ownership of business jets, business jet charter, and (soon) very light jet air taxi services. These services, while impacting a small number of passengers, are important because they skim off premium customers who might otherwise purchase flexible, last-minute, or first-class tickets at high prices.

It is worth emphasizing that any analysis of the threat of (demand-side) substitution must look broadly at all the different ways of performing similar functions for customers, not just at physically similar products. Thus, the airline industry also must reckon with the substitution threat associated with videoconferencing and other Internet-based collaboration tools—although the impact of these technologies as substitutes is counterbalanced by their effects as complements in stimulating business over long distances, which leads to additional demand for travel.[23] And substitutes for pharmaceuticals, broadly construed, might include preventive medical care and hospitalization. Indeed, there may be some truth to the pharmaceutical industry's assertions that one reason for its profitability and growth is the fact that pharmaceuticals represent a more cost-effective form of health care, in many cases, than hospitalization.

Conceptually, analysis of the substitution possibilities open to buyers should be supplemented by considering the possibilities available to suppliers.[24] Supply-side substitutability reduces suppliers' willingness to provide required inputs, just as demand-side substitutability reduces buyers' willingness to pay for products.

Force 4: Buyer Power

Buyer power is one of the two "vertical" forces—supplier power, discussed next, is the other—that influences the appropriation of the value created by an industry. Buyer power allows customers to squeeze industry margins by compelling competitors to either reduce prices or raise the level of service offered without compensating price increases.

Buyers tend to be powerful if there are few of them, if each one purchases in volumes that are large relative to the size of a single vendor, if they have good information about prices and the other attributes of vendors' products (if those products are standardized), and if buyers face few switching costs or can credibly threaten to integrate backwards. Some of these considerations help explain why corporate buyers, through their travel management companies like American Express, have enjoyed considerable leverage in dealing with airlines through corporate volume agreements. Furthermore, buyer power has been enhanced by technology developments such as the ability to conveniently compare airfares via the Internet (reducing search costs) and for companies to monitor traveler compliance with preferred airline policies. And occasionally companies do integrate backwards by chartering aircraft to meet regular demand ("corporate shuttle" services). In contrast, buyer power has historically been limited in the pharmaceutical industry, especially for individual purchasers of branded drugs who often lack the information required to evaluate substitutes (e.g., generic drugs) even when they are available.

It is also often useful to distinguish potential buyer power from the buyer's willingness or incentive to use that power. For example, the U.S. government is potentially a very powerful purchaser of pharmaceuticals through its Medicaid and Medicare programs. Historically, however, it has refrained from exercising its potential power—a fortunate state of affairs for the pharmaceutical industry but an unfortunate one for taxpayers. In fact, the prescription drug benefit added to Medicare in late 2003 is seen as a windfall for the pharmaceutical firms because it explicitly prohibits Medicare from using its purchasing power to bargain for lower prices!

To explain why buyers do or do not have the incentive to use their inherent power, we must look at other, more behavioral conditions. One of the most important factors in this regard is the nature of cost from the perspective of the purchasing industry. In a stark contrast to spending on pharmaceutical products, travel costs are mostly discretionary in nature. Airlines buyers, especially leisure travelers, have strong incentives to exercise their discretion in choosing to travel at specific price points and refusing to do so otherwise. The situation is obviously somewhat different from the perspective of patients faced with disease or sickness.

Another important factor is the perceived risk of failure associated with a product's use. In pharmaceuticals, patients must take into account the high personal cost of any substitute's failure—which is also a consideration for doctors who prescribe drugs given concerns about malpractice suits. The perceived risks associated with generics, in particular, have been increased by scandals involving some firms' substandard manufacturing practices—another reason why high-priced brands have been able to retain significant shares in many product categories even after satisfactory generic substitutes have reached the market.

The pharmaceutical industry example also highlights the importance of studying the decision-making process when analyzing buyer power. The interests and incentives of all the players involved in the purchase decision must be understood if we are to predict the price sensitivity of that decision. Many doctors and patients have traditionally lacked incentives to hold down the prices paid for drugs because a third party—an insurance company—actually footed the bill. These incentives *are* changing, however, as the spread of managed care increases price sensitivity.

Force 5: Supplier Power

Supplier power is the mirror image of buyer power. As a result, the analysis of supplier power typically focuses first on the relative size and concentration of suppliers relative to competitors and second on the degree of differentiation in the inputs supplied. The ability to charge competitors—suppliers' buyers—different prices in line with the differences in the value created for each of them usually indicates that the market is characterized by high supplier power.

None of these considerations was much of a problem for the pharmaceutical industry in the past. For conventional drugs (as opposed to biotechnological products), inputs are usually available from several commodity chemical companies. The U.S. airline industry, in contrast, has struggled in the face of strong labor unions. Given the damage that even limited disruptions can cause to industry economics, airline employees, especially pilots and aviation mechanics were historically able to hold out for wages and benefits to levels well in excess of other industries. In fact, their power has even thwarted industry consolidation on occasions due to the problem of merging crew seniority lists.

We conclude this section by noting that relationships with buyers and suppliers have important cooperative as well as competitive elements. To foreshadow an example that will be looked at in more detail in the discussion of holdup in Chapter 5, General Motors and other U.S. automobile companies lost sight of the cooperative element when they pushed their parts suppliers to the wall by playing them against one another. Japanese car manufacturers, in contrast, committed themselves to long-run supplier relationships that paid off in terms of higher quality and faster new product development. The importance of both **cooperation** and competition is further highlighted by the template for landscape analysis, the value net, that is discussed in the next section.

THE VALUE NET AND OTHER GENERALIZATIONS

The years since Porter first developed his "five forces" framework have seen the rearrangement and incorporation of additional variables (e.g., import competition, multimarket contact, and collaborative institutions such as trade associations) into

EXHIBIT 2.6 The Value Net.

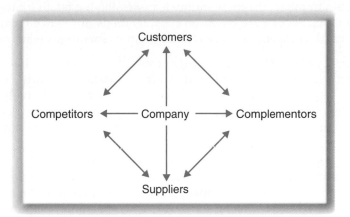

the determinants of the intensity of each of the five competitive forces (rivalry, in the case of these examples). Even more important, the framework itself can be generalized as necessary by bringing new types of players into the analysis. The most successful attempt to do so involves the value net framework devised by Adam M. Brandenburger and Barry J. Nalebuff (see Exhibit 2.6).[25]

The value net highlights the critical role that **complementors**—participants from whom customers buy complementary products or services or to whom suppliers sell complementary resources—can play in influencing business success or failure. Complementors are defined as being the mirror image of competitors (including new entrants and substitutes as well as existing rivals). On the demand side, they increase buyers' willingness to pay for products; on the supply side, they decrease the price that suppliers require for their inputs.

To see why it is important to include complementors in the picture, reconsider the pharmaceutical industry example. Doctors greatly influence the success of pharmaceutical manufacturers through their prescription of drugs, but they cannot, in most cases, be considered buyers: gifts aside, money typically does not flow directly from them to the pharmaceutical manufacturers. Thus they are more naturally thought of as complementors who increase buyers' willingness to pay for particular products.

An even more powerful example is provided by the personal computer landscape, to which we will keep returning for examples in this section. Note that Microsoft's operating systems are worthless on personal computers that lack the appropriate microprocessors from Intel—or AMD—to run them. Yet Microsoft and Intel would not show up on one another's "five forces" screens! Common sense nevertheless suggests that Intel should regard Microsoft as an important player in the business landscape on which it operates, and vice versa. The importance of this insight is reinforced by recent reports of wobbles in the "Wintel" axis as the interests of these two players have diverged. Intel, at least, has incorporated complementors into its analyses of its business landscape.[26]

Chapter 3 will characterize more precisely the value that cooperation with complementors and other types of players can add. Here we will simply emphasize that cooperating with complementors to expand the size of the pie should be combined with some consideration of competing with them to claim slices of that pie. Common sense suggests a number of rules of thumb for assessing the relative bargaining power of complementors. Several are based on considerations of relative competitive intensity: on how much competition there is among complementors, versus among rivals:

- *Relative concentration.*   Complementors are more likely to have the power to pursue their own agenda when they are concentrated relative to competitors and are less likely to be able to do so when they are relatively fragmented. Examples include Microsoft's and Intel's sway over the much more fragmented manufacturers of personal computers; or for that matter, their attempts to support AMD and Linux respectively to weaken each other's hold on the industry.
- *Relative buyer/supplier switching costs.*   When the costs to buyers or suppliers of switching across complementors are greater than the costs of switching across competitors, that increases complementors' ability to pursue their own goals. For instance, the cost of switching software on your personal computer is likely to be significantly higher than the cost of switching your Internet service provider, with clear implications for how much of the economic pie these two classes of players can hope to capture. And within software, switching costs tend to be significantly higher for operating systems than for most types of application programs, which is why many of the latter can be (and are) purchased independently.
- *Relative complementor/competitor switching costs.*   Similarly, the ease with which complementors themselves can switch to working with different competitors versus the ease with which competitors can switch to working with different complementors also matter. In particular, if complementors play a significant role in pulling through demand (e.g., through differentiation) or supply (e.g., through volumes commanded), their power is likely to expand. Intel's "Intel Inside" campaign is a good example of such an attempt to build up independent appeal to buyers.
- *Asymmetric integration threats.*   Complementors tend to have more power when they can threaten to invade competitors' turf more credibly than competitors can threaten to invade theirs. Thus Intel's forward integration into chipsets and even motherboards brings it into more direct competition with personal computer manufacturers, who do not seem to have any offsetting backward integration options.
- *Rate of growth of the pie.*   From a behavioral perspective, competition with complementors to claim value is likely to be less intense when the size of the pie available to be divided among competitors and complementors is growing rapidly. Thus, it is hard not to see some of the heightened tensions between Microsoft and Intel as related to the maturing of demand for high-end personal computers.

Having identified some commonsensical determinants of the relative bargaining power of complementors, it is worth remembering that the point is not to minimize complementors' bargaining power per se, for instance, by setting up a fragmented, undifferentiated complementor network. That would be as bad as U.S. automakers' historical "divide and conquer" strategy toward their suppliers, described at the end of the preceding section. Having independent, differentiated complementors that are motivated to make investments in and support a particular platform has, in fact, proved critical in the personal computer landscape: Microsoft was able to beat Apple with operating systems not normally considered superior partly because, unlike Apple, it encouraged independent software vendors to write applications software to run on its platform.

More broadly, a review of the templates for landscape analysis discussed so far in this chapter—supply-demand analysis, the "five forces" framework, and the value nets—suggests that one way in which each generalizes its predecessor(s) is by bringing new types of players into the analysis. The next question is obvious: can additional improvements in our ability to understand the business landscape be achieved by further broadening the types of players considered?

The answer to this question depends on the case being considered but is sometimes clearly affirmative. For example, it is often important to account for **nonmarket relationships**—such as interactions with the government, the media, activist/interest groups, and the public—that, in addition to involving not-for-profit players, may be distinguished from market relationships by such characteristics as strong norms of fairness, broad participation, and majority rule.[27] Consider the case of the pharmaceutical industry. It depends on the government as a major buyer, regulator, sponsor of basic research, and upholder of patent laws and has increasingly had to worry about the threat to its legitimacy posed by various social as well as political movements, particularly agitation against high pharmaceutical prices and profit margins. As a result, pharmaceutical companies should—and do—pay explicit attention to nonmarket relationships with governments and with nongovernmental organizations instead of looking at them solely in terms of their implications for relationships among groups of market (or for-profit) players. Folding them into the five or six forces will not help them develop integrated strategies that explicitly address both market and nonmarket relationships.[28]

A simple theme should stand out from this discussion: it is impossible to prespecify a single, all-purpose framework or template for analyzing the business landscape. Instead, the framework must be fitted to the landscape—and the decision issue—being analyzed. The successively more general frameworks discussed so far in this chapter remind us that we must think broadly about the other players involved and suggest a process for doing so. The rest of this chapter focuses on that topic.

THE PROCESS OF MAPPING BUSINESS LANDSCAPES

Having reviewed the historical development of different approaches to the business landscape, it is time to discuss how managers can link such thinking to strategic planning and action. The purpose of mapping the business landscape is not (as is often misunderstood) to identify whether one operates on a part of it that is high above or well below economic sea level (in the terms we used in discussing Exhibit 2.1): most managers know whether they are gasping for economic breath or not. Instead, the principal purpose is to understand the reasons for such variations and to incorporate them into strategic action. We lay out a six-step process to make this happen. Although it may be necessary to cycle through these steps more than once, they are most simply considered in turn.

Step 1: Gathering Information

Mapping the business landscape in the kind of detail described in this chapter requires a great deal of information. There is, as a result, a premium on thinking broadly about sources of information. Exhibit 2.7 lists some public sources of

EXHIBIT 2.7   Public Sources of Information for Industry (and Competitive) Analysis.

- Industry studies
  - Books
  - Stock analysts reports
  - Market research reports
  - Business school case studies
  - Trade associations
  - Special interest groups
- Company Sources
  - Annual reports
  - SEC filings
  - Web sites
  - Press releases
  - White papers
- Government Sources
  - Census, legal, or tax documents
  - Antitrust/regulatory documents
- Business Press
  - General publications
  - Specialized industry trade journals
  - Local newspapers
  - Online databases (e.g., Bloomberg, OneSource, Compustat)
- Other World Wide Web
  - Blogs
  - Unarchived stories
- Directories
  - Thomas' Register
  - Dun & Bradstreet
- Miscellaneous
  - Conferences, proceedings (e.g., keynote speeches and Q&A sessions)
  - Trade shows

information for industry (and competitive) analysis. Several broader points should be made about the list.

- The amount of publicly available information in many situations is staggering. As a result, information overload seems at least as significant a problem as information unavailability. And there is often no alternative to information filtering.
- The selection and prioritization of sources of public information must account for variations in their content, quality, and accessibility. For example, while the Internet has clearly transformed information gathering, indiscriminate searches on industry names will likely yield too many hits of too low a quality while missing out on deeper points.
- The need to supplement public information with external private information (from buyers or suppliers, consultants, or even direct or indirect contact with competitors) varies. Generally speaking, however, it is possible to map a business landscape fairly well without depending on costly or hard-to-access external private information of the sort that is more often required for competitive analysis.
- Given the fixed costs of undertaking such analyses from scratch, much emphasis has been placed on systems for scanning the external environment on an ongoing basis. While systems of this sort are costly, their costs can be spread across the types of analysis discussed in the chapters that follow as well as in this one.
- The process of mapping the business landscape should leverage, instead of ignoring, the extensive amounts of information about the external environment generated internally by employees accomplishing their day-to-day activities. It is important to have processes for capturing such information and organizational reinforcement to actually do so.
- The information assembled must be analyzed and must have the potential to influence action to be of any use. The content of what is involved in mapping business

landscapes is reviewed in the analytical steps that follow and the content of competitive analysis (which feeds off the same broad information base, albeit with more of an emphasis on company-level as opposed to group-level analysis) in the chapters that follow.

Step 2: Drawing the Boundaries

Another precursor to the actual analysis is to decide which part of the business landscape to focus on—also known as the problem of **industry definition**. Operationally, the challenge for the strategist is to decide how broadly (or narrowly) to draw the boundaries.

General-purpose industry classification schemes are of some help in this regard but often have to be redrawn to be really useful. For example, one would probably want to split up the most profitable group in Exhibit 2.1, "Household/Personal Care," because buyers, competitors, and even suppliers differ greatly within it.

A different way of drawing boundaries is to take an inside-out approach, starting with a business's served market. Usually, the boundaries of the landscape should be drawn a bit more broadly to include not only the segments that the business serves but also unserved segments with which it shares customers or technologies (or competitors). To make the same point in a different way, substitutability helps determine whether lines of business should be looked at together or separately. And by symmetry, important complements should also be included among the markets covered.

These issues all focus attention on the choice of **horizontal scope** across product markets or segments. This choice is discussed further, in the context of corporate strategy, in Chapter 6. **Vertical scope** and **geographic scope** raise somewhat different analytical issues. As far as vertical scope is concerned, the key issue is how many vertically linked stages of the supplier → buyer chain to consider. For example, can one analyze the mining of bauxite ore, its refining into alumina, the smelting of alumina into aluminum metal, and the fabrication of aluminum products from that metal independently of one another? In general, if a competitive market for third-party sales exists between vertical stages or could be created, the stages should be analyzed separately; if not, they should be analyzed together. In this sense, the tightest coupling in the vertical aluminum chain occurs between bauxite mining and alumina refining, because most refineries can employ only one source of bauxite (as a result of which, most firms participate in both stages or in neither). The loosest coupling arises between aluminum smelting and fabrication, because fabricators can buy aluminum ingot from the London Metal Exchange as well as from different smelters. Issues related to vertical scope are discussed further in the section on holdup in Chapter 5 of this book.

In regard to geographic scope, the key issue is how broadly to define the business landscape in terms of physical locations covered. For example, is it better to look at pharmaceutical manufacturers just in the United States or at the pharmaceutical industry worldwide? Such issues arise around local and regional boundaries in addition to national ones. As before, the degree of market integration—in this case, across geographic boundaries—is key to determining whether geographies should be looked at together or separately. Of course, much also depends on the specific decision at stake: local considerations dominate certain kinds of decisions (e.g., sales force organization in pharmaceuticals) even in industries that are, by most criteria, quite globally integrated. Still, systematic application of the market integration test does suggest, because of increasing cross-border integration, that the complexities of competing across multiple locations affect an ever broader range of decisions. Take the case of prices, which were traditionally set locally in both pharmaceuticals and airlines. In pharmaceuticals, particularly in the lucrative U.S. market, pricing is much more constrained than before by the threat of imports. However, airlines continue to be largely protected from foreign competition with restrictions on cabotage (revenue flights between domestic locations) and limits on foreign ownership. Issues related to geographic scope and global strategy are discussed further in Chapter 7 of this book.[29]

A final remark: given all the scope complexities discussed, there often isn't any perfect way of drawing the boundaries of the business landscape. For that reason, it is more useful to focus on ensuring that the boundaries are drawn clearly and that there is consistency in the treatment of what is in versus out instead of looking for *the* right way of drawing boundaries. And sometimes, both narrow and broad-scope analysis may be necessary, with narrowness focusing attention and breadth guarding against being blindsided.

Step 3: Identifying Groups of Players

The principal groups of players that must usually be considered—direct competitors, potential entrants, substitutes, complements, buyers, and suppliers—and other categories of players that might be added as necessary were discussed in the preceding section. There are, however, some additional procedural guidelines that are worth mentioning here.

- Groups of players need to be clearly and consistently labeled from the perspective of the business for which the analysis is being undertaken. Thus, in case discussions, rivals are sometimes confused with suppliers on the grounds that rivals are suppliers for their own buyers!
- It is often useful to distinguish *within* the groups of players listed above: to explicitly separate out and consider different strategic groups within the set of direct rivals, different buyer segments, and so on. The objective is to pick up variations in bargaining power (the subject of step 4) that more aggregated perspectives might obscure. For example, in airlines, it is useful to distinguish explicitly between labor, with substantial bargaining power, and other input suppliers who typically have much less leverage. Similarly, the bargaining power of different types of buyers of pharmaceuticals varies greatly.
- Finally, there is often a tendency, in mapping business landscapes, to focus on existing players. Deliberate attempts to counteract such biases by explicitly directing attention toward new or potential players may be necessary. Note that this ties in with the theme of thinking dynamically, which is the subject of step 5.

Step 4: Understanding Group-Level Bargaining Power

Building on the preceding steps, we can now discuss the core objective of attempts to map the business landscape: understanding group-level bargaining power. It is useful to concentrate on groups or subgroups of players with particular potential to influence a business's payoffs, for example, suppliers that account for a large percentage of the cost structure, buyers that represent a substantial share of the market, or groups that are outliers on important structural dimensions, such as degree of market concentration.

Not insisting on looking at all groups in equal depth helps keep the amount of analysis manageable. And it is also important to remember that the group-level analysis described in this chapter focuses on "macro" regularities and rules of thumb. Chapters 3 through 5, in contrast, can be seen as going "micro" by burrowing beneath the group level to look at individual businesses in comparison or interaction with each other.

Group-level analysis of the sort discussed in this chapter is driven by the idea that structural analysis can help identify which groups of players will, on average, get how much of the economic pie. The "five forces" framework provides a very helpful checklist in this regard, although it often makes sense to work through the long list rather quickly to focus in on a short list of structural factors to be explored further. The version of the value net developed in the preceding section suggests that similar analytical techniques can also be applied to complementors as a group of players.

Extension of the analysis to at least certain other groups of players (e.g., governments or nonprofits) requires some modifications to the basic approach outlined above, since such players should not, even to a first approximation, be thought of as value-maximizers. It is still possible, however, to think through their interests and the amount of influence that they are likely to bring to bear in pursuing them. And thus their impact on the average profitability of direct competitors in an industry can be identified even though it may not make sense to speak of their own average profitability.

A final point about this step: this is also the juncture at which it is perhaps most useful to test the emerging understanding of the structural determinants of profitability against data about the average profitability of different groups of players or patterns in the decisions that they make. Given the constraints on the information available and the reliance on rules of thumb, there is always judgment involved in assessing group-level bargaining power and, by implication, a need for cross-checking.

Step 5: Thinking Dynamically

The point of the analysis is usually to understand the business landscape *as it will be* rather than as it is or was. **Dynamic thinking** about how the business landscape will change can prove extremely valuable, just as a failure to anticipate changes can be disastrous. For a dramatic example, consider IBM's entry into the personal computer business in 1980. In an apparent rush to get in, it turned to Microsoft for the operating system (as well as to Intel for the microprocessor). Microsoft did not actually have an operating system but bought one called QDOS (Quick and Dirty Operating System) for $50,000, renamed it MS-DOS, and supplied it to IBM. Fatefully, it also secured IBM's permission to sell it to other computer manufacturers.[30] This paved the way for the emergence of a one supplier–many competitors structure dominated by Microsoft's MS-DOS and its successor, Windows, since users preferred to standardize their operating systems. IBM, in contrast, lost market share and, eventually, market leadership in an industry that has experienced sustained overall pressure on average profitability—in large part because of Microsoft and Intel.

In thinking dynamically about the business landscape, it is useful to distinguish explicitly between different time horizons, especially the short run and the long run. Although short-run dynamics pick up on purely transient effects, they also track phenomena such as industry cycles and economy-wide business cycles. Industry cycles are often related to lags in the commercialization of new generations of products or the installation of new, and their duration can vary significantly, even within the same broad sector. Thus, over the last few decades, the industry cycle in semiconductors has averaged 22 quarters or five-and-a-half years in length, but the cycle in personal computers has been one-third shorter, and that in flat panel displays shorter by more than one-half.[31] Comparisons across these industries also afford a number of other insights into industry cycles.

- The amplitude of the industry cycle—its effect on industry output—also varies greatly. Thus, the absolute values of fluctuations in downturns and in upturns averaged 46 percent in the upstream industry of semiconductors versus 17 percent in the downstream industry of personal computers. The difference reflects, in part, the bullwhip effect: Fluctuations in final demand are amplified as they are passed back upstream because of restocking or destocking along the way.
- The amplitude of the industry cycle in flat panel displays is, at 31 percent, also rather large. This reflects not only the bullwhip effect—flat panel displays are incorporated into personal computers, televisions, and other final consumption goods—but also the relative youth of the flat panel display industry, which really emerged only in the 1990s. The effects of industry maturity are considered further when we turn to look at long-run dynamics and, in particular, industry life cycles.
- The extent to which industry cycles parallel economy-wide business cycles is different in different industries. Thus, the correlation between the industry cycle and the general business cycle seems significantly higher in semiconductors than in flat panel displays. Again, differences in industry maturity may be part of the reason.

Economy-wide business cycles also vary greatly in the extent of their impact on different parts of the economy.[32] The service sector generally exhibits less sensitivity to such cycles than the manufacturing sector because of the difficulties of stocking services and their typically lower (physical) capital requirements. Sensitivity to the general state of the economy also tends to be high in mining and construction but is low—perhaps even negative, indicating countercyclicality—in agriculture. And then there are huge variations within sectors. Within manufacturing, for instance, the sensitivity of durable goods output to general economic output has been estimated to be three times as high as that of nondurable goods output and more than five times as high in the case of autos. And transportation and finance, insurance, and real estate significantly exceed the service-sector averages for sensitivity to the business cycle.

In addition to gauging such sensitivity for the industry that you are interested in, it is worth understanding—especially in view of the global economic downturn—two of the ways in which general economic weakness fundamentally reshapes competitive interactions. First, these are the times when financial constraints are most likely to bind a broad range of firms—even large ones from advanced economies. Such financial market imperfections can have strikingly counterintuitive effects on product market competition. For example, debt-laden industries are likely to price countercyclically, that is, to raise markups during downturns, instead of investing in market share by keeping prices lower.[33]

Second, the interactions between labor markets and product markets are also of special interest during a cyclical downturn because firms often look to reduce labor or at least labor costs at such times. During the last contraction in the U.S. economy, in 2001, firms were so aggressive in reducing headcounts that, unusually, labor

EXHIBIT 2.8   Life-Cycle Dynamics.

To understand how common product life cycles are and how dramatic their effects can be, consider findings by Steven Klepper and Elizabeth Graddy. These researchers tracked 46 new products from their early history through 1981—periods covering, in some cases, nearly 100 years.[i] They found that 38 products had experienced some kind of shakeout (i.e., significant reduction in the number of producers), after periods of growth which averaged 29 years, but varied widely. Klepper and Graddy pointed out that the eight remaining products in their sample might still be expected to contract since they were relatively young (as of 1981). Even more striking, the number of producers declined by an average of 52% from the peak for the 22 products that had achieved stability along this dimension (within 11 years of the onset of the shakeout period)!

Klepper and Graddy also found that output rose and prices fell at decreasing percentage rates over time, before stabilizing. Average annual changes in the first five-year interval for the products in Klepper and Graddy's sample were 50% for output and −13% for price. By years 20–30, annual changes along these dimensions had stabilized to averages, respectively, of 2% to 3% and −2% to −3%: a very sharp contrast.

The similarity across landscapes of this constellation of life-cycle related changes—and others, such as a significant shift from product R&D towards process R&D[ii]—is indicative of the importance of reviving the early work on life-cycles put forth by the consulting firm of Arthur D. Little and others.

[i] Steven Klepper and Elizabeth Graddy, "The Evolution of New Industries and the Determinants of Market Structure," *RAND Journal of Economics* (Spring 1990), 27–44.
[ii] W.J. Abernathy and J.M. Utterback. 1978. Patterns of Industrial Innovation. *Technology Review* 80:2–9.

productivity actually rose! But firms in Europe found themselves much more constrained, legally and socially, in this regard.

The long-run cycle that has attracted the most attention is the product/industry life cycle, which hinges on the idea that opportunities for innovation, particularly product innovation, are likely to be depleted as an industry matures. Some researchers have argued that there is actually a typical pattern of structural changes as an industry progresses through its life cycle (see Exhibit 2.8).

Beyond cycles, attention also needs to be paid to long-run trends such as market growth, the evolution of buyer needs, the rate of product and process innovation, and changes in the scale required to compete and in input costs. This short list illustrates that while some trends may emanate from within an industry, others may originate outside it. Exhibit 2.9 supplies a longer list of trends, organized in terms of the "six forces," although it must be noted that broad trends often affect more than one force.

Finally, cycles and trends, while useful in forecasting changes, rely on the continuity of the underlying structure to do so. But discontinuities or shocks of various sorts can lead to a resetting of the structure itself. Thus, while much of the early discussion of the global economic downturn focused on the time until recovery, General Electric's CEO, Jeff Immelt, warned "If you think this is only a cycle you're just wrong. This is a permanent reset."[34] The development of different macrostructural scenarios (e.g., a deglobalization scenario, among others) is one possible response.

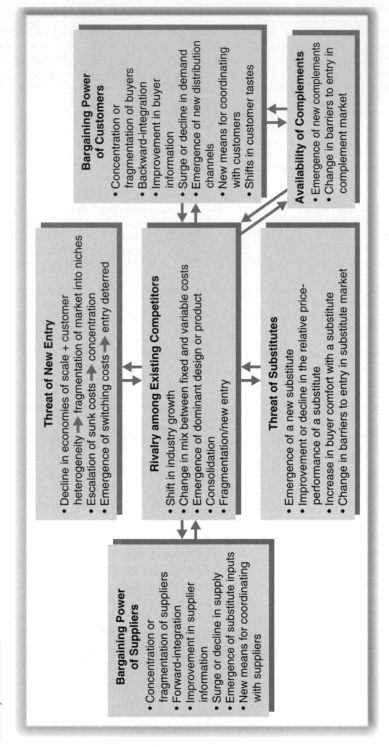

EXHIBIT 2.9   Trends Influencing Industry Structure.
Source: Jan W. Rivkin

Bargaining Power of Customers
- Concentration or fragmentation of buyers
- Backward-integration
- Improvement in buyer information
- Surge or decline in demand
- Emergence of new distribution channels
- New means for coordinating with customers
- Shifts in customer tastes

Availability of Complements
- Emergence of new complements
- Change in barriers to entry in complement market

Threat of New Entry
- Decline in economies of scale + customer heterogeneity → fragmentation of market into niches
- Escalation of sunk costs → concentration
- Emergence of switching costs → entry deterred

Rivalry among Existing Competitors
- Shift in industry growth
- Change in mix between fixed and variable costs
- Emergence of dominant design or product
- Consolidation
- Fragmentation/new entry

Threat of Substitutes
- Emergence of a new substitute
- Improvement or decline in the relative price-performance of a substitute
- Increase in buyer comfort with a substitute
- Change in barriers to entry in substitute market

Bargaining Power of Suppliers
- Concentration or fragmentation of suppliers
- Forward-integration
- Improvement in supplier information
- Surge or decline in supply
- Emergence of substitute inputs
- New means for coordinating with suppliers

For further discussion of how to inject more dynamic thinking into strategy, see Chapters 4 and 5.

To illustrate the potential usefulness of long-run analysis, think of a pharmaceutical company trying to set a strategic agenda for itself. Long-run trends that it might want to consider include

- The increased viability of biotechnology and other unconventional drug-discovery methods and increased outsourcing of drug discovery to them by the major pharmaceutical companies
- The increased dependence of branded pharmaceutical companies on a limited number of blockbusters for profitability and mergers among them as ways of boosting product pipelines and (perhaps) achieving scale economies
- The heightened threat from generic manufacturers and, more generally, imitative, or "me-too," competition
- On the consumer side, pressure from managed care and from import threats (e.g., into the United States from cheaper sources in Canada), counterbalanced by positive changes such as the rapid growth of categories like the "life-style" or behavioral drug segment and, in the United States, relaxation of the rules on direct-to-consumer advertising

The principal long-run cycle of concern, in line with the life-cycle hypothesis, is that the industry's pipeline of potential blockbusters appears to be emptier than before. In terms of shocks, the pharmaceutical companies have individual—often product-specific—concerns (e.g., Merck's recall of its blockbuster, Vioxx in 2004, which wiped out more than one-quarter of its market value) as well as broader ones, most notably, the threat of a backlash against high prices in the United States despite the industry's expensive and generally effective lobbying efforts.

Finally, the pharmaceutical firm might want to consider long-run possibilities other than "business as usual." For instance, given the soaring costs of health care, it is possible to imagine even more extensive governmental involvement in the sector than at present, extending to dimensions on which pharmaceutical firms have at least some freedom currently to compete (R&D, advertising, pricing, etc.).

Step 6: Responding to/Shaping the Business Landscape

Having drawn the industry boundaries and understood the relationships—current and future—between groups of players, the manager's attention must turn to using this knowledge for strategic action. It should be obvious that there are many possible uses of landscape analysis, including:

- Anticipating long-run performance (removing the effects of short-run cycles from current performance)
- Identifying groups of players or forces that must be countered to achieve good performance
- Testing decisions to enter, invest in, or exit from an industry
- Assessing the effects of a major change in the business landscape so as to be able to respond to it
- Identifying ways to shape the business landscape

Some of these uses are obvious or have already been discussed at some length. But the notions of responding to or shaping the business landscape should be elaborated further.

For an example of creative responses, consider the recent changes at the major accounting firms.[35] The profitability of their audit business, in particular, had been eroded over time by the rivalry between what were originally the Big Eight firms, which resembled each other in terms of size and the intent of becoming market leader, and by price pressure from the typical purchaser, a company CFO, for whom the audit fee typically represented the single largest item on the budget. Mergers since the mid-1980s that consolidated the Big Eight into the Big Five helped mitigate some of this pressure. The big payoff, however, came after the collapse of Arthur Andersen, one of what was by then the Big Five, in the wake of the Enron scandal in 2001. After this shock, the remaining Big Four were able to divide Andersen's clients in such a way as to increase their concentrations in many industry sectors and geographies well above the levels that would normally be permitted by the U.S. Department of Justice on antitrust grounds. In addition, they appear to have had some success in shifting the purchase of audit services away from CFOs and toward clients' CEOs and audit committees, which are substantially less price-sensitive given their newfound liability, under the Sarbanes-Oxley Act, for accounting inaccuracies. As a result, the average audit fee increased from 9 basis points in 2000 to 16 basis points in 2002, the year the Sarbanes-Oxley Act was passed. And increases in concentration by industry sector explain about half the observed increases in fees, suggesting that the increases in fees reflect more than just the increased cost of audits. As a partner at one of the Big Four put it, "We regained pricing power after . . . the U.S. government just about blew up a fifth of the industry."

Responding in this fashion, while important, is not the only strategic posture that might be adopted in dealing with the business landscape. A business might, instead, strive more actively to shape its environment. Such shaping is most obvious in fluid environments that are still taking form (e.g., multimedia), but is also evident in older, apparently more mature contexts. Consider De Beers's dominance of the diamond industry.[36]

De Beers grew out of Cecil Rhodes's takeover, in 1888, of South African mines that produced 95 percent of the world's diamonds. Over the course of the next 100 years, South Africa's production share dropped below 15 percent. De Beers nevertheless continued to regulate the flow of new diamonds to the market—and to dominate and shape it—by using its Central Selling Organization (CSO) to buy and, if necessary, stockpile other suppliers' rough diamonds. The CSO cleared markets by deciding who would get which stones; stabilized prices to prevent boom-and-bust cycles from wrecking its suppliers' (or the trade's) finances or customer confidence; sorted diamonds into standard grades; arranged financing, security, and transportation; and built demand by advertising the category and developing new markets (Japan was the most recent major example) and new products (e.g., tennis bracelets). All these functions expanded the total size of the pie available to the industry. In addition, it provided incentives for others to play along: the diamond trade was highly lucrative for the major supplier countries and, at the individual level, for the CSO's several hundred dealers. But suppliers and dealers had to agree to restrictive contracts and intensive monitoring. And there was a note of menace to the scene as well: De Beers had a well-developed reputation for ruthlessness in punishing transgressors, that is, in bringing sticks as well as carrots to bear.

But starting in the late 1990s, De Beers made substantial changes to this strategy in order to reshape a deteriorating industry structure. Rough diamond supply had surged more or less continuously since the early 1980s as additional (primarily non-De Beers) mines came on line, and created chronically large inventories for the CSO. To deal with this problem, De Beers finally stopped supporting the industry by paying for and stock-piling everyone's diamonds and refocused instead, on a strategy of becoming "the supplier of choice" by pumping up advertising and focusing it on its own brand, further tightening controls on the trade, integrating forward into jewelry retailing in a joint venture with Louis Vuitton, capitalizing on its superior infrastructure and information to address social concerns about "conflict diamonds" that fuel civil wars in Africa, and trying to clean up its image with the public and with governments. In other words, De Beers embarked on a strategy of reshaping the diamond business. A postscript: This new strategy appeared, for the most part, to work in its first few years, although by early 2009, forecasts that demand would drop by one-third or even one-half forced De Beers, as in previous downturns, to idle some of its mines, including the very productive ones operated as joint ventures with the Botswanan and Namibian governments.[37]

These changes at De Beers suggest, more generally, a need to move beyond looking at environmental attractiveness—the first of the two determinants of profitability in the profitability grid in Exhibit 1.7—to considering competitive positioning, the second of the two determinants. This move requires a shift from industry-level analysis to firm-level analysis. We can visualize this shift in landscape terms. Instead of looking at the landscape from a high altitude, where only the principal features of its various parts, such as the average height above (or below) sea level, stand out, we will zoom in for a much closer look. Our scrutiny will reveal that the landscape often looks very rugged with a higher degree of resolution as well: variations in the profitability of direct competitors tend to be even larger than the common components of their profitability examined in this chapter. Understanding such differences in competitive positioning and figuring out how to create competitive advantage are the principal topics of Chapter 3.

Summary

Analysis of the business landscape improves on part of the older SWOT (strengths-weaknesses-opportunities-threats) by systematizing analysis of the opportunities and threats that are common to an individual business and its direct competitors.

Landscape analysis is not confined, however, to direct competitors: it usually involves looking beyond them. Supply-demand analysis focuses attention on product markets—that is, on exchange relationships between suppliers and buyers. The "five forces" framework extends the analysis to three-stage (supplier → competitor → buyer) vertical chains and to explicit consideration of substitution possibilities. The value net draws complementors into the picture. Even more groups of players may need to be added, depending on the context. The broader point is that it is important to fit the framework used to the situation being studied rather than the other way around.

Identification of the relevant groups of players paves the way for actually understanding their relative bargaining power and,

at a deeper level, the relationships among them. Both the cooperative and the competitive components of such relationships must be taken into account—otherwise, this task would be a lot simpler. The "five forces" framework offers a number of helpful heuristics with its structural determinants of industry attractiveness. So does the value net, as developed in this chapter. It is also worth emphasizing that any such understanding of group-level profitability must be dynamic, because relationships between groups of players can and do change over time, as a result of cycles, trends, shocks, and other factors.

The ultimate object of such exercises is to affect the actions that businesses take. The analytical frameworks and steps discussed in this chapter are helpful in this regard, but not, by themselves, complete. As the SWOT framework reminds us, perceptions of common opportunities and threats must be integrated with consideration of the strengths and weaknesses of individual players. The next chapter expands on this insight.

Glossary

business landscape
buyer power
complementors
cooperation
demand curve
dynamic thinking
entry barriers
extended competition

"five forces" framework
geographic scope
horizontal scope
industrial organization or IO
nonmarket relationships
oligopolistic competition
price-elasticity of demand
rivalry

strategic groups
substitutes
supplier power
supply curve
supply-demand analysis
value net
vertical scope

Notes

1. This chapter has benefited enormously from the help of Adam M. Brandenburger and Jan W. Rivkin, who developed many of the ideas that it covers, allowed us to draw on their unpublished materials, and offered comments on earlier drafts.

2. See, for example, Richard Schmalensee, "Do Markets Differ Much?" *American Economic Review* 75, no. 3 (June 1985): 341–351; Richard P. Rumelt, "How Much Does Industry Matter?" *Strategic Management Journal* 12, no. 3 (Mar. 1991): 167–185; A. M. McGahan and Michael E. Porter, "What Do We Know About Variance in Accounting Profitability?" *Management Science* 48, no. 7 (Jul 2002): 834–851.

3. Dean Neese of Marakon/Trinsum deserves our thanks for helping make these data available.

4. The landscape metaphor originated in biology more than fifty years ago. See Stuart A. Kauffman, *At Home in the Universe: The Search for Laws of Self-Organization and Complexity* (New York: Oxford University Press, 1995) for a discussion in that context. The last four chapters of his book also discuss applications to issues concerning human organizations. For other applications of landscape-based models to strategy, see Daniel A. Levinthal, "Adaptation on Rugged Landscapes," *Management Science* 43, no. 7 (July 1997): 934–950; Jan W. Rivkin, "Imitation of Complex Strategies," *Management Science* 46, no. 6 (June 2000): 824–844; and Pankaj Ghemawat and Daniel A. Levinthal, "Choice Structures, Business Strategy and Performance: A Generalized Nk-Simulation Approach" (Harvard Business School Working Paper no. 01-012, 2000).

5. This discussion builds on Adam M. Brandenburger's unpublished note, "Models of Markets" (Harvard Business School, January 1998).

6. Jurg Niehans, *A History of Economic Theory: Classic Contributions, 1720–1980* (Baltimore: Johns Hopkins University Press, 1990).

7. Alfred Marshall, *Principles of Economics*, bk. 5 (London New York: Macmillan, 1890).

8. For additional details, see Gary P. Pisano and Maryam Golnaraghi, "Partners Healthcare System, Inc. (A)" (Harvard Business School Case no. 696–062, Boston, 1996). Also note that the implications of a decline in capacity utilization would be even more severe than implied by this cost curve because it includes fixed as well as variable costs in its cost base.

9. Antoine A. Cournot, *Recherches sur les principes mathématiques de la théorie des richesses* (Paris: Hachette, 1838). The rather different characterization of outcomes when duopolists set prices rather than quantities was provided by another French savant, Jean Bertrand, in his review of Cournot's book in the *Journal des Savants* 67 (1883): 499–508.

10. See Edward Chamberlin, *The Theory of Monopolistic Competition*, Harvard Economic Studies, vol. 38. (Cambridge, Mass.: Harvard University Press, 1933), and Joan Robinson, *The Economics of Imperfect Competition* (London: Macmillan, 1933).

11. Economists associated with the University of Chicago generally doubted the empirical importance of this possibility-except as an artifact of regulatory distortions.

12. Mason's seminal work was Edward S. Mason, "Price and Production Policies of Large-Scale Enterprise," *American Economic Review* 29, no. 1 (March 1939): 61–74.

13. Joe S. Bain, "Relation of Profit Rate to Industry Concentration: American Manufacturing, 1936–1940," *Quarterly Journal of Economics* 65, no. 3 (August 1951): 293–324.

14. Joe S. Bain, *Barriers to New Competition* (Cambridge, Mass.: Harvard University Press, 1956), p. 3.

15. See, for instance, Harvey J. Goldschmid, H. Michael Mann, and J. Frederick Weston, *Industrial Concentration: The New Learning* (Boston: Little, Brown, 1974).

16. Michael E. Porter, "Note on the Structural Analysis of Industries" (Harvard Business School Case no. 376–054, Boston, 1975).

17. Richard Schmalensee, "Inter-Industry Studies of Structure and Performance," in *Handbook of Industrial Organization*, ed. Richard Schmalensee and Robert D. Willig (Amsterdam: North-Holland, 1989), chap. 16, pp. 951–1009.

18. Darrell K. Rigby, "Managing the Management Tools," *Planning Review*, September–October 1994.

19. Alfred E. Kahn, "Surprises Of Airline Deregulation," *American Economic Review* 78, no. 2 (1988): 316–322.

20. Alvin J. Silk and Jamie Harper, "American Airlines' Value Pricing (C)" (Harvard Business School Case no. 595–037, Boston, 1994).

21. Alvin J. Silk and Steven C. Michael, "American Airlines' Value Pricing (B)" (Harvard Business School Case no. 594–019, Boston, 1993).

22. The "five forces" framework focuses on the threat of product substitution. The threat of resource substitution is considered in Chapter 5.

23. The impact of complements on industry attractiveness is considered in the next section.

24. Adam M. Brandenburger and Harborne W. Stuart, Jr., "Value-Based Business Strategy," *Journal of Economics & Management Strategy* 5, no. 1 (1996): 5–24.

25. Michael E. Porter's recent resummarization of his work on business strategy ("The Five Competitive Forces that Shape Strategy," *Harvard Business Review*, 86, no. 1 (January 2008): 78–93, esp. p. 86) takes issue with the inclusion of complementors as a sixth force. However, his reason for excluding complementors—in effect, that relationships with them have important cooperative as well as competitive elements—also apply to buyers and suppliers, as noted at the end of the previous section.

26. Andrew S. Grove, *Only the Paranoid Survive: How to Exploit the Crisis Points That Challenge Every Company and Career* (New York: Currency Doubleday, 1996), pp. 27–29.

27. David P. Baron, "Integrated Strategy: Market and Nonmarket Components," *California Management Review* 37, no. 2 (Winter 1995): 47–65, esp. p. 47. See David P. Baron, *Business and Its Environment*, 2nd ed. (Upper Saddle River, N.J.: Prentice Hall, 1996) for an extended treatment of nonmarket strategies.

28. *Ibid*. And for further discussion of nonmarket threats and responses to them in this textbook, see Chapter 5.

29. Also see Pankaj Ghemawat, *Redefining Global Strategy* (Boston: Harvard Business School Press, 2007).

30. Adam Horowitz and the editors of Business 2.0, *The Dumbest Moments in Business History: Useless Products, Ruinous Deals, Clueless Bosses and Other Signs of Unintelligent Life in the Workplace*, compiled by Mark Athitakis and Mark Lasswell (New York: Portfolio, 2004).

31. Hao Tan and John A. Mathews, 2007. "Cyclical Dynamics in Three Industries," DRUID Working Papers 07-07, DRUID, Copenhagen Business School, Department of Industrial Economics and Strategy/Aalborg University, Department of Business Studies.

32. This paragraph is based on Tan and Matthews, op cit., Bruce Petersen and Steven Strongin, "Why Are Some Industries More Cyclical Than Others?" *Journal of Business & Economic Statistics* 14, no. 2 (April 1996): 189–198; Magda Kandil, "Cyclical Fluctuations across Industries of the United States: Evidence and Implications," *Journal of Economics and Business* 47 (1995): 17–37.

33. Judith A. Chevalier and David S. Scharfstein, "Capital-Market Imperfections and Counter-cyclical Markups: Theory and Evidence," *American Economic Review* 86, no. 4 (Sept. 1996): 703–725.

34. Tyler Hamilton, "Crisis Reset Economy: Immelt," *Toronto Star*, Feb 11, 2009, accessed at http://www.thestar.com/Business/article/585510 on March 29, 2009.

35. This description of the accounting industry is based on Emilie R. Feldman, "Arthur Andersen: A Lesson in How Not to Punish an Oligopolistic Competitor" (Harvard College Senior Honors Thesis, 2004); Sharad Asthana, Steven Balsam, and Sungsoo Kim, "The Effect of Enron, Andersen, and Sarbanes-Oxley on the Market for Audit Services" (unpublished working paper, June 2004); and interviews with industry participants.

36. This description of De Beers is based on Pankaj Ghemawat and Sonia D. Marciano, "De Beers at the Millennium," (Harvard Business School Case no. 706–518).

37. Leandi Cameron, "SA Diamond Sector Seeking Ways to Mitigate Economic Downturn," *Creamer Media's Mining Weekly*, March 20, 2009?, accessed at http://www.miningweekly.com/article/sa-diamond-sector-seeking-ways-to-mitigate-economic-downturn-2009-03-20 on March 29, 2009.

CHAPTER

3

Creating Competitive Advantage
Pankaj Ghemawat and Jan W. Rivkin

*If a man . . . make a better mousetrap than his neighbor,
tho' he build his house in the woods, the world will make
a path to his door.*

—RALPH WALDO EMERSON (ATTRIBUTED)

L ecturing in the nineteenth century, Emerson anticipated one of the key pieces of advice that strategists still stress at the beginning of the twenty-first: Strive for an edge over the competition! Since Emerson's time, strategists have explored, in effect, what makes one mousetrap better than others from the point of view of profitability. "Better" involves not just buyers' **willingness to pay** for a firm's mousetrap or the costs incurred to provide the trap, but the difference between the two. In other words, an appreciation of the importance of a competitive edge has been elaborated into an understanding of the economics of what might be called the competitive wedge. A firm is said to have created a **competitive advantage** over its rivals if it has driven a wider wedge between willingness to pay and costs than its competitors have achieved.[1]

The long-standing interest in competitive advantage and its inclusion as the second dimension of the profitability grid in Exhibit 1.7 reflect the sense that while industry- or population-level effects have a large impact on business performance, large differences in performance also appear *within* industries. Consider, for example, the two industries identified as outliers in terms of performance and analyzed in Chapter 2—pharmaceuticals and airlines. Exhibit 3.1 unbundles the spreads between returns on equity and the costs of equity capital in these two industries, competitor by competitor.[2] Note that while pharmaceutical firms have, on average, earned returns higher than airlines, the best performing airlines create economic value while the worst performing pharmaceutical firms destroy it. In other words, while industry matters, it is not destiny.

EXHIBIT 3.1 A   Average Economic Profits in the Airline Industry, 1988–2007.
(*Source*: © 2008 Marakon/Trinsum)   **B   Average Economic Profits in the Pharmaceutical Industry, 1988–2007.**   (*Source*: © 2008 Marakon/Trinsum)
Note: Several familiar airlines such as United, Northwest, and USAir are invisible in Exhibit 3.1 because of negative book equity (bankruptcy). What this means, of course, is that the depiction in the exhibit understates actual value destruction in the airline industry.

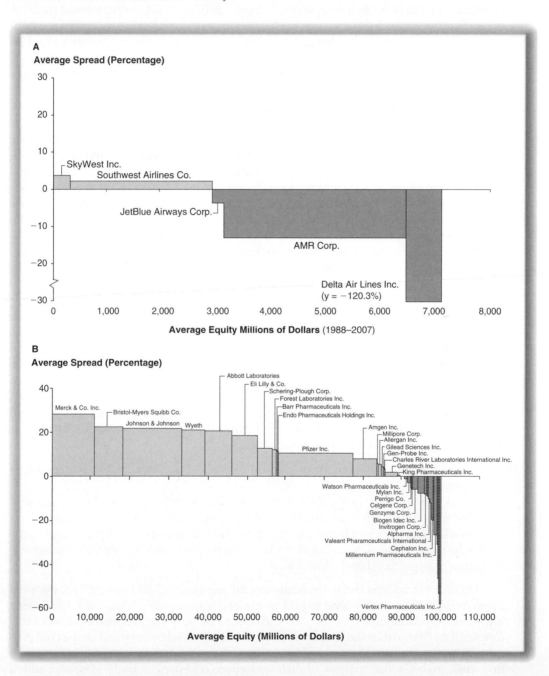

The structure within industries, often described in terms of "strategic groups," helps explain part of these differences in performance. Thus, while the major pharmaceutical firms in Exhibit 3.1 have averaged returns 20 percent higher than their cost of equity capital, biotechnology firms as a group have averaged returns 5 percent lower than their cost of capital. But there is more to the story than just group-level differences. Within the group of biotech companies, Amgen has historically outperformed its peers as has Southwest Airlines (although both have come under pressure recently, foreshadowing the discussions of the dynamics of competitive advantage in Chapters 4 and 5).

More systematic research confirms that such within-industry performance differences are widespread and substantial. The research suggests, in fact, that within-industry differences in profitability are larger than differences in the averages across industries. While industry-level effects appear to account for 10–20 percent of the variation in business profitability in the United States, stable within-industry effects account for 30–45 percent.[3] (Most of the remainder can be assigned to effects that fluctuate from year to year.) Note, however, that this is *not* an argument for ignoring industry-level effects, the other dimension of the profitability grid introduced in Exhibit 1.7 and discussed in Chapter 2. First, industry-level effects *do* account for a significant fraction of the variation in performance observed on average. Second, industry-level effects may have a more persistent influence on business-level profitability than within-industry differences.[4] Third, there is some evidence that industry characteristics play a larger role in determining the room for positive departures from average profitability than their average effects suggest.[5] Finally, market leaders, in particular, often confront important tensions between managing industry structure and improving their own **competitive position** within that structure.

All that said, within-industry differences in profitability do appear to be larger than the differences in the averages across industries—and may loom even larger during downturns. In purely arithmetic terms, a deep downturn that pushes an industry's average player into unprofitability makes a superior competitive position the only basis for profitability. And in terms of strategy, firms are often exhorted to invest during a downturn to improve their long-term competitive positions.[6] Such advice is meant to counteract a tendency by businesses to cut investments during downturns more than can be explained by either changes in relevant (longer-run) economic forecasts or externally-imposed capital constraints. A number of mechanisms may underlie such a pattern, including

- manic depressive behavior of the sort evoked by Keynes in discussing animal spirits
- herd behavior by competitors that can lead to cascading cut-backs across them
- the managerial bias toward internal funding even when external funding is available on efficient terms, implying an internally-imposed capital constraint.
- a focus by managers during downturns on firm survival rather than maximization of expected shareholder value

In order to understand within-industry differences in good times or bad, we must zoom in from the industry level to look at the landscapes within industries. Examining intra-industry landscapes, which also turn out to be very rugged, is the focus of this chapter. The first part of the chapter reviews the historical development of the core concepts in analyzing competitive position (either advantaged or disadvantaged): competitive **cost analysis**, the analysis of **differentiation**, cost-benefit **trade-offs**, and **added**

value. The second part of the chapter draws on these concepts to lay out a process for analyzing competitive positioning, illustrated with an extended example. This tack, which is primarily analytical, is not intended to deny the importance of creativity and insight in the creation of competitive advantage. Rather, it can be read as an attempt to guide entrepreneurial energies by setting up a battery of tests for new business ideas. The topic of creativity in developing new ideas is taken up again in Chapter 4.

THE DEVELOPMENT OF CONCEPTS FOR COMPETITIVE POSITIONING

Starting in the 1970s, academic researchers made a number of contributions to our understanding of positioning within industries. The IO-based approach to strategic groups, initiated at the Harvard Business School by Michael S. Hunt's work on broad-line versus narrowline strategies in the major home appliance industry, suggested that competitors within particular industries could be grouped in terms of their competitive strategies in ways that helped explain their interactions and relative profitability.[7] And a stream of work at Purdue University by Dan E. Schendel and his collaborators explored the heterogeneity of competitive positions, strategies, and performance in brewing and other industries with a combination of statistical analysis and qualitative case studies.[8] The work that seems to have had the most impact on business-strategic thinking about competitive positions in the late 1970s and the 1980s, however, was more pragmatic than academic in its orientation. Consultants once again played a leading role, particularly in the development of techniques for competitive cost analysis.

Cost Analysis

With the growing acceptance of the experience curve in the 1960s, most strategists turned to some type of cost analysis as the basis for assessing competitive positions. The interest in competitive cost analysis survived the declining popularity of the experience curve in the 1970s but was reshaped by it in two important ways. First, greater attention was paid to disaggregating businesses into their components as well as to assessing how costs in a particular activity might be shared across businesses. Second, strategists greatly enriched their menu of **cost drivers**, expanding it beyond just experience.

The disaggregation of businesses into components was motivated, in part, by early attempts to "fix" the experience curve so as to deal with the rising real prices of many raw materials in the 1970s.[9] The proposed fix involved splitting costs into the costs of purchased materials and "cost added" (value added minus profit margins) and then redefining the experience curve as applying only to the latter category. The natural next step was to disaggregate a business's entire cost structure into parts—functions, processes, or activities—whose costs might be expected to behave in interestingly different ways. (To be consistent with later sections of the chapter, we will refer to the parts as "activities.")[10] As in the case of portfolio analysis, the idea of splitting businesses into component activities diffused quickly among consultants and their clients in the 1970s. A template for activity analysis that became especially prominent is reproduced in Exhibit 3.2.

Activity-based analysis also suggested a way of circumventing the "free-standing" conception of individual businesses built into the concept of strategic business units (SBUs).[11] One persistent problem in splitting diversified corporations into SBUs was

EXHIBIT 3.2   McKinsey's Business System.[12]
(*Source:* Pankaj Ghemawat, "Competition and Business Strategy in Historical Perspective," *Business History Review*, 76 (Spring 2002).)

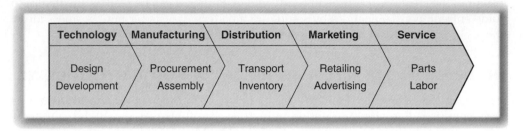

that, with the exception of pure conglomerates, SBUs often shared elements of their cost structure with one another. Consulting firms—particularly Bain & Company and Strategic Planning Associates (SPA)—began to emphasize the development of field maps or matrices that identified shared costs at the level of individual activities that were linked across businesses.[13]

In another important development in competitive cost analysis during the late 1970s and early 1980s, strategists began to consider a richer menu of cost drivers. Scale effects, although officially lumped into the experience curve, had long been studied independently in individual cases. Even more specific treatment of the effects of scale was now forced by activity analysis that might indicate, for example, that advertising costs were driven by national scale, whereas distribution costs were driven by local or regional scale. Field maps underscored the potential importance of economies (or diseconomies) of scope across businesses rather than scale within a given business. The effects of capacity utilization on costs were dramatized by macroeconomic downturns in the wake of the two oil shocks. The globalization of competition in many industries highlighted the location of activities as a key driver of competitors' cost positions and so on. Cost drivers are discussed more comprehensively in the second section of this chapter.

Differentiation Analysis

Increasingly sophisticated cost analysis was followed, after a significant lag, by greater attention to customers in the process of analyzing competitive position. Of course, customers had never been entirely invisible. Even in the heyday of experience curve analysis, market **segmentation** had been an essential strategic tool—but it was often used to chop up markets to "demonstrate" a positive link between segment share and cost advantage rather than for truly analytical purposes. By one insider's recollection (that of Walker Lewis, the founder of Strategic Planning Associates), "To those who defended the classic experience-curve strategy, about 80 percent of the businesses in the world were commodities."[14] In the 1970s, this view began to change.

As strategists paid more attention to customer analysis, they began to reconsider the idea that attaining low costs and offering customers low prices was always the best way to compete. Instead, they focused more closely on *differentiated* ways of competing that might let a business command a price premium by improving customers' performance or reducing their (other) costs.[15] Although (product) differentiation had always occupied center stage in marketing, the idea of considering it in a cross-functional, competitive context alongside cost levels apparently began to emerge in business strategy in the 1970s. Thus one member of Harvard's Business Policy group assigned Joe Bain's writings on entry barriers (see Chapter 2) to students in the 1970s and used the concepts of cost and differentiation—implicit in two of Bain's three sources of entry barriers—to organize classroom discussions.[16] McKinsey began to apply the distinction between cost and value in its consulting activities later in the same decade.[17] The first extensive treatments of cost and differentiation, in Michael E. Porter's *Competitive Strategy* and in a *Harvard Business Review* article by William K. Hall, appeared in 1980.[18]

Porter's 1985 book, *Competitive Advantage,* suggested analyzing cost and differentiation via the **value chain**, a template that is reproduced in Exhibit 3.3. Although Porter's value chain bore some resemblance to McKinsey's business system, his discussion of this construct emphasized the importance of regrouping functions into the activities actually performed to produce, market, deliver, and support products, thinking about linkages among activities, and connecting the value chain to the determinants of competitive position in a specific way:

> Competitive advantage cannot be understood by looking at a firm as a whole. It stems from the many discrete activities a firm performs in designing, producing, marketing, delivering, and supporting its product. Each of these activities can contribute to a firm's relative cost position and create a basis for differentiation. The value chain disaggregates a firm into its strategically relevant activities in order to understand the behavior of costs and the existing and potential sources of differentiation.[19]

EXHIBIT 3.3 Value Chain for an Internet Start-Up.

Exhibit 3.3 illustrates the value chain for an Internet start-up that sells and physically distributes music.

Subsequent advances in the integration of cost analysis and differentiation analysis not only disaggregated businesses into activities (or processes) but also split customers into segments based on cost-to-serve as well as customer needs. Such deaveraging of customers was often said to expose situations in which 20 percent of a business's customers accounted for more than 80 percent (or even 100 percent) of its profits.[20] It also suggested new customer segmentation criteria. Thus, starting in the late 1980s, Bain & Company built a thriving "customer retention" practice based on the notion that it generally cost more to capture new customers than to retain existing ones.

Costs Versus Differentiation

Porter and Hall, the first two strategists to write about both cost and differentiation, argued that successful companies usually had to choose to compete *either* on the basis of low costs *or* by differentiating products through quality and performance characteristics. Porter popularized this idea in terms of the **generic strategies** of low cost and differentiation. He also identified a **focus strategy** that cut across the two basic generic strategies (see Exhibit 3.4) and linked these strategy options to his work on industry analysis:

> In some industries, there are no opportunities for focus or differentiation— it's solely a cost game—and this is true in a number of bulk commodities. In other industries, cost is relatively unimportant because of buyer and product characteristics.[21]

These generic strategies appealed to strategists for at least two reasons. First, they captured a common tension between cost and differentiation. A firm must often incur higher costs to deliver a product or service for which customers are willing to pay more. Most customers are willing to pay more for a Toyota automobile than for a Hyundai, for example, but the costs of manufacturing a Toyota are significantly higher

EXHIBIT 3.4   Porter's Generic Strategies.
Source: (Reprinted with the permission of The Free Press, a Division of Simon & Schuster, Inc., from *Competitive Strategy: Techniques for Analyzing Industries and Competitors* by Michael E. Porter. Copyright © 1980, 1998 by The Free Press. All rights reserved.)

than the costs of making a Hyundai. Toyota's higher profit margins derive from the fact that the price premium Toyota can command is greater than the incremental costs associated with its product.

Second, the generic strategies were also appealing because the capabilities, organizational structure, reward system, corporate culture, and leadership style needed to make a low-cost strategy succeed are, at first sight, contrary to those required for differentiation. For the sake of **internal consistency** and to maintain a single-minded purpose, a firm might have to choose to compete either in one way or the other.

The generic strategies nonetheless provoked a vigorous debate among strategists, for both empirical and logical reasons. Empirically, the tension between cost and differentiation does not appear to be absolute. In the 1970s and 1980s, for instance, Japanese manufacturers in a number of industries found that, by reducing defect rates, they could make high-quality products at lower cost. Exhibit 3.5 traces the interplay between cost and differentiation in an expanded treatment of competitive advantage that recognizes the possibility of **dual competitive advantages**.

How common are companies with dual competitive advantages? Porter argues that dual advantages are rare, typically being based on operational differences across firms that are easily copied.[22] Others contend that rejecting the trade-offs between cost and differentiation—replacing trade-offs with "trade-ons"—represents a fundamental way to transform competition in an industry.[23] The debate continues today.

A second challenge to the notion of generic strategies is logical in nature. Although a desire for internal consistency may drive companies to the extremes of low cost and high differentiation, external considerations may pull firms back toward the center. If most customers want neither the simplest nor the most elaborate product, for instance, the most profitable strategy may be to offer a product of intermediate quality and intermediate costs. Consider Zara, the Spanish fashion retailer. Its offerings are not nearly as upmarket as Gucci's or Armani's, although they sometimes share the same look. But Zara *is* a rung above other mass-market fashion retailers: its emphasis on within-season production and trendiness boosts willingness to pay—and production

EXHIBIT 3.5   Interplay between Cost and Differentiation.

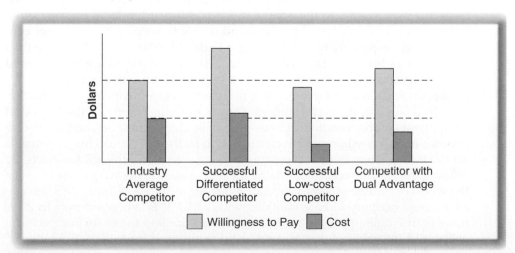

costs as well. Fortunately for Zara, the incremental willingness to pay appears to exceed the incremental costs, making its intermediate position viable.

Strategists have generally stopped being dogmatic about generic strategies of any particular stripe. Instead, they embrace the idea that any analysis of competitive position must consider both relative cost and differentiation and recognize the tension between the two. Positioning, in this view, is or should be about driving the largest possible wedge between cost and differentiation. As differentiation rises, so too does cost in most instances. However, the largest gap between the two need not occur at the extremes of low costs or high price premia. The optimal position, from this perspective, represents a **choice** from a spectrum of trade-offs between cost and differentiation rather than a choice between mutually exclusive generic strategies.[24]

A few examples will help illustrate the richness of positioning possibilities.

- Southwest Airlines has configured itself to focus on budget customers. It has standardized its fleet around fuel-efficient Boeing 737s, concentrates on short-haul point-to-point routes between midsize cities and secondary airports, offers very low ticket prices and no-frills service (no assigned seats, food service, baggage transfer, or connections with other airlines), emphasizes quick turnaround times, and manages to keep its planes in the air one-third longer each day than the average airline. Its stripped-down offering may generate slightly less willingness to pay than the offering of a full-service airline, but it incurs far lower costs than a full-service rival. As a result, Southwest is the only major U.S. airline to have been consistently profitable since deregulation (see Exhibit 3.1), while growing rapidly and maintaining one of the youngest fleets and the lowest debt levels among the majors.

- Accenture is regarded as the leader in information technology (IT) consulting because of its deep experience, reinforced by its research and development, its Knowledge Xchange portal, its stringent hiring and training practices, its close relationships with the CEOs as well as the CIOs of global corporations, and its successful attempts to build its brand. Some of the activities that Accenture undertakes to differentiate itself are clearly costly: R&D and training, for instance, swallow up 5 percent of revenues, even though they have been scaled back in recent years. On the other hand, Accenture often faces no competing bids when it pitches consulting work and is able to keep its revenues per consultant high, especially by maintaining a high utilization rate. This more than compensates for the extra costs it incurs: Accenture has historically earned returns significantly higher than most other large IT services companies.

- Cirque du Soleil is an innovative firm that combines elements of circus and theater. In designing its performances, Cirque excluded many of the high-cost components of the traditional circus—animals, star performers, and three-ring shows—and focused on what it considered to be the three elements responsible for the lasting allure of the circus: the clowns, the tent, and the acrobatic acts. By refining the clowns' acts, glamorizing the tent, and incorporating elements from the world of theater—themes and storylines, for example—Cirque de Soleil created a new category of entertainment with which it is synonymous.[25] In 2006, more than 7 million people paid a total of $620 million to see its live performances, and the value of this privately held firm was estimated at $1.5 billion.[26]

Added Value

In the mid-1990s, Adam M. Brandenburger and Harborne W. Stuart added rigor to the idea of driving the largest possible wedge between costs and differentiation through their characterization of added value.[27] Brandenburger and Stuart considered three-stage vertical chains (suppliers → competitors → buyers) and were precise about the monetary quantities of interest. On the demand side, they mapped differentiation into buyer willingness to pay for products or services; on the supply side, they used the symmetric notion of supplier **opportunity costs** (the smallest amounts that suppliers would accept for the services and **resources** required to produce specific inputs). Given these definitions, the total **value** created by a transaction is the difference between the customer's willingness to pay and the supplier's opportunity cost. The division of this value among the three levels of the vertical chain is, in general, indeterminate. Nevertheless, an upper bound on the value captured by any player is provided by its added value—the maximum value that can be created by all the participants in the vertical chain minus the maximum value that would be created without that particular player.

More precisely, the amount of value that a firm can claim cannot exceed its added value under **unrestricted bargaining**. To see why this constraint applies, assume for a moment that a lucky firm *does* strike a deal that allows it to capture more than its added value. The value left over for the remaining participants is then less than the value that they could generate by arranging a deal among themselves. The remaining participants could, after all, break off and form a separate pact that improves their collective lot. Any deal that grants a firm more than its added value is vulnerable to such breakaway possibilities.

For an illustration of the usefulness of this style of analysis, consider the ill-starred decision in 1986 by the Holland Sweetener Company (HSC) to enter the aspartame industry, then monopolized by NutraSweet.[28] HSC's costs were probably higher, even after its initial capital investment was sunk, than those of NutraSweet because of limited scale and learning. In addition, customers' willingness to pay for HSC's aspartame was probably lower because of NutraSweet's heavy investments in building up its brand identity. HSC decided to enter the market anyway, presumably because the prices that Coca-Cola and PepsiCo were paying NutraSweet were approximately three times as high as HSC's prospective costs.

As things turned out, the big winners from HSC's entry were Coke and Pepsi, which were able to extract much lower prices from NutraSweet. An explanation is suggested in Exhibit 3.6, which graphs in stylized terms the willingness to pay and the relevant post-entry costs. Evidently, HSC's entry depressed NutraSweet's added value (hence the lower prices). HSC, however, could not expect to have added value post-entry (given unrestricted bargaining) because total value created would not be reduced if the firm were to disappear.[29] So HSC would have had to do something more than just jump into this business if it wanted to earn profits from it. One possibility would have been to convince Coke and Pepsi to pay HSC to play up front, instead of relying on their "goodwill" after its entry to amortize its fixed costs.[30] Another approach would have been to communicate that HSC's market-share goals were sufficiently modest that it made no sense for NutraSweet to lower its prices across the board.[31]

Added value is sometimes quantifiable, as was approximately the case in the context of aspartame. Even when it isn't, however, it provides a useful test for judging a

EXHIBIT 3.6   Costs and Willingness to Pay for Aspartame.

firm's strategy: If a firm were to disappear, would someone in its network of suppliers, customers, and complementors miss it? This question is harder edged than older tests in the same vein—come up with a better product (à la Emerson), manage for uniqueness, focus on your distinctive competence, and so on—because it is based on an explicit model of interactions among buyers, suppliers, competitors, and complementors.

The concept of added value also helps tie together intra-industry analysis of competitive advantage and industry-level analysis of average profitability. In an industry with an "unattractive" structure, competitors' added values tend to be low, with exceptions arising only in the case of firms that have managed to create competitive advantages for themselves—that is, driven bigger wedges than most of their competitors between buyers' willingness to pay and costs. In more "attractive" industries, a firm may expect to do better than its competitive advantage alone would guarantee, through two mechanisms. First, the added values of individual competitors tend to be larger than their competitive advantages in such industry environments. Second, some industries seem to make it feasible for competitors to engage in what is politely termed "recognition of mutual dependence" and is less politely described as "tacit collusion" (an important determinant of the degree of rivalry as well as a departure from the assumption of unrestricted bargaining).

A PROCESS FOR ANALYSIS

Having reviewed the development of concepts for competitive positioning, we now discuss a process for linking such concepts to strategic planning and action.[32] How can managers identify opportunities to raise willingness to pay by more than costs or drive down costs without sacrificing too much willingness to pay? Sheer entrepreneurial insight certainly plays a large role in spotting such arbitrage opportunities. Michael Dell, for example, might see that customers are becoming comfortable with computer technology, realize that retail sales channels add more costs than benefits for many customers, and act on his insight to start a direct-to-the-customer computer business.[33] Likewise, a company such as Liz Claiborne might perceive a huge pent-up demand for a collection of medium to high-end work clothes for female professionals.[34] Dumb luck also plays a role. Engineers searching for a coating material for missiles in the 1950s discovered the lubricant WD-40, the sales of which continued to generate a return on equity between 40 and 50 percent four decades later.

Most strategists believe, however, that smart luck beats dumb luck and that analysis can hone insight. To analyze competitive advantage, they typically break a firm down into discrete activities or processes and then examine how each contributes to the firm's relative cost position or comparative willingness to pay.[35] The activities undertaken to design, produce, sell, deliver, and service goods are what ultimately incur costs and generate buyer willingness to pay. Differences across firms in activities—differences in what firms actually do on a day-to-day basis—produce disparities in cost and willingness to pay and hence dictate added value. By analyzing a firm activity by activity, managers can (1) understand why the firm does or does not have added value, (2) spot opportunities to improve its added value, and (3) foresee likely shifts in its added value.

The starting point of positioning analysis is usually to catalog a business's activities. We can often facilitate the task of grouping the myriad activities that a business performs into a limited number of economically meaningful categories by referring to generic templates for activity analysis, such as the ones reproduced in Exhibits 3.2 and 3.3. Porter's value chain, which distinguishes between primary activities that directly generate a product or service and support activities that make the primary activities possible, is particularly helpful in ensuring that one considers a comprehensive array of activities. Generic templates cannot, however, be used blindly for two reasons. First, not all of the activities they identify will be relevant in any given situation. Second, data often come prepackaged so as to favor a particular way of cataloging activities—unless a major effort to "clean up" such data is deemed necessary.

The rest of the analysis usually proceeds in three steps. First, managers examine the costs associated with each activity, using differences in activities to understand how and why their costs differ from those of competitors. Second, they analyze how each activity generates customer willingness to pay, studying differences in activities to see how and why customers are willing to pay more or less for the goods or services of rivals. Finally, managers consider changes in the firm's activities with the objective of identifying changes that will widen the wedge between costs and willingness to pay.

The following subsections discuss these steps in this order, although it is often necessary to iterate back and forth among them in practice. To illustrate their application, we focus on a simple example: the snack cake market in the western part of Canada.[36] Between 1990 and 1995, Little Debbie grew its share of this market from 1 percent to nearly 20 percent. At the same time, Hostess, the maker of such long-time favorites as Twinkies and Devil Dogs, saw its dominant 45 percent share dwindle to 25 percent. An analysis of competitive positioning shows why Little Debbie and Hostess fared so differently and helps suggest a strategy for the latter.

Step 1: Using Activities to Analyze Relative Costs

Typically, competitive cost analysis is the starting point for the strategic analysis of competitive advantage. In pure commodity businesses, such as wheat farming, customers refuse to pay a premium for any company's product. In this type of setting, a low-cost position is the key to added value and competitive advantage. Even in industries that are not pure commodities, however, differences in cost often exert a large influence on differences in profitability.

To begin with our example, in the early 1990s, Hostess's managers struggled to understand why their financial performance was poor and their market share was plummeting. They cataloged the major elements of their value chain and calculated the costs associated with each class of activities. As Exhibit 3.7 shows, although Hostess sold the typical package of snack cakes to retailers for 72¢, raw materials (ingredients and packaging material) accounted for only 18¢ per unit. Operation of automated baking, filling, and packaging production lines (largely depreciation, maintenance, and labor costs) amounted to 15¢. Outbound logistics—delivery of fresh goods directly to convenience stores and supermarkets, and maintenance of shelf space—constituted the largest portion of costs, 26¢. Marketing expenditures on advertising and promotions added another 12¢. Thus, a mere penny remained as profit for Hostess.

After calculating the costs associated with each activity, the managers determined the set of cost drivers associated with each activity, that is, the factors that increase or decrease the cost of an activity. For instance, the Hostess managers realized that the cost of outbound logistics per snack cake fell rapidly as a firm increased its local market share, because delivery costs depended largely on the number of stops that a truck driver had to make. Thus, the larger a firm's market share, the greater the number of snack cakes a driver could deliver per stop. Urban deliveries tended to be more expensive than suburban ones, because city traffic slowed the drivers down. Outbound logistics costs also rose with product variety: the firm's broad product line made it difficult for drivers to restock shelves and remove out-of-date merchandise. Finally, the nature of the product itself affected logistics costs. For instance, snack cakes with more preservatives could be delivered less frequently. Using this information, the managers developed numerical relationships between activity costs and drivers for outbound logistics activities and for the other activities depicted in Exhibit 3.7.

EXHIBIT 3.7   Hostess's Cost Components.

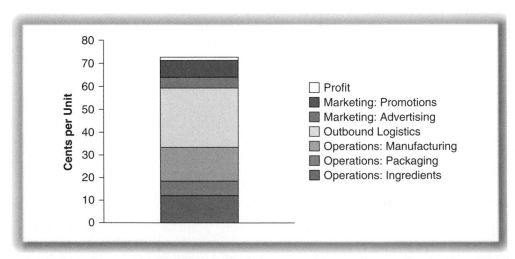

Cost drivers are critical because they allow managers to estimate *competitors'* cost positions. Although one usually cannot observe a competitor's costs directly, it is often possible to study their drivers. Thus, Hostess could observe Little Debbie's market share, the portion of its sales in urban areas, the breadth of its product line, and the ingredients in its products. Using its own costs and the numerical relationships to cost drivers permitted estimation of the competitor's cost position.

The results of the cost analysis were sobering to Hostess's managers. Because Little Debbie used inexpensive raw materials, purchased in bulk, and tapped national-scale economies, its operations costs totaled 21¢, compared with 33¢ for Hostess. Little Debbie packed its product with preservatives so that deliveries could be made less frequently, kept its product line very simple, and benefited from growing market share. Consequently, its logistics costs per unit were less than half those of Hostess. Also, Little Debbie did not run promotions. Altogether, the managers estimated, a package of Little Debbie snack cakes cost only 34¢ to produce, deliver, and market. Exhibit 3.8 illustrates the results of the cost analysis of Hostess and its major competitors. (The comparison with two other major competitors, Ontario Baking and Savory Pastries, was not so discouraging. Indeed, Hostess had a small cost advantage over each.)

This specific example illustrates a number of general points about relative cost analysis:[37]

- Managers often examine *actual* costs—rather than opportunity costs—because data on actual costs are concrete and available. Although the symmetric treatment of suppliers and buyers in the formalization of added value is useful—reminding us that competitive advantage can come from better management of supplier relations rather than solely from a focus on downstream customers—supplier opportunity costs and actual costs are usually assumed to track one another closely. Obviously, this assumption should be relaxed when it does not make sense.
- When reviewing a relative cost analysis, it is important to focus on differences in individual activities, not just differences in total cost. Ontario Baking and Savory Pastries, for instance, had similar total costs per unit. The two firms had

EXHIBIT 3.8   Relative Cost Analysis.

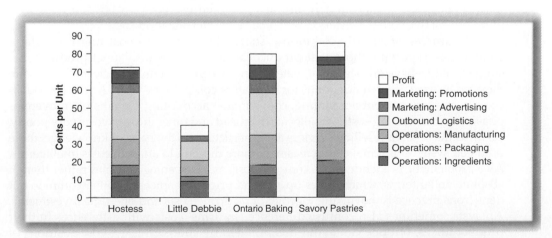

different cost structures, however, and, as we will discuss later, these differences reflected distinct competitive positions.

- Good cost analyses typically focus on a subset of a firm's activities. The cost analysis in Exhibit 3.8, for example, does not cover all the activities in the snack cake value chain. Effective cost analyses usually break out in greatest detail and pay the most attention to cost categories that (1) pick up on significant differences across competitors or **strategic options**, (2) correspond to technically separable activities, or (3) are large enough to influence the overall cost position to a significant extent.
- Activities that account for a larger proportion of costs deserve more in-depth treatment in terms of cost drivers. For instance, the snack cake managers assigned several cost drivers to outbound logistics and explored them in depth. They gave less attention to the drivers of advertising costs. The analysis of any cost category should focus on the drivers that have a major impact on it.
- A cost driver should be modeled only if it is likely to vary across the competitors or in terms of the strategic options that will be considered. In the snack cake example, manufacturing location influenced wages, rates, and, therefore, operational costs. All of the rivals had plants in western Canada, however, and manufacturing elsewhere was not an option because shipping was costly and goods had to be delivered quickly. Consequently, manufacturing location was not considered as a cost driver.
- Finally, because the analysis of relative costs inevitably involves a large number of assumptions, **sensitivity analysis** is crucial. Sensitivity analysis identifies which assumptions really matter and therefore need to be honed. It also tells the analyst how much confidence to have in the results. Under any reasonable variation of the assumptions, Little Debbie had a substantial cost advantage over Hostess.

A number of references discuss cost drivers in greater detail and suggest specific ways to model them numerically.[38] The catalog of potential drivers is long. Many relate to the size of the firm—for example, economies of scale, economies of experience, economies of scope, and capacity utilization. Others relate to differences in firm location, functional policies, timing (e.g., first-mover advantages), institutional factors such as unionization, and government regulations such as tariffs. Differences in the *resources* possessed by a firm may also drive differences in activity costs. A farm with more productive soil, for instance, will incur lower fertilization costs.

A number of pitfalls commonly snare newcomers to cost analysis. Many companies—especially those that produce large quantities of distinct products in a single facility—have grossly inadequate costing systems that must be cleaned up before they can be used as reference points for estimating competitors' costs. As pointed out in courses on management accounting, conventional accounting systems often overemphasize manufacturing costs and allocate overhead and other indirect costs very poorly. As firms move toward selling services and transacting on the basis of knowledge, these outdated systems will make it increasingly more difficult to analyze costs intelligently. Also problematic is a tendency to compare costs as a percentage of sales rather than in absolute dollar terms, which mixes up cost and price differences. Another common but dangerous practice is the mixing together of recurring costs and one-time investments. Analysts sometimes also confuse differences in firms' costs with differences in their product mixes, but one can avoid this problem by comparing the cost positions of comparable products; for example, one should compare Ford's four-cylinder, midsized family sedan to Toyota's four-cylinder, midsized family sedan rather than some imaginary "average" Ford to an "average" Toyota. Finally, a focus on costs should not crowd out consideration of customer's willingness to pay—the topic of the next section.

Step 2: Using Activities to Analyze Relative Willingness to Pay

The activities of a firm do not just generate costs. They also (one hopes) make customers willing to pay for the firm's product or service. Differences in activities account for differences in willingness to pay and subsequently for differences in added value and profitability. In fact, differences in willingness to pay apparently account for more of the variation in profitability observed among competitors than do disparities in cost levels.[39]

Virtually any activity in the value chain can affect customers' willingness to pay for a product.[40] The most obvious effects are those of product design and the manufacturing activities that influence product characteristics—quality, performance, features, aesthetics. For example, consumers pay a premium for New Balance athletic shoes in part because the firm offers durable shoes in hard-to-find sizes. More subtly, a firm can boost willingness to pay through activities associated with sales or delivery—that is, via the ease of purchase, speed of delivery, availability and terms of credit, convenience of the seller, quality of presale advice, and so on. The catalog florist Calyx and Corolla, for instance, can command a premium because it delivers flowers faster and fresher than most of its competitors do.[41] Activities associated with post-sale service or complementary goods—customer training, consulting services, spare parts, product warranties, repair service, compatible products—may also matter. For example, U.S. consumers may hesitate to buy a Fiat automobile because they fear that spare parts and service will be difficult to obtain. Signals conveyed through advertising, packaging, and branding efforts can play a role in determining willingness to pay as well. Nike's advertising and endorsement activities, for instance, affect the premium it commands. Finally, support activities can have a surprisingly large, if indirect, impact on willingness to pay. Thus, the hiring, training, and compensation practices of Nordstrom create a helpful, outgoing sales staff that permits the department store to charge a premium for its clothes.

Ideally, a company would like to have a "willingness-to-pay calculator"—something that indicates how much customers would pay for any combination of activities. For a host of reasons, however, such a calculator usually remains beyond a firm's grasp. In many cases, willingness to pay depends heavily on intangible factors and perceptions that are hard to measure. Moreover, activities can affect willingness to pay in complicated (i.e., nonlinear and nonadditive) ways. And when a business sells to end-users through intermediaries rather than directly, willingness to pay depends on multiple parties.

Lacking a truly accurate calculator, most managers use simplified methods to analyze relative willingness to pay. A typical procedure is as follows. First, managers think carefully about who the *real* buyer is. This determination can be tricky. In the market for snack cakes, for instance, the immediate purchaser is a supermarket or convenience store executive. The ultimate consumer is typically a hungry school-age child. The pivotal decision-maker, however, is probably the parent who chooses among the brands.

Second, managers work to understand what the buyer or buyers want. The snack-cake-buying parent, for example, makes a purchase based on price, brand image, freshness, product variety, and the number of servings per box.[42] The supermarket or convenience store executive selects a snack cake on the basis of trade margins, turnover, reliability of delivery, consumer recognition, merchandising support, and so forth. Marketing courses discuss ways to flush out such customer needs and desires through formal or informal market research.[43] It is important for such research to identify not only what customers *want* but also what they *are willing to pay for.* Moreover, it should reveal the needs that are most important to consumers and determine how they trade them off.

Third, managers assess how successful the firm and its competitors are at ful-filling customer needs. Exhibit 3.9 shows such an analysis for the snack cake market that helps us understand both the statics and the dynamics of the marketplace. Little Debbie stands out on an attribute that customers value highly (low price), while Hostess is not superior on any of the customer needs. This sort of analysis helps explain the large shifts in share observed in the market. Ontario Baking enjoys the best brand image—a position for which it has paid via relatively heavy advertising and promotion. Savory Pastries delivers the freshest product, as reflected in its high manu-facturing and raw materials cost. Further analysis (not carried out in the snack cake example) can actually assign dollar values to the various customer needs. For example, it can estimate how much a customer will pay for a product that is one day fresher.

Fourth, managers relate differences in success in meeting customer needs back to company activities. Savory Pastries' high score on the freshness need, for instance, can be tied directly to specific activities regarding procurement and selection of ingredients, manufacturing, and delivery.

At this point, managers should have a refined idea of how activities translate, through customer needs, into willingness to pay. They should also understand how activities alter costs. Now they are prepared to take the final step—the analysis of dif-ferent strategic options. Before moving on to that step, however, we should highlight some guidelines concerning the analysis of willingness to pay.

A major challenge in analyzing willingness to pay is narrowing the long list of customer needs down to a manageable roster. In general, we can ignore needs that

EXHIBIT 3.9   Relative Success in Satisfying Customer Needs.

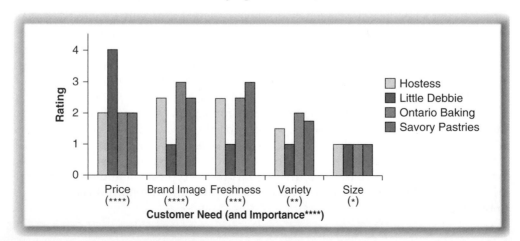

have little bearing on customer choice. Likewise, needs that are equally well satisfied by all current and contemplated products can usually be neglected. If the group of competing products plays a small role in satisfying a need relative to other products outside the group, the need can often be removed from the list as well.

So far, we have treated all customers as identical. In reality, of course, buyers differ in what they want and how badly they want it. Some customers in a bookstore want novels, while others look for business books. (This type of disparity, in which different customers rank products differently, is known as **horizontal differentiation**.) Among those customers who want J. K. Rowling's new *Harry Potter* novel, some will pay for the more expensive hardback edition, while others are content to wait for the less expensive softcover version. (**Vertical differentiation** arises when customers agree on which product is better—the hardback edition, in this example—but differ in how much they will pay for the better product.)

The analysis of willingness to pay becomes trickier, but more interesting, when customers are either horizontally or vertically differentiated. The usual response is segmentation: one first finds clumps of customers who share preferences and then analyzes willingness to pay on a segment-by-segment basis. In our experience, firms that identify segments tend to pinpoint between two and twelve clusters of customers. Diversity in customer needs and ease in customizing the firm's product or service typically increase with the number of segments that the analysis considers. Some observers have even argued that companies should move beyond segmentation to embrace mass **customization**.[44] In this approach, enabled by information and production technologies, companies begin to tailor their products to individual customers. Thus, Blinds To Go receives up to 25,000 custom orders for window blinds and shades per day that it processes within 48 hours. New approaches to customization have enabled the company to build up a business with more than $100 million in revenues and 20 percent net margins.[45]

Finally, we want to emphasize the limits to analyzing willingness to pay. In some settings, it is possible to quantify willingness to pay quite precisely. For example, when a firm provides an industrial good that saves its customers a well-understood amount of money, it is relatively easy to calculate this amount. Calculations become much more difficult, however, when buyer choice includes a large subjective component, when customer tastes are evolving rapidly, and when the benefits that the customer derives from the product are hard to quantify. A wide range of market research techniques— such as surveys, hedonic pricing, attribute ratings, and conjoint analysis—have been designed to overcome such problems. Nevertheless, we remain wary especially when market research asks people to assess their willingness to pay for new products that they have never seen or for the satisfaction of needs that they themselves may not recognize. Fine market research "proved" that telephone answering machines would sell poorly, for instance.[46] In some settings, creative insight may have to replace analysis. In all settings, analysis should serve to hone insight and not to displace it.

Step 3: Exploring Different Strategic Options and Making Choices

The final step in the analysis of cost and willingness to pay involves the search for ways to widen the wedge between the two. To this point, the management team has researched how changes in activities will affect added value. The goal now is to find favorable options. Because the generation of options is ultimately a creative act, it is difficult to lay down many guidelines for it. We can, however, suggest a few patterns from past experience:

1. It is often helpful to distill the essence of what drives each competitor. Little Debbie, for instance, saw that preservatives could substitute for fast delivery. By adding preservatives to its physical product, the company was able to reduce its delivery costs substantially. This approach also reduced customers' willingness to pay, but the reduction was smaller than the corresponding cost savings. Such distillation often suggests new ways to drive wedges between costs and willingness to pay. Savory Pastries, for instance, was tapping a willingness to pay for freshness. The Hostess managers, however, felt that Savory was not exploiting this customer need fully; a product even fresher than what was available from Savory might command a large premium that might serve as the basis for substantial added value.

2. When considering changes in activities, it is crucial to consider competitor reactions. In the snack cake example, Hostess's managers felt that Little Debbie would readily launch a price war against any competitor that tried to match its low-cost, low-price position. They were less concerned about an aggressive response from Savory Pastries, whose managers were distracted by an expansion into a different business. Such reactions and, more generally, notions related to sequencing and dynamics are the topics of Chapter 4.

3. Managers often tend to fixate on a few product characteristics and think too narrowly about benefits to buyers. They rarely consider the full range of ways in which all of their activities can create added value. One way to avoid a narrow focus is to draw out not only one's own value chain but also the value chains of one's customers and suppliers and the linkages between the chains.[47] Such an exercise can highlight ways to reduce buyers' costs, improve buyers' performance, reduce suppliers' costs, or improve suppliers' performance. Some apparel manufacturers, for instance, have found new ways to satisfy department store buyers that have nothing to do with the physical character of the clothes. By shipping clothes on the proper hangers and in certain containers, for example, these manufacturers can greatly reduce the labor and time required to transfer clothes from the department store's loading dock to the sales floor.

4. In rapidly developing markets, it is often valuable to pay special attention to leading-edge customers *if* their demands anticipate the needs of the broader market. Thus, a number of technology companies release test versions of new services to sophisticated users to shake down software and sense the future needs of the wider market.[48] Similarly, underserved customer segments often represent a significant opportunity. And the Southwest example reminds us that overserved customers can offer an opportunity as well.

5. More generally, one of the most potent ways that a firm alters its added value is by adjusting the *scope* of its operations—that is, changing the range of customers it serves or products it offers within an industry.[49] Broad scope in an industry tends to be advantageous when there are significant economies of scale, scope, and learning (including vertical bargaining power based on size), when customers' needs are relatively uniform across market segments, and when it is possible to charge different prices in different segments. Of course, broader is not always

better: there may be diseconomies rather than economies of size, and attempts to serve heterogeneous customers may introduce compromises into a firm's value chain or blur its external or internal message by creating cognitive conflicts in the minds of customers or employees.[50] And even when broader *is* better, there tend to be a variety of ways in which a firm can expand its reach, some of which (such as licensing, franchises, or strategic alliances) fall short of an outright expansion of scope. Chapters 5 through 7 discuss scope-related issues in detail.

6. We have laid out a process in which a management team develops a comprehensive grasp of how its activities affect costs and willingness to pay, and *then* considers options to widen the wedge between the two. In practice, it is often efficient and effective to reverse this process: to start with a set of options, articulate what each option implies for activities, then analyze the impact of each alternative configuration of activities on the wedge between costs and willingness to pay. By reverse-engineering the analyses they do from the options they face, managers can focus on the analyses that truly matter. Of course, this alternative process works best when managers start with a good grasp of the options available to them.

In general, a firm should search through its business system for, and eliminate, activities that generate costs without creating commensurate willingness to pay. It should also search for inexpensive ways to generate additional willingness to pay, at least among a segment of customers.

THE WHOLE VERSUS THE PARTS

The analysis described in the preceding section focuses on decomposing the firm into parts—that is, discrete activities. In the final step of exploring options, however, the management team must work vigilantly to build a vision of the whole. After all, competitive advantage comes from an *integrated set* of choices about activities. A firm whose choices do not fit together well is unlikely to succeed.

The importance of internal consistency can be visualized, once again, in terms of our metaphor of the business landscape. What particularly complicate the search for high ground—or added value—on this landscape are the interactions among choices: production decisions affect marketing choices, distribution choices need to fit with operations decisions, compensation choices influence a whole range of activities, and so forth. Graphically, the interactions make for a **rugged landscape** characterized by lots of local peaks, each of which depicts a coherent bundle of mutually reinforcing choices.[51]

The ruggedness of the business landscape has several vital implications. First, it suggests that incremental analysis and incremental change may not lead an established firm to a new, fundamentally higher position. Rather, the firm may have to consider changing many of its activities in unison to attain a higher peak. To improve its long-run prospects, it may even have to step down and tread through a valley. (Consider the wrenching and far-reaching changes required to turn around IBM, for instance.)

Second, ruggedness implies that more than one internally consistent way to do business often exists within the same industry. Although only a limited number of viable positions are available, more than one high peak usually appears when the interactions among choices are rich. In the retail brokerage business, for instance, both Merrill Lynch and Edward Jones succeeded historically but did so in very different ways. Merrill Lynch operated large offices in major cities, provided access to a full range of securities, advertised nationally, offered in-house investment vehicles, and served corporate clients as well. Edward Jones operated thousands of one-broker offices in rural and suburban areas, handled only conservative securities, marketed its services through door-to-door sales calls, produced none of its own investment vehicles, and focused almost exclusively on individual investors.[52]

Third, the landscape metaphor reminds us that the creation of competitive advantage involves *choice.* In occupying one peak, a firm forgoes an alternative position. Relatedly landscape imagery can be used to visualize the role of competition. There is often more added value to occupying one's own separate peak than from piling on to a heavily populated summit. Claiming a distinctive peak may even insulate a new player in an industry from effective retaliation. Consider how Google entered the market for applications such as word processing and spreadsheet software. Had it simply copied Microsoft's approach of selling packaged software to be installed on individual computers, Google would have faced an unrestrained, aggressive response from Microsoft. Instead, Google adopted an altogether different set of choices—scaled a distinct peak: It made word processing and spreadsheet software available online through a Web browser, with documents stored online, with an emphasis on making documents available to collaborators, and without an upfront payment. To follow Google's distinctive approach, Microsoft would have to forego lucrative sales of its own packaged software, Word and Excel. Moreover, it would have to legitimize a Web-based model of computing in which a user's operating system mattered little—an unattractive move for Microsoft, the world's dominant maker of operating systems. Google's focus on a distinctive peak has muted Microsoft's retaliation. Moreover, its approach toward software applications has reinforced its broader strategy of shifting users from a Microsoft-dominated world in which computer processing power resides mostly on personal computers toward a world of "cloud computing," in which users tap into the processing power of centralized servers via Web browsers. Such "new game" strategies and barriers to effective competitive response are discussed further in Chapters 4 and 5.

Finally, the landscape metaphor provides additional perspective on the techniques for industry analyses that were discussed in Chapter 2. It suggests, at least to us, additional emphasis on deaveraging: somewhat less emphasis on analyzing average industry attractiveness—which might be envisioned as the average height of the landscape above sea level—and more emphasis on understanding the industry features that influence the locations of peaks and troughs in the landscape and their evolution over time. The question of how a competitive advantage or disadvantage—related, respectively, to the height of a peak and the depth of a trough—will evolve over time is the focus of the next two chapters of the book, dynamics.

Summary

The analysis in this chapter helps systematize part of the older SWOT (strengths-weaknesses-opportunities-threats) paradigm for strategic planning because strengths and weaknesses often vary substantially, even among direct competitors. As a result, within-industry differences in performance tend to be significant, and businesses that aim to be very successful must typically position themselves to create competitive advantages within their industries.

Competitive advantage depends on driving a wider wedge between costs and buyers' willingness to pay than one's competitors can. The concept of added value helps integrate considerations of competitive advantage/disadvantage and industry-level conditions into assessments of the likely profitability of individual businesses. A business has added value when the network of customers, suppliers, and complementors in which it operates is better off with it than without it—that is, when the firm offers something unique and valuable in the marketplace.

To achieve a competitive advantage or a higher added value than its rivals, a business must do things differently from them on a day-to-day basis. These differences in activities, and their effects on relative cost position and relative willingness to pay, can be analyzed in detail and used to generate and assess options for creating competitive advantage.

In addition to decomposing the business into activities, however, its managers must also craft a vision of an integrated whole. Much power can be derived, in particular, from positive, mutually reinforcing linkages among activities that make the whole more than the sum of its parts.

Finally, we must emphasize the discussions of positioning risk being static instead of dynamic. Some of this risk flows from the terminology itself. It would probably be better to talk about targeting a path for continuous improvement than to discuss settling into a position for all time. Additionally, positioning has a connotation of choosing from a preset, well-specified set of possibilities, whereas coming up with new positions—fundamentally new ways of competing—can have very high payoffs and therefore demands strategic attention. And perhaps most important, while achieving lower costs or delivering greater benefits than competitors can lead to competitive advantage, how is a competitive advantage—or disadvantage—likely to evolve over time? This question occupies center stage in Chapters 4 and 5, which focus, respectively, on competitive dynamics and evolutionary dynamics.

Glossary

added value
choice
competitive advantage
competitive position
cost analysis
cost drivers
customization
differentiation
dual competitive advantage

focus strategy
generic strategies
horizontal differentiation
internal consistency
opportunity costs
resources
rugged landscape
segmentation
sensitivity analysis

strategic options
trade-offs
unrestricted bargaining
value
value chain
vertical differentiation
willingness to pay

Notes

1. For further discussion of the definition of competitive advantage, see Steven Postrel, "Competitive Advantage: A Synthesis" (paper presented at the Atlanta Competitive Advantage Conference, Atlanta, June 17, 2004).
2. Dean Neese of Marakon/Trinsum deserves our thanks for helping make these data available.
3. Richard P. Rumelt, "How Much Does Industry Matter?" *Strategic Management Journal* 12, no. 3 (March 1991): 167–185, and Anita M. McGahan and Michael E. Porter, "How Much Does

Industry Matter, Really?" *Strategic Management Journal* 18 (July 1997): 15–30.
4. Anita M. McGahan and Michael E. Porter, "The Persistence of Shocks to Profitability: Comparing the Market-Structure and Chicago Views," *Review of Economics and Statistics* 81 (1999): 43–53.
5. Richard E. Caves and Pankaj Ghemawat, "Identifying Mobility Barriers," *Strategic Management Journal* 13 (1992): 1–12; Jan W. Rivkin, "Reconciliable Differences: The

Relationship Between Industry Conditions and Firm Effects," manuscript, Harvard Business School (1997).

6. See, for instance, Pankaj Ghemawat, "The Risk of *Not* Investing in a Recession," *Sloan Management Review* 34, no. 2 (Winter 1993): 51–58, reissued with updated commentary in *Sloan Management Review* 50, no. 3 (Spring 2009): 31–38; or David Rhodes and Daniel Stelter, "Seize Advantage in a Downturn," *Harvard Business Review* 87, no. 2 (February 2009): 31–40.

7. See Michael S. Hunt, "Competition in the Major Home Appliance Industry" (D.B.A. thesis, Harvard University, 1972). Two other dissertations at Harvard—Howard H. Newman, "Strategic Groups and the Structure-Performance Relationship: A Study with Respect to the Chemical Process Industries," and Michael E. Porter, "Retailer Power, Manufacturer Strategy and Performance in Consumer Good Industries"—elaborated and tested the notion of strategic groups. A theoretical foundation for strategic groups was provided by Richard E. Caves and Michael E. Porter, "From Entry Barriers to Mobility Barriers: Conjectural Decisions and Contrived Deterrence to New Competition," *Quarterly Journal of Economics* 91, no. 2 (May 1977): 241–262.

8. See, for instance, Kenneth J. Hatten and Dan E. Schendel, "Heterogeneity within an Industry: Firm Conduct in the U.S. Brewing Industry, 1952–71," *Journal of Industrial Economics* 26, no. 2 (1977): 97–113.

9. This conclusion is based on Pankaj Ghemawat's experience working at BCG (Boston Consulting Group) at the beginning of the 1980s.

10. Michael E. Porter, *Competitive Advantage: Creating and Sustaining Superior Performance* (New York: Free Press, 1985), chap. 2.

11. For a review of activity-based analysis from the perspective of cost accounting, see Robin Cooper and Robert S. Kaplan, "Profit Priorities from Activity-Based Costing," *Harvard Business Review* 69, no. 5 (May–June 1991): 130–135.

12. Adapted from Carter F. Bales, P. C. Chatterjee, Donald J. Gogel and Anupam P. Puri, "Competitive Cost Analysis," McKinsey Staff Paper (January 1980), p. 6.

13. Interestingly, the founders of both Bain and SPA had worked on a BCG study of Texas Instruments that was supposed to have highlighted the problem of shared costs. See Walter Kiechel III, "The Decline of the Experience Curve," *Fortune*, October 5, 1981, p. 139.

14. Quoted in ibid.

15. The term "differentiated" is often misused. When we say that a firm has differentiated itself, we mean that it has boosted the willingness of customers to pay for its output and can command a price premium. We do not mean simply that the company is different from its competitors. Similarly, it is a common error to say that a company has differentiated itself by charging a lower price than its rivals. A firm's choice of price does not affect how much customers are intrinsically willing to pay for a good—except when price conveys information about product quality.

16. Interview with Joseph Bower, April 25, 1997.

17. Interview with Fred Gluck, February 18, 1997.

18. Michael E. Porter, *Competitive Strategy: Techniques for Analyzing Industries and Competitors* (New York: Free Press, 1980), chap. 2; William K. Hall, "Survival Strategies in a Hostile Environment," *Harvard Business Review* 58, no. 5 (September–October 1980): 75.

19. Porter, *Competitive Advantage*, p. 33.

20. Talk by Arnoldo Hax at Massachusetts Institute of Technology, April 29, 1997.

21. Porter, *Competitive Strategy*, pp. 41–44.

22. Ibid., chap. 2. Michael E. Porter, "What Is Strategy?" *Harvard Business Review* 74, no. 6 (November–December 1996): 61–78.

23. Adam M. Brandenburger and Barry J. Nalebuff, *Co-Opetition* (New York: Doubleday, 1996), pp. 127–130.

24. See, for instance, Pankaj Ghemawat, *Commitment: The Dynamic of Strategy* (New York: Free Press, 1991), chap. 4. For some empirical studies that seem to support this conclusion, see Lynn W. Phillips, Dae R. Chang, and Robert D. Buzzell, "Product Quality, Cost Position and Business Performance: A Test of Some Key Hypotheses," *Journal of Marketing* 47, no. 2 (Spring 1983): 26–43; Danny Miller and Peter H. Friesen, "Porter's (1980) Generic Strategies and Performance: An Empirical Examination with American Data. Part I: Testing Porter," *Organization Studies* 7, no. 1 (1986): 37–55.

25. W. Chan Kim and Renée Mauborgne, "Blue Ocean Strategy," *Harvard Business Review* 82, no. 10 (October 2004): 76.

26. "Montreal's 50 Leaders: Guy Laliberté: Shining Star," *Montréal Centre-Ville*, January, 2007 available at http://mtlcentreville.v1.myvirtualpaper.com/magazine/2007072701/?page=24

27. Adam M. Brandenburger and Harborne W. Stuart, Jr., "Value-Based Business Strategy," *Journal of Economics & Management Strategy* 5, no. 1 (1996): 5–24.

28. Adam M. Brandenburger, Maryellen Costello, and Julia Kou, "Bitter Competition: The Holland Sweetener Co. Vs. Nutrasweet (A)" (Harvard Business School Case no. 794-079, Boston, 1993).

29. This conclusion assumes, of course, that NutraSweet would continue to expand its capacity in line with rapidly growing demand—something that might have appeared quite uncertain to HSC. One limiting feature of added value analysis in its current form is that it doesn't allow for informational complexities of this sort, although it may turn out to be generalizable.

30. In the event, HSC was able, later on, to get paid to stay.

31. Such expedients have variously been referred to as "judo economics" and the "puppy-dog ploy." See Judith R. Gelman and Steven C. Salop, "Judo Economics: Capacity Limitation and Coupon Competition," *Bell Journal of Economics* 14, no. 2 (Autumn 1983): 315–325; Drew Fudenberg and Jean Tirole, "The Fat-Cat Effect, the Puppy-Dog Ploy, and the Lean and Hungry Look," *American Economic Review* 74, no. 2 (May 1984): 361–366.

32. This section draws heavily on ideas first developed in Porter, *Competitive Advantage,* especially chaps. 2–4. Also see Ghemawat, *Commitment,* chap. 4.

33. Das Narayandas and V. Kasturi Rangan, "Dell Computer Corp." (Harvard Business School Case no. 596-058, Boston, 1995).

34. Nicolaj Siggelkow, "Change in the Presence of Fit: The Rise, the Fall, and the Renaissance of Liz Claiborne," *Academy of Management Journal* 44, no. 4 (August 2001): 838–857.

35. Porter, *Competitive Advantage,* chaps. 2–4; Porter, "What Is Strategy?"

36. The authors thank Roger Martin, formerly of Monitor Company, for this example. Details about the companies and other items have been altered substantially to protect proprietary information.

37. See Ghemawat, *Commitment,* chap, 4, for a more extensive list of general guidelines.

38. Porter, *Competitive Advantage,* chap. 3; David Besanko, David Dranove, and Mark Shanley, *The Economics of Strategy* (New York: John Wiley, 1996), chap. 13.

39. Richard E. Caves and Pankaj Ghemawat, "Identifying Mobility Barriers," *Strategic Management Journal* 13, no. 1 (January 1992): 1–12. Of course, this general pattern may not hold up in a particular setting.

40. Porter, *Competitive Advantage,* chap. 4; Besanko, Dranove, and Shanley, *The Economics of Strategy,* chap. 13.

41. Walter J. Salmon and David Wylie, "Calyx & Corolla" (Harvard Business School Case no. 592-035, Boston, 1991).

42. We present "low price" as an attribute that buyers seek. This statement should not be misunderstood as meaning that price determines willingness to pay. Rather, price is included as an attribute in surveys of customer needs so that one can calibrate the willingness of customers to pay a price premium for the other attributes in the survey (such as freshness).

43. See, for instance, Philip Kotler, *Marketing Management: Analysis, Planning, Implementation, and Control,* 8th ed. (Englewood Cliffs, N.J.: Prentice-Hall, 1994).

44. B. Joseph Pine II, *Mass Customization: The New Frontier in Business Competition* (Boston: Harvard Business School Press, 1992).

45. Larry Menor and Ken Mark, "Blinds To Go: Invading the Sunshine State" (Richard Ivey School of Business Case no. 901D04, 2001).

46. Oren Harari, "The Myths of Market Research," *Small Business Reports* 19, no. 7 (July 1994): 48–52.

47. Porter, *Competitive Advantage.*

48. Marco Iansiti and Alan MacCormack, "Developing Products on Internet Time," *Harvard Business Review* 75, no. 5 (September–October 1997): 108–117.

49. Scope has a number of dimensions—horizontal, vertical, and geographic—which were discussed in Chapter 2. The discussion here focuses on horizontal and geographic scope. Vertical scope within an industry, which raises a different set of issues, is discussed at greater length in Chapter 5, in the context of holdup. Horizontal scope that stretches across industries and geographic scope that stretches across national borders are discussed, respectively, in Chapters 6 and 7.

50. Porter, "What Is Strategy?"

51. Daniel A. Levinthal, "Adaptation on Rugged Landscapes," *Management Science* 43, no. 7 (July 1997): 934–950; Jan W. Rivkin, "Imitation of Complex Strategies," *Management Science* 46, no. 6 (June 2000): 824–844. The landscape metaphor is derived from evolutionary biology, especially Stuart A. Kauffman, *The Origins of Order: Self-Organization and Selection in Evolution* (New York: Oxford University Press, 1993).

52. Richard Teitelbaum, "The Wal-Mart of Wall Street," *Fortune,* October 13, 1997, pp. 128–130.

Anticipating Competitive Dynamics

Bruno Cassiman and Pankaj Ghemawat

*Know your enemy, know yourself, and you can fight a
hundred battles with no danger of defeat. When you are
ignorant of the enemy but know yourself, your chances of
winning and losing are equal. If you don't know your
enemy or yourself, you are bound to perish in all battles.*

—Sun Tzu, *The Art of War*

Mapping the business landscape and pursuing a peak or advantaged position
on it are necessary but not sufficient for business success over time. Unless a
business can count on all its competitors being inept or inert, it needs to recognize that even as it tries to maximize its own payoffs, competitors may be similarly
engaged, with significant implications for what it ought to do. Interactions with buyers,
suppliers, and other players striving to improve their own positions can have similar
implications. Strategists are confronted, therefore, with the challenge of anticipating
important interactions with all these types of players. That said, most of the discussion
in this chapter will focus on anticipating interactions with direct competitors, although
many of the same principles apply to dynamics involving other types of players. The
chapter is intended to provide a better answer to the broad question: "What moves or
strategy shifts are identifiable competitors—or significant others—likely to make?"

The conceptual importance of such dynamic thinking is clear but managers
still do not seem to engage in much of it. According to one survey, for example, while
70–75 percent say they consider competitors in making product and pricing decisions,
only 8 percent report thinking through *future* competitive behavior in the context of
product introductions and 15 percent in the context of price changes.[1] The most

commonly cited reason is that the real world is far too uncertain for such anticipations to be folded into action. But even if this were correct—and there is no evidence that it is—competitors do not stand still, which suggests that ignoring their moves is *not* the answer. It seems better to make use of the available techniques for anticipating competitive dynamics, even though they are partial, on the grounds that in the land of the blind, the one-eyed can be king. And if competitors also display strategic foresight, failing to look ahead is even more likely to be problematic. Put differently, the advantages of anticipating competitive dynamics do *not* depend on those advantages being widely overlooked—a theme that we return to toward the end of this chapter.

The obvious way to analyze competitive dynamics among a few players is to use detailed information about them to forecast what they will do, with a view to preventing moves that harm one's interests while promoting those that help. This requires managers to put themselves in the shoes of other players instead of viewing competitive situations solely from the egocentric perspectives of their own businesses. This chapter focuses, for the most part, on two broad approaches that have been proposed for this purpose: **game theory** and **competitor profiling**. Game theory takes an economic perspective by focusing on incentives under conditions of competition, whereas competitor profiling takes more of a behavioral perspective by trying to identify competitors' predispositions. Put differently, game theory tries to answer this question by focusing on what competitors *should* do under some (reasonable) baseline assumptions, while competitor profiling brings in considerations related to what competitors really want, what they might—given their beliefs—see themselves doing to accomplish their goals, and what they have tended to do historically in similar situations.

While they obviously involve very different kinds of analysis, the two approaches are generally complementary: game theory is worth considering unless you expect your competitors to succumb to their predispositions with probability one, and competitor profiling unless you expect them to be economically rational all the time.

The chapter begins by using detailed examples to illustrate how to apply game theory to the challenge of forecasting what competitors will do and how to fold the insights afforded into one's own choice of strategy. It then discusses competitor profiling and ways of melding it with game-theoretic analysis to increase predictive power by decreasing the uncertainty surrounding competitive dynamics. The chapter concludes by proposing some ways of opening up the process of analyzing competitive dynamics in order to enhance its applicability to real-world situations involving a small number of identifiable players. Situations in which players are numerous or faceless are addressed in Chapter 5.

SIMPLE GAMES

Game theory is the study of interactions among players whose **payoffs** depend on one another's choices and who recognize the interdependence in trying to maximize their respective payoffs. The historical development of game theory is outlined in Exhibit 4.1. In this chapter, we focus on *non-cooperative* game theory.[2] A real-world application, to a pricing study for a major pharmaceutical company, will illustrate the building blocks of the theory, its perspective on interactions, and guidelines for applying it.

Consider, therefore, the pharmaceutical case study. One of the most profitable products sold by the incumbent (hereinafter, *I*) dominated its category but faced the

EXHIBIT 4.1   The Historical Development of Game Theory.

The Jewish Talmud supplies what is apparently the first application of game theory when it discusses the death of a man whose estate is too small to cover the (different) payments specified in separate marriage contracts with his three wives. The Talmud recommends apparently different ways of dividing the estate—depending on the size of the shortfall—that have perplexed scholars for the better part of two millennia. Two decades ago, game-theorists realized that the Talmudic solutions correspond to a particular solution concept from **coalitional** (or what is sometimes known as **cooperative) game theory**.[3]

The notion of coalitional games was formalized in 1944 in the celebrated book *The Theory of Games and Economic Behavior* by John von Neumann, a mathematician also regarded as the father of modern computing, and Oskar Morgenstern, an economist.[4] Von Neumann and Morgenstern also advanced the analysis of **strategic** or **non-cooperative game theory**—the theory of moves (as opposed to combinations) that has attracted more attention in the formal development of game theory. Specifically, they supplied a general theory of the purely adversarial case of two-person **zero-sum games**, in which one player's gain is exactly equal to the other player's loss (e.g., chess).

Very few games in business—or elsewhere—seem to be strictly zero-sum, however, so modern game theory has come to focus on nonzero-sum or, more accurately, **nonconstant-sum games** that afford opportunities for cooperation as well as competition. While we still lack a general theory of such games, a broad organizing principle is provided by the work of mathematician John F. Nash, who won the Nobel Prize in economics in 1994 and whose life was exposed to a broader audience in the book/movie *A Beautiful Mind*. In two papers published in 1950 and 1951, Nash proved the existence of a strategic equilibrium for non-cooperative games—the **Nash equilibrium**—and proposed that cooperative games be studied by reducing them to non-cooperative form.[5]

Subsequent theorizing has focused mainly on refinements and extensions of the Nash equilibrium. Thus, Nash's co-winners of the Nobel Prize, for work done in the 1960s, were Reinhard Selten, who suggested using the refinement of subgame perfection (backward induction or looking ahead and reasoning back) to select from the frequently large number of Nash equilibria in dynamic games, and John C. Harsanyi, who developed the concept of a Bayesian Nash Equilibrium for games with incomplete information, thereby laying the foundations for a vast literature on signaling and, more broadly, information economics.[6]

Harsanyi and Selten also collaborated in the 1980s to develop a general theory of equilibrium selection in non-cooperative games.[7] Work on this broad topic continues. In addition, recent years have seen an interest in learning, evolutionary processes, and the incorporation of behavioral and experimental insights into game theory, as discussed in the latter sections of this chapter.

introduction of a substitute product by a major competitor. As the late mover, the entrant (hereinafter, *E*) was expected to launch its own product at a very large discount. It was uncertain exactly how low *E*'s launch price would be, and whether *I* should reduce its own prices in anticipation or reaction. The cash flows involved were large enough, however, to compel careful analysis of *I*'s options.

The analysis began with the specification of the **players** in the game: *I* and *E*. In fact, there were a total of five players, including *E*, in the product category. However, two players were excluded from the analysis on the grounds that they were marginal players without a discernible impact on market outcomes, and a third, because unique product characteristics insulated it from interactions between *I* and *E*. The broader point here is that the number of players can sometimes also be reduced—and game-theoretic analysis greatly simplified—by aggregating players with similar economics and objectives.

The second step in applying game theory to this problem involved specifying the possible actions of both players: their **strategies**.[8] The final analysis focused on four strategies involving different levels of discounting for E's launch price and four strategies for I's own (relative) price.[9] The latter were bounded by the alternatives of holding I's price level constant (which would entail a very large price advantage for E) and neutralizing E's price advantage.

As a third step, payoffs were assigned to the different combinations of strategies for I and E. This involved, first of all, assessing the two players' objectives: was E likely to maximize profits, or would it emphasize growth and gaining share? (Based on considerations discussed in the section on competitor profiling, E was deemed to be a profit-maximizer, like I.) Next, players' objectives were mapped into numerical payoffs associated with each outcome from each player's perspective. Experts gauged the market shares implied by each pair of prices and combined them with knowledge of I's costs and estimates of E's to calculate the net present values (NPVs) of the two products for the two players. (The estimation of product market payoffs is illustrated in more detail in the next section, in the context of a different example.) Note that if E had been deemed to be a sales maximizer, for example, further analysis might have been couched in terms of NPVs for I and some measure based on sales revenue for E.

Because there were only two players, the information on their strategies and payoffs could conveniently be captured in a **payoff matrix**, as depicted in Exhibit 4.2, with the rows representing I's strategic options, and the columns E's. The first entry in each cell corresponds to the estimated NPV, in millions of dollars, for I, and the second entry to the estimated NPV for E. Within this set-up, firms select strategies—rows or columns—and not individual outcomes, as in particular cells. It is in this sense that payoff matrices capture the dependence of each firm's payoff on its rival's strategy as well as its own.

Use of the payoff matrix to derive strategic recommendations required additional specification of the **rules** of the game. In this game, as in many others, the timing of moves was critical: were the players making **simultaneous moves**, or was

EXHIBIT 4.2   The Pharmaceutical Payoff Matrix (millions of dollars for *I, E*).[i]

Incumbent's (*I*'s) Price	Entrant's (*E*'s) Price			
	Very Low	Low	Moderate	High
No Price Change	358,190	507,168	585,129	624,116 (Business Plan)
Large Price Advantage for *E*	418,163	507,168	Infeasible	Infeasible
Small Price Advantage for *E*	454,155 (Nash Equilibrium)	511,138	636,126	Infeasible
Neutralization of *E*'s Price Advantage	428,50	504,124	585,129	669,128

[i]The first entry in each cell of the payoff matrix corresponds to the estimated NPV, in millions of dollars, for I, and the second entry to the estimated NPV for E. Three of the cells were ruled out as arithmetically infeasible. Also note that in the last column, payoffs are higher in the bottom cell because it assumes price increases in excess of inflation, unlike the top cell.

there more of a dynamic structure to their interactions? As a first cut, it was assumed that *I* and *E* would simultaneously and independently choose their pricing strategies—although *I* revisited the assumption of simultaneity as opposed to sequentiality later in the analytical process.

This structure provided the basis for *I* to think through its interactions with *E* *before* *E* entered the market. In particular, the payoff matrix raised questions about the business plan that firm *I* had in place, which assumed that *E* would launch with a high price and that *I* would not change its price at all. The matrix suggested that this "base case" was unlikely to materialize. Specifically, if *E* launched with a high price, leaving its price unchanged was *not* a **best response** for *I*. Instead, *I* could, by neutralizing *E*'s price advantage, achieve an expected NPV of $669 million versus $624 million in the base case. Similarly, the base case also failed to coincide with a best response for *E*. With no price change anticipated on the part of *I*, *E* had a large incentive to charge a very low price instead and achieve an estimated NPV of $190 million versus $116 million in the base case. Since neither firm would actually be using its best response to the other, this base case is a highly implausible outcome.

The game-theoretic idea of eliminating **dominated strategies**, strategies that do not maximize payoffs for one player no matter what the other player does, was used to further narrow the possible outcomes. In the payoff matrix in Exhibit 4.2, charging a high price was a dominated strategy for *E* because, irrespective of *I*'s choice among the rows, *E* would do better, in terms of its choice among the columns, by setting a moderate price instead of a high price. The implication is that *I* should not expect *E* to set a high price—in other words, that it should eliminate the outcomes in the last column of the payoff matrix from the space of possibilities.

The idea of **iterated elimination** of dominated strategies was used to push farther: once the high launch-price strategy was ruled out for *E*, *I*'s dominant strategy, the strategy that maximized *I*'s payoffs no matter what *E* did, became leaving *E* a small price advantage regardless of *E*'s choice among the three remaining columns. Note the effect that this has of narrowing the space of possible outcomes to the first three cells in the third row, in which *I* concedes *E* a small price advantage.

Pressing forward, another round of iterated elimination of dominated strategies, this time from *E*'s perspective, pinned down—in this case, but not necessarily in general—a unique **Nash equilibrium**: a strategy pair, one for each player, from which neither player had an incentive to deviate unilaterally. Note that if *E* launched with a very low price, and *I* conceded *E* a small price advantage, each player would be playing its best response to the other's strategy: given *E*'s strategy, *I* would have no incentive to change its own strategy, and vice versa. As a result, unilateral deviations from this strategy pair would be costly—imposing a penalty of at least $17 million in NPV terms on each player (= $155 million – $138 million for *E*), up to nearly $100 million on *I* ($454 million – $358 million for *I*), depending on the precise deviation.

But this was the only Nash equilibrium that did not make it very enticing from the perspective of *I*'s managers, some of whom saw it as threatening to their careers. After all, compared to the (admittedly unrealistic) business plan, it implied payoffs only 73 percent of the NPV of $624 million in the original business plan—which despite its unrealism, remained an aspiration. In response, *I*'s managers began to explore whether they could make a **credible precommitment** to a (relative) pricing strategy for their product before *E* committed to a particular launch price. If feasible, this would effectively change the rules of the game from simultaneous moves to sequential moves, with

I becoming the **first mover**. In particular, a credible precommitment to ceding a large price advantage to *E* might, given the payoff matrix, persuade *E* to launch with a low price rather than a very low price (*E* stood to make a bit more money with the former strategy) and increase *I*'s payoffs from 73 percent of the original business plan to 81 percent (i.e., to $507 million). And a credible precommitment to neutralizing *E*'s price advantage was even more likely to persuade *E* not to launch with a very low price: it stood to make an extra $73–$79 million, more than doubling its NPV, by entering with a low-to-moderate price instead. In particular, if *I* committed to neutralize and *E* entered with a low price, *I*'s payoffs would approximate 81 percent of the original business plan; if *E* entered with a moderate price instead, *I*'s payoffs would increase by another $80 million, to 94 percent of the original business plan. Subsequent work centered on the legal and practical feasibility of credibly communicating the "neutralization strategy" to *E*.

In addition to illustrating the payoffs from modeling business situations as simple, quantifiable games, the pharmaceutical example highlights the broader contribution that game theory can make to business strategy: game theory forced *I*'s managers to think about the launch price that would maximize *E*'s profits—*E*'s best response—instead of fixating on the high launch price that they would have *liked* to see *E* set. And *E*, too, stood to gain from thinking through *I*'s best response—that is, recognizing that *I* might react to *E*'s entry instead of leaving its price unchanged. In effect, each firm had to derive a **reaction function** identifying its rival's best responses to different pricing choices that it might make. Such reaction functions, by themselves, offer useful insights into competitors' incentives. In particular, if one player is able to move first, as *I* aspired to do by the end of the study, it can try to maximize its payoffs by selecting the point that it prefers off its rival's reaction function instead of waiting for things to settle down at an intersection of the reaction functions of *I* and *E* respectively—the predicted outcome of a simultaneous move game. The next section focuses on such explicitly **dynamic games**.

DYNAMIC GAMES

Strategic decision-making takes place over time, not once for all time. Game theory also lets us structure and study strategic interactions over time, as dynamic games with multiple moves over time, as uncertainty about competitor behavior or other elements of the environment is progressively resolved. While the dynamics complicate matters—by requiring strategies that consider different actions over time and also key off updated information—the game-theoretic concepts discussed in the previous section *can* be extended to more explicit dynamic competitive interactions. This dynamic extension is essential to studying such issues as timing advantages, credible threats and promises, and the implications of commitment or irreversibility for strategy.

We illustrate the application of game theory to a dynamic context with a second detailed example. Our discussion of it begins by defining the structure of the dynamic game and the interactions between the players. We then attach payoffs to the possible outcomes to the game and characterize the equilibrium outcome. We also discuss how this structure can be used to understand the impact of environmental changes on the players and even to help players attempt to change the game. The specific application is to the "Sirius Content" game within the U.S. market for satellite radio: Sirius's decision about whether to ramp up investment in acquiring content to overcome XM's early lead.[10] The broader intent is to illustrate the application of game theory to competitive dynamics without insisting on impossible amounts of information or advanced math.

Structuring the Game

In 1997, the FCC auctioned off the digital audio radio service spectrum, and Sirius and XM Radio each obtained renewable licenses, paying $80–$90 million apiece. Sirius launched three satellites costing more than $1 billion in 2000, and XM two satellites, costing about $900 million, in 2001. Both players also began signing up automobile manufacturers to pre-install satellite radio receivers in new cars: both expected that by 2006, growth would be driven by such pre-installations and "conversion" (i.e., actual subscription) rates of over 50 percent. XM, assisted by lower-priced models, also entered in partnerships (through sales of shares) with General Motors (GM) and Honda and eventually signed exclusive deals covering 60 percent of U.S. production with GM, Honda, and Toyota, while Sirius signed agreements with Ford, Volkswagen (VW), DaimlerChrysler, and BMW. In November 2001, XM was the first to go on air. We begin by focusing on this point in time, with Sirius yet to go on air and considering whether to ramp up investment in acquiring content to overcome XM's lead.

Up until this point, most analysts covering the development of the satellite radio market had assumed that satellite radio content would be much cheaper than that of satellite TV, where programming costs absorbed 35–45 percent of revenues. Specifically, many assumed that in satellite radio, programming costs would be close to the classical broadcast radio model and would mostly be accounted for by music royalties that added up to 6–7 percent of revenues. But content escalation was a strategy alternative that may allow a firm to expand total volume and its share of it—especially among the after-market segment of potential "switchers." This segment is of particular interest since major car manufacturers were locked in through long-term contracts, and further competition to pre-install hardware was likely to be limited.

The first step in applying game-theoretic reasoning to these events is to specify the structure of the game. A **game tree** provides a representation that is useful in this regard. (This, like the matrix representation in the preceding section, is simply a visual aid to better understand the structure of the game and play it more effectively.) Node 1 in the game tree in Exhibit 4.3 focuses on Sirius's choice between escalating investment by acquiring its own content or following the classical broadcast radio model of licensing content and paying royalties. Note the simplification of what is in reality a continuum of choices into just two options (one of which is the estimation of the present value, at decision time of the escalated investments in content that Sirius actually chose to undertake). This simplification illustrates the broader principle of crystallizing what is usually an infinite number of possible futures into a limited number of scenarios, selected to be interestingly different, and are then analyzed in some depth.

Once Sirius has made its choice on the decision to escalate investment in content, XM can observe it and decide if it should also escalate its own investments (nodes 2 and 3 in Exhibit 4.3). Note, again, the simplification of having two options. This implies four possible product-market outcomes.

Estimating Payoffs

While drawing a game tree helps clarify the structure of moves and countermoves, "solving" it game-theoretically also requires that payoffs be attached to the possible outcomes. The numbers at the (right-hand) end of the game tree in Exhibit 4.3 are estimates of the net present values (NPVs), at decision time, of the product-market

EXHIBIT 4.3   The Sirius-XM Satellite Radio Game: Present Values of Expected Operating Profits ($ millions).

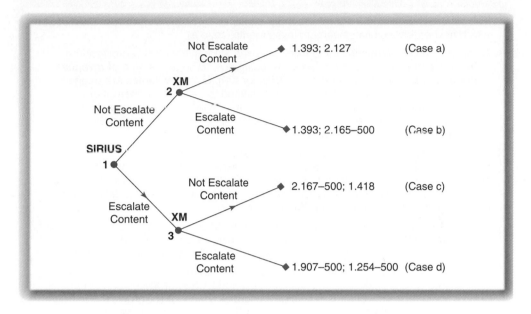

payoffs for the two players (in each case, the first NPV is for Sirius and the second for XM). More specifically, the NPV estimates are gross payoffs of (i.e., do not net out) the costs already sunk into satellites, licenses, and establishing a business infrastructure.

The specific assumptions underlying the estimated NPVs in Exhibit 4.3 are summarized in Exhibit 4.4. Here it is useful to discuss some of the underlying principles. Remember that NPVs are evaluated by applying a discount rate to a stream of estimated cash flows. While finance focuses on the denominator of the analysis, that is, the discount rate, strategy helps with the numerator, which consists of the cash flow estimates themselves. Specifically, it helps calibrate the two components of value, margins and volume.

One *could* imagine average long-run margins in satellite radio ranging from zero (if cut-throat competition collapsed prices to marginal costs) to the profit-maximizing level that a monopolist would select. From the standpoint of the Sirius content game, assuming average product-market margins of (close to) zero if one or more players escalates content investment is not very interesting: in such a world, escalation would not make sense because it would not begin to pay off. We find it more interesting to assume that margins may drop as a result of content escalation–as the bar for ongoing expenditures on content is raised—but do not vanish, at least not when measured in terms of EBITDA (earnings before interest, taxes, depreciation, and amortization). This assumption also fits with large switching costs for subscribers due to incompatible hardware: despite aggressive competition to build market share in the industry's growth phase, maturity should be expected to lead to more relaxed product market competition with a shift in focus toward milking largely distinct customer bases.

In regard to volume, we calibrate the long-run effects of Sirius and XM's content-related choices in terms of the total number of subscribers to U.S. satellite radio in

EXHIBIT 4.4   Sirius versus XM in Satellite Radio: Product-Market Payoffs.

The payoffs in Exhibit 4.3 are most simply explained by beginning with the case in which neither firm escalates content investments (case a).

Case a: EBITDA (earnings before interest, taxes, depreciation and amortization) margins are predicted, based on analysts' estimates, to be about 40% of revenues in this base case (42% for Sirius and 40.5% for XM). Overall volumes are pegged at 15 million subscribers by 2010 and are assumed to grow at 3% thereafter (a steady-state growth rate that also applies to the other cases discussed below). The total subscriber base is assumed to be split 60:40 between XM and Sirius since XM leads in going on air and in appeal to auto manufacturers.

Case b: If XM escalates content investments after Sirius chooses not to, EBITDA margins drop for XM as content becomes more expensive and margins are taken to be 26.5% for XM and 42% for Sirius. In terms of volumes, the total subscriber base in 2010 grows to 20 million as a result of better content and increased advertising by XM and is split 70:30 between XM and Sirius.

Case c: If Sirius escalates content investments but XM chooses not to, EBITDA margins are taken to be 28% for Sirius and 40.5% for XM. In terms of volumes, the total subscriber base in 2010 grows to 20 million and is split 70:30 between Sirius and XM.

Case d: If Sirius escalates content investments and XM reacts by doing so as well, EBITDA margins are taken to be 23% for Sirius and 21.5% for XM as content prices are bid up. In terms of volumes, the total subscriber base in 2010 grows to 25 million and is split 60:40 between Sirius and XM (with Sirius assumed to have an edge on the grounds that as first-mover, it should be able to cherrypick better content).

The payoffs at the tips of the game tree represent the (forward-looking) net present values or NPVs at the end of 2001 of the two businesses. More specifically, the EBITDA margin in 2010 is extended into perpetuity, volume is assumed to grow at 3%, and a discount factor of 12.5% (based on the capital asset pricing model with a risk-free interest rate around 5% in 2001 and a historical beta for these firms of about 1.5) is applied to discount both companies' EBITDA streams back to end-2001. Also note that these NPVs are gross of incremental investments in content escalation, which are specified separately in the cases where one or both firms decide to engage in such escalation. To simplify matters, let us assume that a company deciding to escalate in content acquisition is investing about $500 million *more* in terms of end-of-2001 NPV over the ramp-up period (the amount that Sirius actually ended up spending).

For example, the NPV of the business for Sirius when both players escalate content investments (case d) is $1.4 billion, based on a terminal value of $5.5 billion in 2010. In this case the market is assumed to reach 25 million subscribers by 2010 and Sirius has a 60% market share. The corresponding numbers for XM Radio are an NPV of $754 million in 2001 based on a terminal value of $3.6 billion.

2010 and summarize Sirius and XM's relative appeal to new subscribers in terms of shares of that total volume. Our specific assumptions about overall long-run volume are significantly closer to how the subscriber base has actually evolved than to the much higher forecasts bandied about by industry analysts at the time—even though they hadn't thought through the option of escalating investment in content.

This long-run scenario is actually tacked onto a period of investment in and build up of the market between 2002 and 2010 and steady-state competition (subject to a modest growth rate) thereafter. To keep the analysis tractable, we model the effects of increasing the investment in programming content during the 2002–2010 period in terms of a different steady-state payoff that is reflected in the terminal value. As a result, the only difference during the ramp-up period between the strategy options is related to the investment in programming content. The broader strategic principle here is that an alternative to modeling the evolution of margins and volumes in detail year by year, is to pick a **reference horizon** by which things are assumed to reach a steady state and interpolate between here and there.

Solving the Game: Equilibrium

After setting up the (highly simplified) structure of the game and estimating payoffs for the possible outcomes (Exhibit 4.3), we can solve it using the cardinal principle of dynamic game theory: **look ahead and reason back**.

First, look ahead at the possible responses of XM to an investment decision by Sirius (nodes 2 and 3). If Sirius escalates in content, XM can decide to respond in kind by escalating content investment or continue along the "normal" programming trajectory (Node 3). The first option has an NPV in 2001 of $754 million ($1,254 − $500) and the latter of $1,418 million. Clearly, XM should opt for the latter if Node 3 is reached. And if Sirius decides not to escalate content investments, XM faces a similar decision problem (Node 2). Escalation by XM has an expected NPV of $1,665 million while not escalating content investments yields returns of $2,127 million. Again XM has little incentive to escalate content investment and therefore, not doing so is its **dominant strategy**. In the game tree, we indicate with an arrow the option that XM is predicted to select at each of nodes 2 and 3.

Next, reason back in an attempt to anticipate what Sirius will do (Node 1). If Sirius escalates content investments, it should not, based on the reasoning above, expect XM not to follow, and should therefore expect an NPV of $1,667 million ($2,167 − $500). Alternatively, Sirius can decide not to escalate content investments, anticipating that XM will also not escalate as well, implying an NPV for Sirius of $1,393 million. Given these expected payoffs, Sirius should opt for content escalation. Once again, the game tree indicates with an arrow the option Sirius is expected to select at Node 1.

The key insight from the game is that Sirius has more incentive to engage in content escalation, both because Sirius needs to come from behind as XM already launched commercially and because XM's incentive to escalate is muted if Sirius moves first to lock up the best programming. Sirius is therefore predicted to escalate, and XM not to follow. This predicted outcome coincides broadly with what has actually happened in the U.S. market for satellite radio. Both companies started signing important deals for sports, music, and talk radio content. However, Sirius was the one that seriously increased investments, to a level in excess of $100 per subscriber in the peak year of 2006 (representing more than half a billion dollars in absolute terms and 82 percent of Sirius's revenues that year), while XM's expenditure levels stayed close to $20 per subscriber. NASCAR auto racing provided one example: a five-year deal for $15 million with XM was followed by a five-year deal for $107 million with Sirius. Sirius's five-year, $500 million contract with "shock jock" talk radio host, Howard Stern, was another. The week it was announced, Sirius's shares jumped by 18 percent and XM shares dropped by 9 percent. Overall, in terms of numbers of subscribers, Sirius did start at a disadvantage by being later to go on air but made up ground by adding subscribers faster without triggering a matching response by XM.

Leveraging the Game

The game-theoretic apparatus developed so far can easily be adapted to address a broader range of problems. Consider some of the possibilities:

- *Varying the assumptions.* The characterization of the equilibrium outcome in the previous subsection embodied some specific assumptions, for example, steady-state volume and when it would be achieved. If steady-state volume were much higher—in line with analysts' forecasts rather than reality—or achieved by, say, 2006 instead of 2010, the basic conclusion that Sirius should escalate continues to hold. The point of more general interest is that the game-theoretic apparatus developed in this section provides a (somewhat) flexible structure for thinking about a broader range of problems than the one analyzed above.

- *Reasoning farther back.* Another way to extend the structure developed above is to embed it in a more extended game that goes farther back in time, that is, to use it for the "look ahead" part of applying "look ahead and reason back" to the extended game. For instance, extend the Sirius content game backwards, to firms' prior decisions to enter the market, with XM the more plausible first-mover and Sirius making its decision knowing that it will be part of a duopoly if it does enter. Adding on the content "subgame" analyzed above, Sirius's billion-plus dollar entry cost is rationalizable (in present value terms) if Sirius can count on escalating content without being matched—but perhaps not otherwise.[11] So, predicting the outcome to the content subgame could have helped with Sirius's even more momentous initial decision about whether to enter the market as a duopolist. And, the extension to include entry as well as content decisions also illustrates the point that when looking at decisions across multiple variables, variables whose values can only be changed in the long run should be modeled, in a tree-like representation, as being chosen before variables whose values can be changed in the short run.

- *Changing the game.* In early 2007, after extended speculation, XM and Sirius announced that they were entering a merger of equals. Approval was obtained in 2008 from the U.S. Justice Department and the Federal Communications Commission. A benign interpretation is that with a smaller market than expected and higher content costs, monopoly had become essential to economize on equipment development, advertising, and content. A cynical interpretation is that merger was planned early on: that the second mover entered to claim a share of the merged monopoly rather than to compete. Either way, the merger clearly goes beyond the game tree in Exhibit 4.3, reminding us that care in setting up and solving game trees is ideally a complement to rather than a substitute for creativity in thinking about changing the game—a topic to which we return in the section after the next one. For now, simply note that game theory is somewhat helpful in this regard as well: it tells us that games of chicken—games where players stake out an unprofitable position in the hope that the other players will exit, leaving it with a profitable monopoly—are particularly dangerous games to play and that it therefore makes sense to look particularly hard for ways to get out of them.[12]

- *Allowing for uncertainty.* The flexibility of the structure also allows the injection of fundamental uncertainty into the analysis. Thus, after the Sirius XM merger was finally approved, the global downturn led to a collapse in the auto industry—and in the demand for satellite radio. As a result, Sirius XM was forced to sell off a 40 percent stake in the company to Liberty Media in early 2009 in exchange for a $530 million loan. Uncertainty about demand could have been added explicitly to the structure developed above by thinking of "Nature" as the third player in the Sirius content game, with an independent influence on whether demand was high or low. This is a reminder, of course, that the quality of game-theoretic insights is dependent on the appropriateness of the setup and the quality of the information plugged into it.

COMPETITOR PROFILING

So far, we have focused on interactions among players who see the business landscape in the same way and relentlessly maximize their expected net present values. While these are attractive baseline assumptions, we can obtain additional insights by relaxing them. Competitors may not be out to maximize firm value, or they may hold different beliefs about the (shifting) business landscape or may behave in ways that have a hard-wired component, reflecting **inertia** rather than purposeful choice. Attempts to predict their behavior should take such possibilities into account.

Thus, when deciding what to do in satellite radio, Sirius should have paid attention not only to value-maximizing courses of action for XM Radio but also to XM's noneconomic predispositions. While XM was—like Sirius—a new company rather than one with a long track record, some of its predispositions were evident early on. In particular, XM's top management team, including its head of content, mostly had backgrounds in telecommunications and traditional radio and TV broadcasting which, especially in the United States, had tended to focus on technological platforms or channels rather than on the content transmitted through them. The background of Sirius's top management team was more balanced across channels and content. One might expect this difference to make XM more likely to compete as a traditional radio broadcaster (based largely on licensed music) and Sirius more likely to come up with a new game strategy with more of a focus on content. This reinforces the conclusions derived from the game-theoretic analysis in the previous section in this particular case. But alignment between such behavioral predispositions and the pure economic incentives that game theory focuses on cannot, in general, be assumed. Instead, behavioral predispositions and their effects warrant additional analysis.

Competitor profiling systematizes such analysis. It uses an in-depth examination of competitors' **goals**, **beliefs**, and **routines** to address questions concerning

- What competitors really want
- How they might see themselves as pursuing their goals
- What they have tended to do historically

Exhibit 4.5 lists some of the elements of the goals-beliefs-routines framework. Compared to the formal apparatus of game theory, it clearly has a miscellaneous character. Instead of running through each of the elements of the framework, we will focus on discussing its basic logic in a way that emphasizes piercing the veil of what competitors say about themselves to uncover what really drives them, and to understand, in particular, the role of their top management.

The importance of thinking through a competitor's goals is directly related to the scope for deliberate departures from firm value maximization. Such departures

EXHIBIT 4.5 Framework for Competitor Profiling.

Questions	What do competitors really want?	How do competitors see themselves as pursuing their goals?	What have competitors actually tended to do historically?
Components	**Goals,** Stated and Latent	**Beliefs,** Explicit and Tacit	**Routines** and other Sources of Inertia
Markers of Importance	–Organizational Charter/ Ownership/Governance Structure *(Scope for Deliberate Departures from Value-Maximization)*	–Ambiguity/Divergence –Embeddedness *(Differences in Mental Models and Their Implications)*	–Size/Maturity/Complexity/ Bureaucratization/Thick Culture/ Insularity/Poor Information/ Continuity at the Top *(Inertia Indicators)*
Top Management	–Compensation/Incentives –Clout/Credibility/Reputation –Superordinate Goals/Intrinsic Commitment –Emotions	–Life Experiences –About Management Tools/Practices/Principles –Consultants/Advisors –Role Models/Analogies	–Sunk Cost Fallacy –Self-Justification –Focus on Confirmatory Evidence –Advocacy instead of Inquiry
Businesses/ Segments	–Business/Segment Mix –Status of/Linkages across Businesses/Segments	–About Profit Pools/ Industry Evolution –About Cross-Business/Segment Scope Economies/Diseconomies	–Patterns in Choice of Scope –Endowment Effects/Organizational Attachments –Aversion/Dead Zones/ Blind Spots
	–Type of Competitive Advantage –Share/Rank in Terms of Sales, Assets or Profits –Relative Price	–About Relative Costs/ Willingness-to-Pay –About Drivers: Scale etc. –About Competitor Behavior	–Illusion of Control –Groupthink –Politics –Coalitions/Deadlocks
Strategies	–Capability Development Intent	–About Key Capabilities/ Competences (Activities/Functions/Processes) –About Improvement Possibilities	–Capability/Competency Traps
Performance	–Profitability: ROS/ROA/ROE/ ROCEÉ –Growth: Revenue vs. Volume –Risk/Aggressiveness/ Inter-temporal Tradeoffs –Social/Noneconomic Goals	–About Financial Markets and Capital Costs –About Sources and Uses of Funds –About Risk and Its Management –About Nonmarket Opportunities/ Threats	–Satisfactory/Slowly Declining Performance –Resistance to Reducing Growth Targets (Hysteresis) –Loss-Aversion: Losses that loom larger than gains –Past Social/Noneconomic Commitments

(Left margin vertical letters spelling ELEMENTS: E L E M E N T S) may reflect an organization's charter (e.g., public enterprise, nonprofit), ownership structure (e.g., family-owned and -oriented), or **agency problems**, with managers pursuing personal goals at the expense of firm value. When there *are* agency problems, top managers tend to be the ones who matter the most in determining the direction of the departure from firm value-maximization. It is useful to recognize that their motivations are often complex: purely self-serving behavior, while perhaps more in evidence than pure saintliness, is far from universal. At an organizational level, attention may also usefully be paid to a corporation's desired portfolio of businesses/segments, to the competitive position and other operating or competitive goals it is pursuing within a business, and to its stated financial targets. (Public companies' statements about financial goals are more believable than many other promises they might make because of pressure from investors to deliver on them.)

Beliefs represent the second component of the framework for competitor profiling. The importance of thinking through a competitor's beliefs rests on room to see the world in different ways because of either the inherent **ambiguity** of a situation or **embedded beliefs** that are so deeply or broadly held that do not change much with new information. It is often useful to try to synthesize differences in beliefs into different **mental models**: semi-permanent, simple, and often partly subliminal maps of the world that guide choices. (Of course, if beliefs are too incoherent to lend themselves to such a synthesis, that is of interest as well.) Competitors' top managers provide, once again, a very good pool in which to fish for insights into beliefs as well as to seek to pin down overall mental models.

The importance of thinking through the final component of the competitor profiling framework, competitor's routines, is contingent on the possibility that the competitor's behavior may not be entirely purposeful even in relation to its true goals and beliefs. Philip Selznick started this line of analysis nearly 50 years ago by proposing that "Commitments to ways of acting and responding are built into the organization."[13] In other words, organizations exhibit inertial tendencies, numerous markers of the importance of which are listed in Exhibit 4.5. The precise mechanisms underlying inertia are diverse, encompassing not only the (active but "mindless") routines evoked by Selznick but also passivity/inactivity and systematic **biases**, individual and group-level, that are observed even when choices *are* made mindfully.[14] These myriad individual mechanisms make the broader point that a competitor's past routines may have considerable power to predict its future behavior.

One way to grasp the overall goals-beliefs-routines framework for competitor profiling as well as its individual elements is to apply it to an organization that you have worked for or otherwise know well. Another approach, pursued here, is to use a relatively detailed example—based on a consulting study—to illustrate the application of the framework.

An Application: Accenture's India Strategy

The process and content of competitor profiling will be illustrated with the example of Accenture, an information technology (IT) consulting, software services, and business process outsourcing (BPO) firm.[15] The analysis was undertaken for a major Indian software services firm in 2003. It focused on reports that Accenture would begin to make large BPO-related investments in India. If Accenture was serious, it could seriously affect Indian software firms that still mostly arbitraged the cost differences between software professionals in India and in developed countries.

Too much information was available on Accenture for it all to be reviewed. So, in keeping with the principles for gathering information listed under Step 1 in Chapter 2, the analysis began with a deep dive into the SEC (U.S. Securities and Exchange Commission) filings and analysts' reports. Other sources, including private ones such as customers and former employees of Accenture, industry observers, and the client, were used to fill out the picture.

Accenture's strategic intent was analyzed with a modified version of the goals-beliefs-routines framework: given the interest in figuring out whether the company was serious about a strategy shift, the analysis emphasized changes, particularly in beliefs and routines, rather than continuity. But to begin with goals, BPO had already contributed significantly to Accenture's growth after the technology bubble burst and IT consulting slumped, and management had publicly pinned hopes for satisfying future revenue growth goals on it. So the commitment to BPO itself was relatively clear.

There was, however, the question of how committed Accenture was to India as a platform for its BPO business. Accenture's announced strategy cast India as the anchor of a new offering that Accenture had traditionally turned up its nose at: a "lift & drop" offering that would relocate work without any consulting or transformation. This change could be related to Accenture's mental model of its businesses as a pecking order, with IT consulting ranking highest in terms of strategic value for clients (and margins and stickiness for Accenture), and lift & drop the lowest (see Exhibit 4.6). Accenture had managed to establish leadership in IT consulting and systems integration without getting into lift & drop. But the emphasis on BPO as the growth driver focused attention on a business much closer to lift & drop. As a senior manager pointed out, "We cannot ignore the needs of nine out of ten clients. If we don't give them a solution that meets their needs, they will go to the Indians. If they go

EXHIBIT 4.6   Accenture's Business Hierarchy.

to the Indians, we will be shut out of any high-value work that comes along in the future." Based on such reasoning, Accenture apparently decided to offer lift & drop out of India as a loss leader instead of simply trying to sell clients on work with more of a consulting component. It clearly held stronger *beliefs* than a few years earlier about the importance of BPO, of having an Indian component to a BPO offshoring story, and of countering the long-run threat posed by Indian software competitors.

Given what a departure the lift & drop offering was for Accenture, it also made sense to look for evidence of *changes in routines* rather than of their continuity to see whether the new offering might actually get off the ground. Commitment to the new direction seemed to have been cemented by a management shake-up in spring 2003, in which nearly one-half of Accenture's leadership team was replaced (although skeptics had not been entirely sidelined). Since then, there had been numerous initiatives to build up the Indian operations. Thus, three of the eight BPO lines had been moved to India, with promises that more would follow, and the Financial Services business had agreed to spearhead the shift of work there. It was apparently also decided that all large outsourcing contracts would have an Indian component. Marketing pitches began to emphasize Accenture's Indian initiative and were supplemented with new sales and marketing training materials designed to increase internal awareness. In October 2003, management announced that 4,500 consultants and 1,700 partners had been trained with the new materials. So, while the focus on India was recent, it had considerable momentum.

The implications for the Indian software firm that was the client were crystallized by a point that Accenture executives had made to outsiders (including a client executive): by investing in India, Accenture would not only cut its costs but decrease Indian competitors' margins as well. More specifically, reports circulated that Accenture would let its Indian operations price at (operating) cost for at least their first two or three years. Such reports could not be completely verified, but they seemed worth taking seriously, because they fit with the loss-leader positioning of lift & drop within Accenture and also helped explain its extremely aggressive bidding in some recent head-to-head encounters with Indian competitors.

Assuming that Accenture would enter in a big way and would price at operating cost sounded some alarms at the client organization. Given its initial operating margins of 30 percent, head-to-head competition with Accenture pricing at cost could—even if Accenture were not differentiated—wipe out all or one-half of the initial margin, depending on whether Accenture's cost disadvantage was 0 percent or 20 percent. If Accenture enjoyed a sustainable price premium because of its differentiation as described in the preceding chapter, then that made matters even worse from the client's perspective, as did the likelihood that large-scale foreign entry would push up the costs of Indian software personnel. As a result, the analysis received considerable attention—especially since Accenture has indeed built up its Indian operations, to the point where they already employ 20 percent of its worldwide workforce—more than any other country, including the United States—and continues to grow rapidly.

Integration

Game theory and competitor profiling embody not only different styles of analysis but also different behavioral assumptions. Game theory, as discussed above, generally assumes symmetric value-maximization, similar beliefs, and zero inertia or routinized behavior. Competitor profiling relaxes these (reasonable) baseline assumptions by bringing in considerations related to what competitors really want, what they might—given their beliefs—see themselves doing to accomplish their goals, and what they have tended to do historically in similar situations. How should we think about the relationship between game-theoretic effects and the kinds of considerations flagged by competitor profiling?

It is useful to begin by noting that the broader assumptions about goals, beliefs, and routines brought up by competitor profiling can, in fact, be accommodated within the formal structure of game theory—so that there is no fundamental incompatibility.[16] This is clearest with regard to goals other than value-maximization. Thus, if Sirius thought, say, that XM was maximizing revenues rather than profits, it could replace the (present values of) profits for XM in Exhibit 4.3 with revenues and then proceed to solve the game exactly the same way as before. Differences in beliefs have been analyzed extensively by game theorists in the decade since John C. Harsanyi developed his theory of games of incomplete information. In particular, there is a large body of literature on information signaling and information jamming, as discussed briefly below. And finally, routines can also be embedded into game-theoretic models in the form of preprogrammed behavior in certain situations or by certain types of players—the focus of considerable research in evolutionary game theory, for example.[17]

We can go even further: competitor profiling is not only conceptually consistent with game-theoretic analysis but is complementary to it. As a purely statistical matter, predictive power should not go down as a result of considering both kinds of analyses rather than just one. And in fact, it will often go up rather than remain unchanged. Recognizing as much is the pragmatic way of resolving the feud about whether organizations are rational or irrational.

That is the conceptual logic for integrating insights from game theory and competitor profiling. How is integration actually to be achieved? It is sometimes possible—but not always advisable—to seek to boil considerations of both sorts down to a quantitative common denominator. Even when complete quantification is not feasible, however, things remain simple if game theory and competitor profiling point in the same broad direction, as in the discussion above of how the backgrounds of XM's and Sirius's top management reinforced the prediction from the game-theoretic analysis. There is no integration challenge here.

Cases in which the effects predicted by competitor profiling and game theory do not line up neatly with each other *and* cannot be compared quantitatively are much more difficult. One approach is to quantify what one can of the competitor's perceived value from doing one thing as opposed to another, and then implicitly weigh the results of the quantitative comparison against the qualitative differences it might perceive among strategic options. The logic is that understanding the economic cost of satisfying a noneconomic predisposition is helpful in deciding whether it will be satisfied or not. A useful practical device in this context, as Benjamin Franklin pointed out more than 200 years ago, is to draw up a balance sheet of pros and cons:

> When these difficult Cases occur . . . [I] divide half a Sheet of Paper by a Line into two Columns, writing over the one *Pro,* and over the other *Con.* Then, during three or four Days Consideration, I put down under the different Heads short Hints of the different Motives that at different Times occur to me for or against the Measure. . . . And tho' the Weight of Reasons

cannot be taken with the Precision of Algebraic Quantities, yet when each is thus considered separately and comparatively, and the whole lies before me, I think I can judge better, and am less likely to make a rash Step.[18]

Finally, the kind of integration that is probably most important is not between different types of analysis but between analysis and action. The follow-up to the competitor profile on Accenture may help make this point more vividly than an abstract discussion. The client's senior management team discussed the threat from Accenture's Indian initiative at a day-long workshop. Both adaptation by the client to large-scale entry by Accenture and how, if at all, the client might shape those entry plans were of interest. As a result, "loose bricks" in Accenture's strategy and possible disadvantages vis-à-vis the client (e.g., the liabilities of foreignness or newness, lack of focus, mixed motives, limited internal commitment, etc.) had to be examined along with its advantages. Additionally, some weight had to be attached to preserving industry structure as well as to improving relative position, compelling consideration of cooperative as well as competitive approaches. Certain avenues of action seemed worth exploring irrespective of the approach adopted for dealing with Accenture: rethinking the supply side to keep costs under control, broadening the marketing pitch by placing more emphasis on nonprice dimensions, and increasing cross-selling. The detailed analysis of Accenture was specifically helpful in this regard because it afforded insights into relationship marketing, which was an area that had proven challenging for the client. And finally, given the perceived utility of the analysis and the areas that it identified as worth monitoring, the client decided to set up a competitor intelligence system to track Accenture and other competitors continuously as opposed to sporadically.

OPENING UP THE ANALYTICAL PROCESS

The first three sections of this chapter implied a specific process for analysis:

- Start with the decision at stake and identify the players whose actions/reactions matter for the focal firm's payoffs
- Understand the other players' objectives and beliefs, and explore what they are likely to do or not do on past form
- Pick the best of one's own strategic options based on predictions about where things are likely to settle down given these assessments of competitors' actions/reactions

In addition, the preceding section broadened the bases of the analysis by looking beyond economic incentives to competitors' goals, beliefs, and routines.

A further broadening is suggested by the fact that classical game theory presupposes a "closed world" in which it is possible both to prepare a complete list of possible states, strategies, payoffs and probabilities and to rule out unforeseen contingencies.[19] The real world, however, is "open"—and therefore too complex to consider exhaustively. Recognition of this reality suggests room for creativity in coming up with strategic options and applying a broader range of modes of analysis to them. So the first and second principles below can be seen as reformulating the first two bulletpoints from the list immediately above in ways that are more "open-minded." The third principle is meant to help keep the analysis manageable—and enhance the likelihood of useful action—in the face of all this opening up.

Principle 1. Think Broadly about the Set of Strategic Options

The first two sections of this chapter, in particular, assumed choice from a predetermined set of strategic options—that is, they assumed a closed world. But in an open world, being creative in coming up with the strategic options to be evaluated is often a premium. Creativity can never completely be systematized, but both game-theoretic thinking and competitor profiling can help enrich the set of strategic options considered. Consider both types of analysis in turn, starting with the large body of literature on the business applications of game theory.

VARIABLES   Game-theoretic models now span a very broad array of variables: see Exhibit 4.7 for a (partial) list of fifty. Checklists of this sort can help a company consider more of the relevant competitive variables than it otherwise might.

ASYMMETRIES   Game theory identifies the effects of various **asymmetries**—most often leaders versus followers, incumbents versus entrants, or others related to size—on interactions across a broad array of strategic variables. It may thereby help surface nonobvious options for developing or unwinding such asymmetries. For example, game-theoretic models suggest that, as demand declines in capacity-driven industries, small players should at least consider hanging on and forcing larger players to shoulder most of the early capacity reductions—an outcome that, while counterintuitive, describes the Nash equilibrium.[20]

COMMITMENT POSTURES   In addition to emphasizing long-run **commitments** or choices about variables that are hard to reverse and can change the terms of subsequent competitive (sub)games, game theory offers various typologies of commitment postures. For example, depending on the circumstances, it can make sense to behave like a "Top Dog" to force rivals to retreat, like a "Fat Cat" to make them less aggressive as well, or like a "Puppy Dog" to convince larger rivals not to act aggressively. These generic postures can be helpful in devising new strategic options; and so can the underlying distinction between **strategic substitutes**, for which the best response to more aggressive play by one player is less aggressive play by its rivals, and **strategic complements**, for which aggression is met with aggression.[21] Note that the specificity of competitor profiling helps pin down whether strategic substitution or strategic complementarity is likely, making up for some of the fragility of inferences based on pure economics.

INFORMATION   In addition to recognizing the possibility of asymmetric information, game theory places considerable emphasis on bluffs, feints, and, more generally, strategic misrepresentation or concealment of **information**. Such initiatives often seem important to the pursuit of strategic purpose even when they are not the main course.

Competitor profiling can also help generate new options and variations on existing ones in some of the same ways. An in-depth analysis of competitors may highlight additional **variables** that the competitor is leveraging that the company doing the analysis is not. It can shed more light on critical asymmetries: both where the competitor is vulnerable or sensitive ("loose bricks") and where it is strong

EXHIBIT 4.7 Fifty Varieties of Game-Theoretic Modeling.

General/Competitive Positioning
Vertical Differentiation
Market Share/Leadership
Investment/Disinvestment in Resources, Capabilities
Raising Rivals' Costs/Reducing Rivals' Willingness-to-Pay
Signaling/Signal-Jamming

Customer/Business Scope
Customer Selection/Horizontal Differentiation
Multimarket Contact and Tacit Collusion
Strategic Substitutes versus Complements
Vertical Integration and Foreclosure

Firm Organization and Infrastructure
Organizational Structure
Centralization/Decentralization
Accounting Systems
Incentive Systems
Flow of Internal Communications
Disclosure/Public Relations
Government Lobbying

Product Positioning/Scope
Product Attributes (Quality, Durability, etc.)
Product Line
Product Variety
Product Integrality vs. Modularity
Provision of Complements

Sales and Marketing
Product Pricing
Price Discrimination/Volume Discounts
Most Favored Nation Clauses
Branding (e.g., Product vs. Umbrella)
Advertising
Couponing
Sampling
Warranties/Service Agreements
Locations
Sales Force/Service Structure
Distributor Relationships
Vertical Restraints
Slotting Allowances
Retailer Information Exchange

Procurement/Input Markets
Financial Leverage and Debt
Input Pricing/Contracting
Supplier Relationships

Operations
Quantities versus Prices
Capacity Expansion
Learning Curves
Flexibility
Inventories
Backlogs

Technology Development
Product Innovation
Process Innovation
Technology Races
Standards/Platform Competition
Innovation versus Imitation
Correlated vs. Uncorrelated Strategies
Patenting
Licensing, Contracting, etc.

*This list of 50 dimensions/lines of analysis in the game-theoretic modeling of business competition is meant to be illustrative rather than exhaustive and focuses on modeling activities in industrial organization (IO) economics and in marketing. While many models along these lines are unidimensional, some do look at interactions across different dimensions, further enriching the palette. Detailed textbook treatments of many of the types of models/issues listed can be found in Tirole, Cabral and McAfee.[22] Also note that given the focus on IO, the list of internal and nonmarket issues under Firm Organization and Infrastructure is particularly abbreviated: such issues are addressed at great length by other branches of economics (which supply most of the game-theoretic treatments) as well as by other disciplines.

("foundations"). And as mentioned above, it helps with the articulation and evaluation of a range of *commitment postures* by helping answer the following questions:

- What kinds of commitments will provoke the greatest and most effective retaliation by the competitor (hot buttons)?
- What will evoke the most cooperative response?
- What commitments will the competitor have the most trouble matching (because of goals, beliefs, and routines as well as capabilities)?
- What future moves or strategy shifts is the competitor likely to make, and to what effect? Can they and should they be influenced?

And finally, competitor profiling can trigger new thinking by challenging the information or mental models of the company doing the analysis. For this and other purposes, it can even be helpful to commission a competitor profile of one's own company from the outside.

Of course, game theory and competitor profiling are not the only ways of enriching the set of options considered. Other ways of stretching strategic thinking include the following:

- *Scope changes.* Broadening and shifting the scope of the strategic scanning effort can help put one in the shoes of players other than direct competitors, direct attention to weak signals from the periphery, and foster thinking across multiple businesses or geographies through questions such as "Where else would this work?"
- *Shifts in perspective.* Strategic thinking can often be stretched even further through radical shifts in perspective. Ways of inducing such shifts include thinking about how one might solve a particular problem if starting afresh or, if money were no object, identifying the unwritten rules that drive the industry and competitor behavior and trying to break them, emphasizing threats (e.g., via devils' advocates or worst-case scenarios) as well as opportunities in order to increase receptivity to change, and following outside-in paths—from possible answers to the issues facing a business that they might address, as well as inside-outside paths—from issues to answers.[23] It is also helpful to bring a "can change" attitude to bear on the status quo by asking yourself "Why not?"[24]
- *Organizational enablers.* A final way to stretch thinking about strategic options involves moving beyond the "one big brain" model of strategic innovation by exploiting what we know about creativity. Recommendations include brainstorming (but with some structure), cultivating open-mindedness, risk taking, and a commitment to learning; emphasizing rich information flows; countering known biases (e.g., the "not invented here" syndrome); and continuously revitalizing, challenging, and even unsettling the organization. Of course, organizational attributes along these dimensions affect the evaluation of new options as well as their generation.

Principle 2. Augment the Toolkit for Dynamic Analysis

The preceding sections focused on game theory and competitor profiling as ways of anticipating competitive dynamics. However, in a complex, open world, it makes sense to supplement them with insights from other tools for dynamic analysis. We shall simply mention some of these alternate possibilities and refer the interested reader to more elaborate treatments to each of them.[25] One alternative, already discussed at some length in Chapter 2 of this book, is provided by **structural analysis**, particularly analysis of the effects of the sorts of long-run dynamics laid out in Exhibits 2.8 and 2.9. A specific line of development that is especially worth citing in a dynamic context is **scenario analysis**, which uses structural reasoning to build distinct but internally consistent representations of the future of an industry (or company or technology).[26]

Simulation represents a tried-and-tested technique for dynamic analysis about which there seems to be some fresh excitement. For example, simulations of concentrated, capacity-driven industries facing rapid growth in demand consistently indicate a tendency toward overexpansion.[27] A bonus, proponents argue, is that building and running such simulations actually helps correct flaws in mental models (in this case, misperceptions of feedback, among others) as well as offers insight into the consequences if they go uncorrected.

Wargaming and roleplaying represents another established approach to sorting through competitive dynamics that rubs shoulder with but is less rigidly structured than simulations and in which unforeseen contingencies and actions represent a real possibility as a result. This approach actually spans a number of subapproaches that can be arrayed in terms of the extent to which they incorporate the specifics of the situation into which insight is being sought. At one extreme, there are the "massively multiplayer online role-playing games" which, despite unfolding in virtual worlds, may help sharpen dynamic decision-making and other leadership skills in the real world of business.[28] Roleplaying games that involve team effort to accumulate resources (e.g., Eve Online) or orchestrate supply chains or demand (e.g., Star Wars Galaxies) seem to be of particularly direct interest in this regard.

At the other extreme, there are wargames that actually attempt to capture much of the complexity and richness of specific real world situations. A particularly high-stakes example is cited by retired General Anthony Zinni, former commander of U.S. Central Command (CENTCOM), with military responsibility for the Middle East, East Africa and Central Asia:[29]

> I decided to organize a "war game" that presented several post-Saddam Iraq scenarios. The game—called "Desert Crossing"—was conducted in the Washington, D.C., area late in 1999 at Booz Allen, the contractor; experts from all the relevant branches of government took part. The scenarios looked closely at humanitarian, security, political, economic, and other reconstruction issues. We looked at food, clean water, electricity, refugees, Shia versus Sunnis, Kurds versus the other Iraqis, Turks versus Kurds, and the power vacuum that would surely follow the collapse of the regime (since Saddam had pretty successfully eliminated any local opposition). We looked at all the problems the United States faces in 2003 trying to rebuild Iraq. And when it was over, I was starting to get a good sense of their enormous scope and to recognize how massive the reconstruction job would be. Desert Crossing gave us the ammunition we needed to define the post-Saddam problem.

An impressive achievement—or it would have been if the insights had actually been applied. According to Zinni, who retired in 2000, "As far as I can tell, the plan was pigeonholed. And by the time Iraqi Freedom [the invasion of Iraq in 2003] rolled around, nobody in CENTCOM had ever heard of it. There's no longer any corporate memory of it." Plugging this and other tools for dynamic analysis into organizations in a way that actually enhances the likelihood of action is discussed briefly under the next principle.

To round out the discussion of this principle, there is the possibility of **market testing** or, more broadly, taking actions in the real world, as opposed to in some simplified representation of it, in order to generate real data. Particularly when implementation is staggered (e.g., across distinct geographic submarkets) or sequenced for other reasons, there is the possibility of learning about competitive dynamics by looking, for instance, at the pattern of actions and responses in the first few submarkets entered and making adjustments in the course of a **sequenced rollout**. On the other hand, learning by doing of this sort is costly, both in direct operating terms and, for instance, in terms of what it may disclose about one's own plans.

Consider, for example, the cookie wars of the 1980s when Nabisco's dominance was challenged by the introduction of Grandma's cookies by Frito-Lay and Duncan Hines by Procter & Gamble. Based on their results in their test markets (Kansas City in both cases), these entrants apparently caught Nabisco unprepared. However, given the constraints on their manufacturing capacities and their narrow product scope, Nabisco managed to counterattack in time by repositioning all its existing lines of cookies and launching a new one; using its superior scale and profitability to launch aggressive advertising, promotion, and trade programs; and bolstering its direct-to-store-door distribution system. In retrospect, while Frito-Lay and Procter & Gamble both learned a lot from their test marketing, Nabisco learned more—or at least enough to hang on to its dominance.

To summarize, as we move from scenario analysis and simulation toward wargaming and testing, we move from relatively schematic modes of representing the world toward more realistic ones and from offline/off-the-shelf modes of learning toward online/experiential learning. But the prejudice that this represents some sort of progression should be resisted: the cookie war example reminds us that taking the most "real" approach is not always a good idea. Rather, the choice of which tools to apply will depend on the industry and company context, as discussed next.

Principle 3. Match the Analytics to the Industry and Company Context

The first two principles suggested, respectively, many sources of new ideas and additional tools for dynamic analysis. But given the risk of analysis-paralysis, it is also important to be able to narrow down this many possibilities. The third principle emphasizes an obvious way of doing so: by matching the analytics to the industry and company context. An emphasis on matching meshes well with the conclusions from more than two decades of game-theoretic modeling: precise conclusions from models of interactions depend on, and are often very sensitive to, the details of the context. Matching also helps build a bridge between analysis and action.

Consider first how the industry context helps guide choices from the menus of possibilities provided by Principles 1 and 2. In regard to Principle 1, industry attributes, such as whether an industry is intensive in labor, physical capital, marketing, or R&D, help delimit the variables, asymmetries, commitments, and even communication strategies that are likely to be of most interest in a particular case. And as far as Principle 2 is concerned, the most important effect of industry context operates through the number (and size distribution) of competitors in an industry. Game theory and competitor profiling, in particular, tend to have a comparative advantage under conditions of industry concentration.

Turn next to the company context. This obviously conditions where a company falls along some of the dimensions discussed under Principle 1, as well as the directions that it might (realistically) pursue. Less obviously, it also affects the usefulness of the various tools for dynamic analysis discussed under Principle 2 and in the preceding sections. Very large efficiency gaps among competitors sometimes limit the value of thinking through their interactions strategically, as opposed to purely on the basis of relative efficiency. More broadly, companies are not always as receptive to offline learning from relatively abstract representations of the world (e.g., classical game theory or simulations) as they are to more textured representations or online/experiential learning (e.g., competitor profiling or wargaming). It is usually better to acknowledge and, if possible, take advantage of variations in a company's cultural receptivity to different analytical tools than to ignore them.

It is interesting to juxtapose these possibilities against actual practice. Interviews in 2007 with thought leaders at three of the four largest management consulting firms about their clients indicated very limited usage of game-theoretic thinking and mixed assessments of the other tools for dynamic analysis discussed in this chapter. The few users of game theory seem to be large firms that also use other sophisticated analytical techniques and tend to cluster in certain industries (e.g., pharmaceuticals and telecom services). Such sophisticates offer the most immediate prospects for incorporating game-theoretic modeling and the other more abstract dynamic tools discussed in this chapter into strategic decision making. Without such sophistication, it generally makes more sense to treat game theory, in particular, as a source of insights and analogies than as a basis for serious modeling.

How long is this state of affairs likely to persist? There is often a pointed subtext to this question: If game theory and the other tools discussed above are so potentially valuable, why haven't they caught on more quickly? There are at least three possible types of responses.

First, the S-shaped curves, described in the context of product substitution in Chapter 2 and also used to study the diffusion of ideas, are known to be prone to long, slow take-offs. Thus, even simpler tools that have diffused widely (e.g., discounted cash-flow analysis) took decades to move from the classroom to the executive suite.

Second, several dynamics seem to favor the diffusion of dynamic tools: developments in computer technology and pedagogy as well as in the tools themselves, the cumulation of examples and expertise in academia and consulting, and greater general visibility, as exemplified by the Economics Nobel Prizes given in1994 and 2005 to game theorists, and *A Beautiful Mind*, the book and film about one of them.

Third, a more fundamental force for the diffusion of dynamic tools is related to the observation that *thinking through actions and responses is, in a sense, a dominant strategy*. The incentives to use the tools and approaches discussed in this chapter, and in Chapter 5, to sharpen thinking dynamically do *not* depend on their not being widely grasped or adopted. In fact, strategic complementarities seem more likely than substitution: as more competitors apply such tools to strategy, not doing so may become even more costly.

Summary

The analysis in this chapter has added a dynamic dimension to the discussion of competitive advantage and added value in Chapter 3 by examining ways of anticipating how interactions among small numbers of players will unfold. Its range of coverage can be summarized in terms of a few recommendations. Always start with a sense of relative competitive position, the general attractiveness of the industry environment, and the trends to which it is subjected to. Based on this understanding, try to anticipate the moves that competitors might initiate as well as how they might react to moves that you make. Anticipation typically requires integrated analysis of competitors' economic incentives and noneconomic predispositions, with game theory shedding light on the benchmark case of firms as symmetric economic maximizers, and competitor profiling adding texture in terms of their noneconomic predispositions. And both help overcome egocentric biases. Finally, because analysis without action is not very valuable, explicitly think through bridges to action by reflecting on the industry and company context *before* making basic choices about which analytical tools to employ and how to apply them.

In terms of the domain of coverage, this chapter focused on the dynamics of situations in which there are a small number of identifiable players. The next chapter takes a rather different approach to dynamics: it focuses, in a complementary way, on generic threats to the sustainability of superior performance and strategic responses to them.

Glossary

agency problems	game theory	reference horizon
ambiguity	game tree	routines
asymmetries	goals	rules
beliefs	inertia	scenario analysis
best response	information	sequenced rollout
biases	iterated elimination	simulation
coalitional game theory	look ahead and reason back	simultaneous moves
commitments	market testing	strategic complements
competitor profiling	mental model	strategic substitutes
cooperative game theory	Nash equilibrium	strategies
credible precommitment	nonconstant-sum games	structural analysis
dominant strategy	non-cooperative game theory	variables
dominated strategies	payoff matrix	wargaming and roleplaying
dynamic games	payoffs	zero-sum games
embedded beliefs	players	
first mover	reaction function	

Notes

1. Joel E. Urbany, David B. Montgomery, and Marian Moore, "Competitive Reactions and Modes of Competitive Reasoning: Downplaying the Unpredictable?" (Marketing Science Institute Report No. 01-121, 2001).

2. In *Co-opetition* (New York: Doubleday, 1996) Adam M. Brandenburger and Barry J. Nalebuff generate insights from both *cooperative* and *non-cooperative* game theory for business strategy, but with a focus on the former. Avinash Dixit and Barry Nalebuff provide interesting and more general applications of game theory in *Thinking Strategically: The Competitive Edge in Business, Politics and Everyday Life* (New York: W.W. Norton, 1992).

3. Robert J. Aumann and Michael Maschler, "Game Theoretic Analysis of a Bankruptcy Problem from the Talmud," *Journal of Economic Theory* 36, no. 2 (1985): 195–213.

4. John Von Neumann and Oskar Morgenstern, *Theory of Games and Economic Behavior* (Princeton, N.J.: Princeton University Press, 1944).

5. John F. Nash, Jr., "Equilibrium Points in N-Person Games," *Proceedings of the National Academy of Sciences of the United States of America* 36 (1950): 48–49, John F. Nash, Jr., "Non-Cooperative Games," *Annals of Mathematics* 54 (1951): 286–95. These ideas were actually first applied more than a hundred years earlier by Augustin A. Cournot, who focused on duopoly and used a restricted version of Nash equilibrium as his solution concept. See his *Recherches sur les principes mathématiques de la théorie des richesses* (Paris: L. Hachette, 1838). English translation: *Researches into the Mathematical Principles of the Theory of Wealth.* (New York: Macmillan, 1897. Reprinted New York: Augustus M. Kelley, 1971).

6. Reinhard Selten, "Spieltheoretische Behandlung Eines Oligopolmodells Mit Nachfragetragheit," *Zeitschrift fur die gesamte Staatswissenschaft 121* (1965): 301–24 and 667–68; John C. Harsanyi, "Games with Incomplete Information Played by 'Bayesian' Players, I–III. Part I. The Basic Model," *Management Science* 14, no. 3 (Nov. 1967): 159–82, "Games with Incomplete Information Played by 'Bayesian' Players, I–III. Part II. Bayesian Equilibrium Points," *Management Science* 14, no. 5, (Jan. 1968): 320–34; "Games with Incomplete Information Played by 'Bayesian' Players, I–III. Part III. The Basic Probability Distribution of the Game," *Management Science* 14, no. 7 (Mar. 1968): 486–502.

7. John C. Harsanyi and Reinhard Selten, *A General Theory of Equilibrium Selection in Games* (Cambridge, MA: MIT Press, 1988).

8. In keeping with game-theoretic usage, strategies are defined in this section and the next discusses complete specifications of what players will do in all contingencies, whether those contingencies actually arise or not. This is somewhat different from the way they are defined elsewhere in the book.

9. Note that these strategies imply a sustainable level of product differentiation. Technically speaking, firm *I* is choosing its capacity level of production ("Cournot" game) where the optimal level of capacity depends on the perceived level of product differentiation due to marketing and sales effort by firm *I*.

10. We are grateful to Hugh Courtney for steering us toward this situation and for sharing with us analyses by his students that persuaded us to undertake our own relatively detailed analysis of this case example.

11. This is a hypothetical calculation since we do not know that the initial Sirius entry was actually made with the intent of escalating content investments later on.

12. David Besanko and Ronald R. Braeutigam (2005) describe the competitive dynamics between XM and Sirius as a simple static game of chicken and advance a merger as a possible outcome. David Besanko and Ronald R. Braeutigam, *Microeconomics*, 2nd ed. (New York: John Wiley & Sons, 2005).

13. Philip Selznick, *Leadership in Administration: A Sociological Interpretation* (New York: Harper & Row, 1957).

14. Pankaj Ghemawat, *Commitment: The Dynamic of Strategy* (New York: Free Press, 1991), pp. 23–25.

15. The discussion in this section is a highly abridged and somewhat disguised version of a competitor analysis prepared for a client's private use by Ken A. Mark under the supervision of Pankaj Ghemawat.

16. Goals refer to what your competitor maximizes (i.e., its objective function), beliefs are related to the weights your competitor puts on various possible actions or outcomes, and routines imply constraints on or opportunities for your competitor's optimization problem that make certain choices infeasible or more likely.

17. Richard Nelson and Sidney Winter's *An Evolutionary Theory of Economic Change* (Cambridge, Mass.: Belknap Press, 1982) is a seminal book on routines and business behavior.

18. Benjamin Franklin, letter to Joseph Priestley, September 19, 1772. Available at The History Carper: *www.historycarper.com/resources/twobf3/letter11.htm* (accessed September 30, 2004).

19. Leonard J. Savage, *The Foundations of Statistics*, 2d rev. ed. (1954; New York: Dover Publications, 1972) and Ken Binmore and Adam M. Brandenburger, "Common Knowledge and Game Theory," in *Essays on the Foundations of Game Theory*, Ken Binmore, ed. (Oxford: Basil Blackwell, 1990). In this context, it is interesting to read Savage's original discussion of "small worlds" versus "grand worlds" and Binmore and Brandenburger's critique of Savage's subjective expected utility theory for assuming a "closed universe."

20. Pankaj Ghemawat and Barry J. Nalebuff, "Exit," *RAND Journal of Economics* 16 (1985): 84–94; and Pankaj Ghemawat and Barry J. Nalebuff, "The Devolution of Declining Industries," *Quarterly Journal of Economics* 105 (1990): 165–186.

21 See Jean Tirole, *The Theory of Industrial Organization* (Cambridge, Mass.: MIT Press, 1988), pp. 323–328, for a formal treatment of these effects.

22. Jean Tirole, *The Theory of Industrial Organization* (Cambridge, Mass.: MIT Press, 1988); Luis M. B. Cabral, *Introduction to Industrial Organization* (Cambridge, Mass.: MIT Press, 2000); R. Preston McAfee, *Competitive Solutions: The Strategist's Toolkit* (Princeton: Princeton University Press, 2002).

23. See, for example, Edward De Bono, *Lateral Thinking for Management: A Handbook of Creativity* (New York: American Management Association, 1971).

24. Barry J. Nalebuff and Ian Ayres, *Why Not? How to Use Everyday Ingenuity to Solve Problems Big and Small* (Boston: Harvard Business School Press, 2003).

25. On the importance of dynamics for strategy analysis see Pankaj Ghemawat and Bruno Cassiman, "Introduction to the Special Issue on Strategic Dynamics," *Management Science* 53 no. 4 (April 2007): 529–537. Strategic Dynamics is an area of active research as the dedication of an entire issue of Management Science illustrates. The papers selected for this special issue clearly demonstrate a wide array of approaches to thinking in interesting ways about strategic dynamics and cover a wide set of methodologies for building dynamic effects into the strategy analysis.

26. On industry scenarios, see Michael E. Porter, "Industry Scenarios and Competitive Strategy under Uncertainty," Chapter 13 in *Competitive Advantage* (New York: Free Press, 1985). See Peter Schwartz, *The Art of the Long View* (New York: Currency Doubleday, 1991), for a broader discussion of scenario thinking and Hugh Courtney, *20/20 Foresight: Crafting Strategy in an Uncertain World* (Boston: Harvard Business School Press, 2001), for an even broader discussion of McKinsey & Company's work on strategy and uncertainty. This is also the most apposite place to mention the literature on real options and strategy (e.g., Timothy A. Luehrman, "Strategy as a Portfolio of Real Options," *Harvard Business Review* 76, no. 5 (September 1998): 89–99. Although it is sometimes too prone to perceive anything and everything as a real option, real option analysis can actually be seen as a baseline for the kind of competitive overlay discussed in this chapter because, while dynamic, it generally has trouble handling competitor interactions in nonmechanical ways.

27. See Paul A. Langley, Mark Paich, and John D. Sterman, "Explaining Capacity Overshoot and Price War: Misperceptions of Feedback in Competitive Growth Markets," unpublished working paper, Sloan School of Management, MIT (1998), on this specific point. For broader discussions of simulation and business dynamics, see John D. Sterman's textbook, *Business Dynamics: Systems Thinking and Modeling for a Complex World* (New York: Irwin/McGraw-Hill, 2000) and Michael Schrage's *Serious Play: How the World's Best Companies Simulate to Innovate* (Boston: Harvard Business School Press, 2000).

28. Byron Reeves, Thomas W. Malone, and Tony O'Driscoll, "Leadership's Online Labs," *Harvard Business Review* 86, no. 5 (May 2008): 58–66.

29. Excerpt from *"Battle Ready,"* book written by Tom Clancy with General Tony Zinni and Tony Koltz, 2004. Available at http://www.americanprogress.org/issues/2004/05/b88973.html (accessed June 10, 2008).

Sustaining Superior Performance

But many that are first shall be last; and the last first.

—MARK 10:31

This chapter, like Chapter 4, focuses on dynamics. It takes a different track, however, which can best be illustrated by expanding upon the advice offered at the beginning of Chapter 3, to build the better mousetrap. We need to take that advice a step further and look at **sustainability** in the face of **imitation**. Because garages seem to feature many small mousetrap manufacturers as well as mice, an innovator will gain little from anticipating its interactions with any one rival in the kind of dynamic detail discussed in Chapter 4. But it *can* add a useful dynamic dimension to the analysis by recognizing that better mousetraps that have succeeded in the marketplace in the past (e.g., repeating traps and glueboards) haven't greatly enriched their respective innovators, partly because better mousetraps attract imitators as well as mice.

Recognizing the threat of imitation is the first step in thinking through whether barriers to imitation exist or can be erected around the innovation. And even if imitation cannot be blocked, its likely scope and speed should be accounted for in deciding whether to develop the better mousetrap in the first place. This chapter discusses imitation and other generic threats to the sustainability of superior performance as well as strategic responses to those threats.

Data on performance dynamics help illustrate the importance of thinking through issues of sustainability. Historically, such dynamics were understudied because they did not form part of the traditional strategy agenda laid out in the profitability grid in Exhibit 1.7. But in the last 15 years, evidence has accumulated that points to the folly of focusing on achieving superior performance while forgetting about its sustainability. This evidence suggests that above-average performance tends to subside toward the average *much more rapidly* than many managers assume.

Consider, for example, an analysis of the return on investment (ROI) reported over a 10-year period by a sample of nearly 700 business units.[1] When this sample was divided into two equally sized groups based on initial ROI, the top group's ROI in year 1 was 39 percent and the bottom group's was 3 percent. If businesses were kept in the groups in which they started out and tracked over a decade, what changes would you predict to the 36-point ROI spread between the group averages by year 10?

When managers are confronted with this question, they often guess that the initial ROI spread between the two groups shrank by between one-third and two-thirds by year 10. In fact, as shown in Exhibit 5.1, the shrinkage was actually greater than 90 percent! In another recent study, only 2 percent of the firms in a large sample managed to sustain superior performance over at least a 10-year period.[2] Such data clearly imply that in most cases, the sustainability of superior performance cannot be taken for granted.

But one should not conclude that just because sustainability is elusive, it is not worth examining. There are at least four reasons why. First, even if initially superior returns can be expected to subside to the average level by year 10, the degree to which they can be sustained in the interim—the shaded area in Exhibit 5.1—is surely of interest. Second, convergence actually *was not* complete by the tenth year for the sample: the initially top group still had an ROI advantage of 3.5 percent. This is a significant difference in long-run spreads that can, in many situations, spell the difference between significant value creation and value destruction. Third, the convergence of returns overstates the convergence of what is actually of interest: (economic) returns times volume. A business posting an ROI of 39 percent—again, the initial average for the top group—probably should not insist that all new investments deliver returns

EXHIBIT 5.1   The Limits to Sustainability.

Source: Pankaj Ghemawat, *Commitment* (New York: Free Press, 1991).

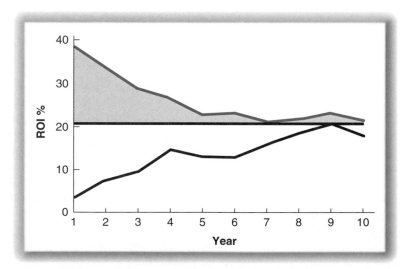

that high. And finally, if you are still taken aback by the extent to which the group averages in Exhibit 5.1 converged, remember that they mask tremendous amounts of variation. It is easy to cite companies that have beaten the averages by large margins over much longer periods (e.g., Wal-Mart). Understanding how they have done so will help illustrate the range of possible strategic responses to threats to sustainability.

To that end, the next section classifies threats to the sustainability of superior performance and relates them to the analytical frameworks and perspectives developed in earlier chapters. Each of the four sections that follow focuses on (1) a threatening evolutionary dynamic and (2) possible strategic responses to it. The final section uses the example of Wal-Mart to review the discussion.

SUSTAINABILITY AND RESOURCES

In classifying threats to sustainability, it is useful to split observed performance into the two components suggested in Chapters 2 and 3, industry-level performance effects and within-industry performance differentials. Recent research suggests that superior performance that *is* sustained over the long haul is due, in large part, to stable industry-level effects, and that performance advantages over the competition tend to be less sustainable.[3] Industry-level effects were discussed in some detail—from a dynamic as well as a static perspective—in Chapter 2 and therefore will not be taken up here, beyond the reminder that dynamics such as demand saturation, technological maturation, and resource depletion do need to be taken into account. The discussion in this chapter will focus, instead, on threats to the sustainability of superior within-industry performance and ways of dealing with them.

Research in industrial organization (IO) economics is helpful in this regard: it suggests that commitments to durable, specialized resources—what might be called **sticky resources**—are generally needed to sustain within-industry profit differences.[4] The deregulation of the U.S. airline industry and its subsequent experiences illustrate this link. The U.S. airline industry was deregulated in 1978 in the belief that the threat of "hit-and-run" entry would keep prices and profitability in check even in city-pairs that ended up being monopolized. Individual city-pairs were supposed to be **contestable**, that is, easy to enter and exit, on the grounds that if prices exceeded relevant costs, an entrant could fly its capital into a market and, if threatened with retaliatory price cuts, could fly it out again. (As Alfred Kahn, who headed the Civil Aeronautics Board at the time of deregulation, put it, airplanes were "marginal costs with wings.") But more than 25 years later, the U.S. airline industry still continues to exhibit significant, sustained within-industry differences in profitability. So the logic of contestability is revealed to be wrongheaded in the industry that was once supposed to be its leading exemplar. But the airline industry is worth examining, nonetheless, to see why differences in profitability have not disappeared.

The summary answer is that the contestability theory overlooked a range of sticky resources that have turned out to be important in the deregulated airline industry. Actually, two distinct phases can be discerned in the industry's evolution since deregulation. Through the 1980s and part of the 1990s, the established airlines fended off entrants much more effectively than the deregulators had anticipated, largely by building and leveraging such resources as hub fortresses, computerized reservations systems, and customer stickiness based on frequent-flyer programs. But as prices have continued to fall—to less than half the real levels of the mid-1970s—the not-so-efficient resources that the incumbents continue to be stuck with, particularly expensive unionized workforces, have loomed ever larger and are, in several cases, the focus of their current struggles to survive. The discount carriers that have challenged the traditional incumbents can also be looked at through the resource lens. Southwest, by far the largest creator of economic value in the airline industry after deregulation, has a uniquely standardized and fuel-efficient fleet of planes and has historically managed to keep them flying one-third longer each day than its competitors. And even the pressures that it has recently experienced related to *its* employee costs draw attention, once again, to sticky resources.

This emphasis on resources has a long tradition in the field of strategy as well as in IO economics.[5] A resource-based perspective does, however, depart from the emphasis in the previous chapters, particularly Chapter 3, on the activities that a business performs. To clarify, the present chapter shares with the others in this book an underlying stocks-and-flows conception of resources and activities. Specifically, resource stocks that can be varied only in the long run—in keeping with the traditional economic conception of resources as fixed inputs—determine the flows of activities that a business can undertake in the short run and these activities, in turn, help shape the evolution of resource stocks over time. Reinterpreted in these terms, Chapter 3 exploited the idea that even when the underlying resources are key, an activity lens may still be useful because it is hard to value fixed inputs except in terms of the flows of services they generate. In other words, activities are easier to measure and, therefore, often a better basis for analysis. But for explicitly dynamic purposes, such as understanding the determinants of sustainability, it is important to look directly at long-run factors. This involves shifting the focus from activities that can be varied in the short run to the underlying resource stocks that are fixed in the short run.

Resource-based research in strategy was slow to capitalize on these insights, partly because of an early tendency to define virtually anything as a resource.[6] As a result, traditional resource-based frameworks for thinking about sustainability often lack a clear conceptual basis.[7] Contemporary resource-based research advances matters by confirming the intuition that in thinking about the conditions under which resources will or will not continue to sustain superior performance, it is useful to distinguish between their added or **scarcity value** and their **appropriability**, or capture, of (some of) that value by the focal firm.[8] Note that these two kinds of conditions—one related to competition and the other to bargaining—are meant to be overlaid: the sticky resources that underpin superior performance at a point in time must continue to be scarce to sustain superior performance, *and* the owners of the firm must be able to appropriate some of that sustainable scarcity or added value.

The discussion in the rest of this chapter will be organized in terms of two threats to scarcity or added value and two threats to appropriability. Specifically, it will work through the **tetra-threat framework** for diagnosing the sustainability of superior within-industry performance that is laid out in Exhibit 5.2:

- *Imitation* of the resources underpinning superior performance to the point where they are no longer scarce is a direct threat to the sustainability of added value. Imitation can be thought of as diminishing the extent to which the player being imitated would be missed if it simply disappeared—a rough measure of added value, as noted in Chapter 3.

EXHIBIT 5.2   The Tetra-Threat Framework for Sustainability Analysis.

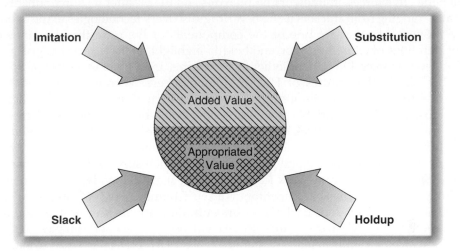

- *Substitution* of the resources underpinning superior performance is an indirect threat to the sustainability of added value, driven by displacement rather than duplication. That said, substitution-related threats to scarcity are often even harder to address than threats of imitation.
- *Holdup* is a threat to the appropriation, or capture, of sustainable added value that is often rooted in resource **cospecialization**. Cospecialization can be essential to value creation, but it does create a problem: as a firm and its complementor (for instance) cospecialize, their added values overlap, making it impossible for both of them to appropriate the full amount. Each then faces the threat of being held up by the other.
- *Slack* is the internal threat to the appropriation, or value capture, that reflects a persistent tendency to dissipate potential economic surplus. The scope for slack depends on past success or current added value: firms without much of either have a hard time surviving while persistently suboptimizing.

Since the tetra-threat framework is superficially similar to the "five forces" framework (imitation ↔ rivalry, substitution, holdup ↔ supplier/buyer power), the differences are worth illustrating. Compare the application of the two frameworks to the pharmaceutical industry, which was analyzed with the help of the five forces framework in Chapter 2. A list of rivalry determinants would flag high levels of concentration, particularly within therapeutic categories, significant product differentiation, rapid growth, and so on as contributing to the pharmaceutical industry's high average profitability. But looking at where the big money is made *within* the industry focuses attention on the blockbuster drugs that have come to dominate big pharmaceutical companies' sales and profits. Why aren't these imitated more effectively than they seem to be? Addressing this question requires attention to patents and other barriers to imitation, also rooted in underlying resources, which actually limit the number of sellers of such drugs.

Similarly, there is a big difference between the product-substitution threats which the "five forces" framework emphasizes and the broader resource substitution threats—ranging from entrants using new drug-discovery technologies to the open science movement—that are one of the components of the tetra-threat framework. Considerations of cospecialization and holdup highlight reliance on a range of suppliers of key resources: biotech and other focused firms, individual inventors, academia, and the National Institutes of Health, among others. Without such a focus on resources, five forces analyses of supplier power in pharmaceuticals tend to split attention across suppliers of variable as well as fixed inputs—or sometimes even ignore the latter entirely. And finally, slack has no counterpart in the "five forces" framework.

In addition to these differences in focus, the two frameworks also differ in terms of concreteness about the behavioral processes that threaten sustained superior performance. The "five forces" framework leans heavily on statistical tendencies and regularities (e.g., the concentration of competitors as a key determinant of profitability), whereas the behavioral foundations of the tetra-threat framework are clearer (e.g., the usual assumption that imitation of a scarce resource will occur if the effort can pay for itself).[9] In other words, tetra-threat analysis operates at a level in between the macro/statistical perspective of the "five forces" framework and the microperspective, involving detailed, grounded analyses of individual players in specific situations, that was presented in Chapter 4. Given differences in the issues flagged, analysis at multiple levels is warranted, and hence this chapter should be seen as a supplement to the earlier ones.

THE THREAT OF IMITATION

Imitation is not always bad for an innovator. It can sometimes lend credibility to a new product (e.g., when network externalities or second-sourcing is an issue). In addition, the imitation of certain types of marketing moves, such as loyalty schemes and meet-the-competition clauses, does not necessarily undermine their effectiveness.[10]

Still, imitative development of scarce resources is usually bad news in added-value terms. And it seems to be endemic. Attempts by one player to increase its capacity, for example, often trigger additions by competitors intent on preserving their capacity shares. Attempts to build one's customer base tend to prompt competitors to defend or develop their own. Furthermore, attempts at product differentiation based on R&D as opposed to marketing are vulnerable on several counts; studies indicate that competitors secure detailed information on most new products within one year of their development, patent-based strategies usually fail to deter imitation, and imitation tends, on average, to cost one-third less than innovation and to get to market one-third faster. And process innovations seem, if anything, to be even more imitable than product innovations.[11]

The upshot is that the threat of imitation has to be taken seriously, even in contexts where the barriers to imitation might seem to be high. The pharmaceutical industry, for example, is characterized by product patents that are unusually effective at choking off imitation for periods exceeding a decade. But the big pharmaceutical firms still have to worry about imitation of the limited number of blockbuster drugs—typically less than five—on which their fortunes depend. (This dependence was dramatized by Merck's 2004 recall of Vioxx, its fourth-best seller in 2003 with $2.5 billion in revenues, triggering a $27 billion, or 27 percent, drop in Merck's market value the day the recall was announced.)

Some imitative pressures reflect the big pharmaceutical companies' practice of tweaking each other's innovative blockbusters to come up with slightly different molecules that are not protected by the original patents, which they then patent and sell under their own brands. But the effects of such copycat molecules are moderated by the branded manufacturers' ability to contain price competition among themselves, perhaps because they recognize their mutual dependence, as in the pharmaceutical pricing game described at the beginning of Chapter 4. What are much more threatening to high prices are the generic manufacturers who enter with 30–90 percent discounts after patents expire, and typically manage to wrest the bulk of category volume away from the original patent holder in a matter of months.[12] Concerns about generic competition loom particularly large among branded manufacturers as of this writing due to impending patent expirations and an anticipated dearth of new blockbusters over the next few years.

The diverse ways in which branded pharmaceutical companies have tried to mitigate the threat of imitation illustrate a variety of barriers to imitation, often involving early-mover advantages, that extend well beyond a prespecified period of patent protection and are at least partly endogenous, meaning that they can be influenced. The following barriers should not be seen as mutually exclusive: strong defenses against imitation typically rely on more than one of them.

Private Information

To the extent that superior information or knowledge can be kept private—to the extent that it is costly for would-be imitators to tap into it—imitation will be inhibited. Although being tight-lipped can sometimes ensure privacy, many other channels of potential informational leakage exist, including customers, employees, and other suppliers, spinoffs, reverse-engineering, and even patent documents. As a result, privacy is most likely to be sustainable when information is tacit rather than specifiable (i.e., doesn't lend itself to blueprinting), and when no one party can carry it out of the organization. Thus, Wyeth has managed to monopolize a lucrative hormone-replacement submarket with its Premarin drug, made from the urine of pregnant mares, for more than 60 years now even though the drug's patent expired decades ago. A two-decade-long attempt to develop a synthetic generic version of the drug has been thwarted by the fact that nobody knows exactly what is *in* Premarin.[13]

Switching Costs/Relationships

The severity of imitation threats may be blunted by signing enforceable contracts or, more commonly, creating switching costs or cultivating relationships that secure superior access to customers, suppliers, or other important types of players. The branded pharmaceutical companies have been particularly imaginative in engaging doctors, for example.[14] They induce trials by doctors (and hospitals) of their newest and most expensive products by distributing billions of dollars of free samples. In addition, they give doctors personal gifts, provide them with generous "research" grants, and offer them consulting, speaking, and even publishing opportunities. This largesse can be thought of as leaving a residue of goodwill with doctors, with effects that linger on in their prescription decisions even after generics become available.

Size Economies

Size economies refer to the (possible) advantages of being large. They come in at least three different varieties: scale economies, which are the advantages of being large in a particular business at a particular point in time; economies associated with **learning** by doing, which imply advantages to being large in a particular business over time; and scope economies, which are the advantages of being large across inter-related businesses and which are discussed in more detail in Chapter 6.[15] If there *are* size economies, a firm may be able to deter imitation by precommitting itself to exploiting them. Deterrence depends on the possibility that if the would-be imitator tried to match the incumbent's size or resource mass, enough excess capacity might result to make it regret the effort. The pharmaceutical majors' sales forces stand out in this context: there are indications that would-be entrants shy away from categories in which they would have to achieve similarly broad reach (typically ones in which drugs have to be promoted to legions of primary-care physicians). Scale economies are also evident in the shift from print to TV advertising of prescription drugs after the rules on direct-to-consumer TV ads were relaxed in 1997.

Threats of Retaliation

Incumbents may also be able to deter imitation by threatening massive **retaliation**. But talk of retaliation is cheap. To be credible, it must be backed up by both the ability and the willingness to retaliate. The ability to retaliate is facilitated by the creation of a competitive advantage and by the maintenance of resource reserves, such as liquidity, excess capacity, "warehoused" product upgrades, and positions in competitors' other businesses, that can be used to put pressure on them. The credibility of retaliation is greatest when it is payoff-maximizing for the retaliator, but it *can* be boosted in several ways: by writing contracts that make retaliation more attractive than accommodation, otherwise binding oneself (e.g., "burning one's bridges"), cultivating a reputation for retaliating in spite of immediate losses to oneself, and so on. Thus, branded pharmaceutical companies threatened with patent expiry now often license their drugs to makers of "authorized generics" or sell their own generics through subsidiaries so as to disrupt the six months of exclusivity that are granted to the first generic manufacturer under U.S. law and are often critical to the pioneering generic manufacturer recouping its investments.[16]

Imitation Lags

Even if the barriers to imitation discussed earlier do not apply, imitation typically takes time. Guesstimates of the average lead times in taking various types of actions will help underscore the importance of such lags.[17] As a rule of thumb, prices and marketing communications are among the few variables that can be changed significantly in less than one year. Changes to resource stocks tend to take longer. It takes two years or more to build and start up the typical manufacturing plant. Building a new distribution system or altering an existing one seems at least as time-consuming. Studies indicate that the mean lag in returns from R&D tends to be on the order of four to six years. And the lags in implementing major changes in human resource practices and restructuring corporate portfolios may stretch out over the better part of a decade—or longer! Changes along multiple dimensions are likely to take longer (and have a higher probability of failure), especially if they have to be executed in sequence.

In pharmaceuticals, the key lags concern generic entry, with each day of delay potentially being worth millions of dollars to the owner of a blockbuster. Instead of treating their time-in-market before generics enter as given, the pharmaceutical majors have taken a range of actions to lengthen it: "evergreening" their patents by tweaking molecules, uses, or formulations, suing generic manufacturers for patent infringement (which automatically delays approvals of generic drugs in the United States by thirty months), exploiting other loopholes that extend patent protection, such as testing drugs on children, which is worth six months, lobbying for the general lengthening of pharmaceutical patents, pressing the Food and Drug Administration to speed up the drug-approval process, and so on. The results? It has been estimated that the effective time-in-market for brand-name drugs before generic entry increased from about eight years in 1980 to 14 years in 2000.[18]

Upgrading

Another significant barrier to imitation is based on continuous upgrading of the organization's own added value. Operationally, this involves driving a wider wedge between customers' willingness to pay and suppliers' opportunity costs over time, and often requires significant resource commitments. Thus, the pharmaceutical majors continue to make major commitments to developing and introducing new blockbusters at costs that are now estimated at $1.7 billion per successful drug and have also been paying more attention in recent years to upgrading their product and process development capabilities (see Exhibit 5.3 for some additional discussion of commitments and capabilities). Note that upgrading makes a business a moving target in a way that compounds the difficulties or delays for potential imitators and may even permit the upgrader to break away from the pack. One way to calibrate the need to upgrade is to track the rate at which an industry's real prices, adjusted for quality, change over time. If an industry's average prices decrease by more than a threshold rate (3 percent per year, according to Jeffrey Williams), it is a "fast-cycle" environment in which advantages tend to be short-lived rather than sustainable, and more or less continuous upgrading is required.[19] The bias toward action built into upgrading also reminds us that barriers to imitation are not just forms of protection that lucky firms are blessed with; they *can* be built.

Numerous other types of barriers to imitation have also been proposed. Several are rooted in considerations of **complexity**, including **causal ambiguity**,[20] as evoked by Wyeth's Premarin, **social complexity**[21] that is supposed to put certain resources—corporate culture is the favorite example—beyond the reach of systematic management, and the challenges of achieving **cross-sectional fit**, or coherence, across many different types of choices.[22] But while insurmountable complexities can help explain barriers to imitation *ex post,* their implications for action *ex ante* are often unclear. For instance, even if it is more difficult for an imitator to copy a whole set of coherent choices instead of just one or two, is it obvious that the innovator had an easier time coming up with the coherent set in the first place? If not, there is no point to pursuing sustainability (as opposed to advantage) through intricate alignment of choices because there are no early-mover advantages to be gained thereby.

In summary, imitation is a direct threat to the sustainability of added value whose severity is inversely related to the height of barriers to imitation. Such barriers often revolve around early-mover advantages. But while moving early may reduce the threat of imitation, it can also raise costs and risks. As a result, the only sensible

EXHIBIT 5.3 Making Commitments and Building Capabilities.

The resource-based view of strategy takes a historical perspective by stressing that the resources a business has assembled determine its menu of opportunities at any point in time. In this sense, it links what the business did in the past to what it can do well today. But to stop there would be to confine attention to the exploitation of "legacy" resources—which would be seriously incomplete, since the value of the resources that firms already have in place is often estimated to account for less than one-half or even one-quarter of their market value.[23] Thus, in pharmaceuticals, while it is extremely important for firms to exploit their legacies—blockbusters still under patent—for all they are worth, it is also essential to invest for the future by making large, relatively discrete **commitments** of resources to developing, testing, and marketing new drugs as well as more diffuse commitments to improving their R&D and manufacturing capabilities, among others.

By implication, a fully dynamic approach to strategy must not only link what a business did in the past to what it can do well today but also what it does today to what it can do well in the future. This involves explicitly considering both lumpy commitments and **capabilities** as ways for it to upgrade or shift its opportunity set. Lumpy commitments are a good way of thinking about not only market entry (and exit), major new-product introductions, significant capacity expansion/modernization, and so on, but also some less obvious categories of change, such as cultural transformation and even shifts in strategy. Thus, when Coors switched from a regional to a national strategy in the U.S. beer market in the 1970s, it had to open its first new manufacturing facility in a century, establish relationships with distributors in 39 new states, improve acrimonious relationships with unions and minorities that were stronger in the new states, build a national clientele by spending more per barrel on advertising than entrenched competitors (two of which, Anheuser-Busch and Miller, also benefited from greater national scale), upgrade its marketing capabilities, and change a production-focused culture. The Coors case also illustrates the four markers of irreversibility, the true measure of significance of lumpy commitments:

- sunk costs that would be unrecoverable if going national did not work out
- opportunity costs that induce lock-out instead of lock-in, as illustrated by Coors locking itself out of certain opportunities by moving very late to go national
- time lags of longer than a decade in completing the switch to a national position
- organizational commitment to or momentum behind the new course of action that would make it hard to reverse even if reversal turned out to make economic sense

Lumpy commitments are individually important enough to warrant the full power of the analytical techniques discussed in this book—assessing fit with or influence on industry structure, and implications for competitive position, interactions, and sustainability.[24]

The development of capabilities, in contrast, involves choices that are individually small and frequent rather than individually important and infrequent. The idea is that firm-specific opportunities to perform activities more effectively than competitors or to make commitments on better terms than them can be built gradually and reinforced over long periods of time.[25]

For a vivid example, consider the success of Japanese automakers in the U.S. market. It is hard to explain this success in terms of superior product market positioning: sedans like the Honda Accord and the Toyota Camry were priced and targeted similarly to the domestic automakers' core offerings. More explanatory power is provided by the estimate that by the 1980s, Japanese automakers had upgraded their product-development capabilities to the point where they could design and introduce a

(continued)

EXHIBIT 5.3   *Continued*

new model in about *half the time* and with *half the engineering resources* required by their U.S. counterparts. This allowed them to update their products more frequently. They, especially Toyota, also managed to produce their products more cheaply and with better quality because of differences in manufacturing facilities and processes. The still unmatched Toyota Production System is protected by knowledge that is tacit and rooted in complex organizational processes, economies of plant scale (particularly in Japan), relationships with suppliers that are elaborated on in the section on holdup, time lags for imitators to build up comparable resources, and a deep commitment to continuous improvement.

Many different kinds of capabilities can be identified, associated with differences in product and process development efficiency, learning, speed, flexibility, mobility (across lines of business), and so forth.[26] "Metacapabilities" associated with integration, reconfiguration, and transformation have also attracted some interest but are quite hard to measure. But measurement and comparisons with competitors are important because in their absence, hubris and politics are likely to lead to excessively high self-ratings and a tendency to designate anything one cares about as a key organizational capability.[27]

Another challenge relates to the incremental nature of capability development: firms must prevent the overall coherence of such efforts from being nibbled away, choice by choice, by drop-in-the-bucket biases, and the like. Somewhat paradoxically, this makes the choice of which capabilities to develop, and how, a relatively lumpy choice, just like conventional resource commitments, since commitment to a major capability-development thrust also exhibits lock-in, lock-out, lags, and organizational commitment. As a result, just like specific commitments, specific capabilities also imply specific rigidities that can, in an uncertain world, result in inferior rather than superior performance.[28] In other words, capability development and commitment may be necessary for sustained success, but are certainly not sufficient. Which is why they must be analyzed.

conclusion about early versus late timing is the one drawn long ago by Alfred P. Sloan: If you are late, you have to be better.

THE THREAT OF SUBSTITUTION

Added value may be threatened by substitution as well as by imitation. Substitution should be thought of here in terms of resource substitution, rather than the product substitution highlighted in Chapter 2. Resource substitution tends to reduce added value by displacing scarce resources instead of duplicating them, that is, by reducing the demand for their services instead of expanding their supply. And while substitution can sometimes blur into imitation at the margin, it can also have rather more drastic effects, as emphasized more than half a century ago by the economist Joseph Schumpeter, who compared the threats of substitution and imitation "as a bombardment is in comparison with forcing a door."[29]

Substitution seems to command much more attention among business strategists today than it did in Schumpeter's era. Particularly popular are discussions of **disruptive technologies**.[30] Substitution is a related but broader idea. Thus, technological substitution encompasses not only disruptive technologies that, while suboptimal for the requirements of existing customers, are improving more rapidly, but also technological threats from above (as opposed to below). Thus, in the first 20 years of the videogame market, each new generation of consoles led to a new competitor becoming the market leader. Of course, the even more radical change associated with Nintendo's wireless handheld controller and dual-screen system *could* be seen as a threat from below, underlining the point that substitution threats can come from both directions. Furthermore, as a threat to added value, substitution encompasses much more than just technological change. Other "supply-side" triggers of substitution include changes in input prices or availability and deregulation (as in the airline industry). On the "demand side," shifts in customer preferences, previously unmet needs, and changes in the customer mix can shake up things.

For a detailed example of a threat of substitution and responses to it, consider the growth of online book retailing in general and Amazon in particular from the perspective of the leader in traditional (bricks-and-mortar) book retailing, Barnes & Noble. Amazon's online store threatened to largely dispense with and displace two of the key resources that Barnes & Noble was stuck with: approximately 10 million square feet of physical selling space in stores whose value, properly capitalized, exceeded the company's annual revenues, and 15,000 in-store employees (1998). What Barnes & Noble did and did not do illustrates the broad array of possible responses to substitution threats: acquiesce, defend, straddle, switch, and innovate.

Not Responding

One way of dealing with substitution dynamics is by not responding at all. This is *not* what Barnes & Noble did: within a year of Amazon's founding, it decided to launch its own online operation. Still, one can imagine some plausible arguments in favor of inaction:

- Online book retailing may prove to be just a flash in the pan
- Even otherwise, online will amount to only a small niche
- The online model underserves purchasers because it does not let them handle books or provide the physical ambiance emphasized by Barnes & Noble's superstores
- Online will cannibalize the physical stores, which are already under pressure
- Barnes & Noble does not have the skills and expertise to make an online initiative work

These objections typify the arguments that are used more broadly to limit consideration of substitution threats.[31] But the general sense—bolstered by recognition of such corporate sins as arrogance, myopia, bureaucracy, and sloth—is that paying too little attention to substitution threats is often more hazardous to a company's health than paying too much.

Migrating/Harvesting

Migrating and harvesting, often employed in tandem, are less passive forms of acquiescence. Migration involves redeploying resources to uses that are less vulnerable to substitution threats or more attractive overall in light of them. Harvesting requires a shift toward milking existing resources instead of building or even maintaining them. Research into disruptive technologies suggests that while harvesting is the most common response of incumbent firms, it is often accidental, at least in the early stages of the process.[32] On the other hand, it is also easy to imagine cases in which harvesting would have made sense but was not attempted. For example, questions can be raised about whether Barnes & Noble should have continued to invest in expanding its network of physical stores despite persistently poor returns.

Defending

Defending against substitution threats means that the threatened business must either increase its willingness to pay or decrease its costs. The obvious danger with this approach, especially in the context of technological threats, is that the threats may have fundamentally faster improvement dynamics.[33] An implication from Chapter 3 that may be less obvious is also worth emphasizing: defense can be achieved not only by improving one's own economic fundamentals but also by impairing the fundamentals of competitors. Thus, Barnes & Noble attempted to squeeze competitors, particularly Amazon, in a number of ways, most notably by announcing, in November 1998, that it would acquire Ingram, which accounted for more than half of book wholesalers' sales in the United States and was also a major supplier to Amazon and others. This deal had to be called off, however, after complaints from publishers and book retailers prompted the U.S. Federal Trade Commission to launch an investigation.

Straddling

Straddling involves responding to a substitution threat by establishing a foothold in both camps. Straddling may be either a transitional hedge or a long-term strategy. Straddles can also be distinguished in terms of whether they are relatively balanced between the old and the new or are imbalanced between the two (e.g., offer only a toehold in the substitute form of competition). Perhaps the biggest risks inherent in straddling are excessive commitment to an old form of competition that may no longer be viable and an unwillingness to make tough choices. Straddling seemed to be Barnes & Noble's principal strategy between 1996 and 2000: it moved to set up Bandn.com as a leading online retailer (rather than a toehold) by drawing on talent and content resources from outside the company, but kept the online venture separate, organizationally and operationally, from its traditional operations.

Switching

Switching is a more radical response to substitution threats than straddling because it involves a wholesale shift to the substitute. Despite its obvious attraction in terms of speed—and the enthusiasm for it in the disruptive-technology literature—switching is, especially in fast-moving environments, like changing horses in mid-stream: there is sometimes no alternative, but the maneuver *is* often subject to spills. Switches also raise questions that should be asked and answered *before* the fact about how the business that is switching will add value after doing so. Given its sense that online retailing would continue to be a niche within the broader book market, it is not surprising that Barnes & Noble chose not to switch.

Recombining

Switching involves adoption of a model of how to compete that is already "out there." In many cases, however, recombining elements of existing ways of competing with some of the new possibilities implicit in substitution threats seems to work better than wholesale switching. Recombination or hybridization possibilities tremendously expand the range of possible responses to substitution threats.

Barnes & Noble should probably have paid more attention earlier on to such possibilities, particularly to the obvious ones of combining its unmatched store network with elements of online book retailing by, for example, using the stores to facilitate orders, delivery, and returns for the online business. The company finally began to move in this direction in late 2000 by introducing Internet Service Counters in the stores and allowing Bandn.com products to be returned there—but this move came too late to allow it to challenge Amazon for leadership online.

Leapfrogging

Leapfrogging is the most radically innovative response to a threat of substitution: it involves trying to outsubstitute the substitution threat by looking for a performance improvement or value innovation that promises even better performance.[34] Thus in 1999/2000, as it became clear that Bandn.com's Amazon-like approach was not gaining ground on Amazon, Barnes & Noble invested more than half a billion dollars in two attempts at leapfrogging: an e-book initiative that required expensive software but could potentially displace physical distribution and a print-on-demand initiative that required expensive printing machinery but could potentially displace some of publishers' traditional roles. Given their desperate character, it is not very surprising that neither initiative panned out.

In summary, there are no foolproof responses to substitution threats. Nevertheless, recognition of the variety and seriousness of such threats and the array of possible responses to them should help companies go beyond the fight-or-switch dichotomy.

THE THREAT OF HOLDUP

Even if an organization can protect its added value from the threats of imitation and substitution, the ability of its owners to appropriate that added value cannot be taken for granted. There are two systematic threats to value appropriation over time: holdup and slack. Holdup, discussed in this section, threatens to divert sustained added value to buyers, suppliers, complementors, and the like, whereas slack—discussed in the next section—threatens to dissipate it.

For a simple example of holdup, consider the privately owned Ambassador Bridge, which links Detroit in the United States and Windsor in Canada and handles nearly 30 percent of the annual trade between the two countries, which are the world's largest trading partners. Since the nearest competing bridge is 80 miles away, and farther from the region's economic center, the Ambassador can charge a significant premium: nearly twice as much for a gas tanker, according to a comparison from 2003.[35] Given the significant escalation in fuel prices since then, the Ambassador Bridge's locational advantage has expanded rather than eroded.

The scarcity value of the Ambassador Bridge is threatened by plans to build a second bridge close by to relieve congestion caused by the tightening of borders after September 11, 2001. But while plans for this new bridge are still being finalized, the owners of the Ambassador Bridge have invested significantly in amenities such as more customs booths and better highway connections, and have secured some of the permissions required to add a second six-lane span to the existing bridge—all the while projecting that total traffic will remain flat over the next 40 years.[36]

The Ambassador Bridge's ability to hold up and appropriate some of the value created through cross-border trade is easy to analyze because the size of the pie is relatively fixed and the balance of power in determining how it is sliced is very one-sided. Holdup assumes more complex forms when players' actions affect the size of the pie as well as the way in which it is sliced up and when they exhibit interdependence, often reflecting underlying resource cospecialization.[37] Bilateral monopoly represents the extreme case in which the added value of each player is equal to the total value that the two create by transacting with one another.

To reflect on these complexities, consider the relationships between automakers and their parts suppliers. Currently, efficiency requires substantial tangible and intangible investments by both automakers and their suppliers, with underinvestment potentially raising costs and reducing differentiation by limiting quality and innovation, lengthening development cycles, and even raising recall risks. The required investments are often relationship specific and hard to reverse or recoup. But a supplier that modifies its designs, machinery, or processes to cater to a specific automaker's requirements runs some risk of being held up by it. Conversely, an automaker can leave itself vulnerable to holdup by its suppliers. Fears of holdup can, as a result, shrink the total size of the pie by reducing the amount of investment or by distorting it (by, for example, forcing inefficient reductions in investment specificity).

The evolution of automaker–supplier relationships over the last 100 years also illustrates a range of approaches for dealing with complex holdup threats.

Contracting

At the beginning of the twentieth century, U.S. automakers relied on older, more established suppliers to the bicycle and carriage industries.[38] As parts suppliers became more committed to the automobile industry and automakers undertook more coordination, the two sides shifted from transaction-by-transaction interactions toward longer-term relationships governed by contracts. Specialization subjected market-based, arm's-length transactions to market failures of the sort discussed in Chapter 6 and mandated alternative governance mechanisms. Contracting was one solution, but only a partial one, since completely comprehensive contracts enforceable at zero cost—contracts of the sort that could entirely eliminate fears of holdup—are typically impractical.[39]

Integrating

A second response to holdup threats, integration, came to the fore with the rapid expansion and consolidation of the U.S. automobile industry. Total production more than quadrupled between 1909 and 1914, and Ford achieved market dominance by increasing its volume more than 25-fold with its inexpensive Model T. Ford also rethought its supplier relationships over this period. In 1909, its operations involved mounting a body, wheels, and tires (sourced from others) on a complete chassis supplied by the Dodge brothers. But by 1914, the Dodges were using their profits from the Model T to enter auto assembly, while Ford was vertically integrating backwards into parts and inputs, partly to reduce dependence on a few suppliers but also as part of a broader cost-leadership strategy. Vertical integration was meant to help efficiency by ensuring large-scale investments that suppliers were reluctant to make, easing coordination, exploiting the potential for speed unlocked by Ford's assembly line innovation, and reducing the risk of disruption (no small concern, since Ford's operations were often within a half-hour of suspension because of tardy deliveries). By the mid-1920s, Ford's vertical scope extended all the way back into mines, plantations, forests, and even sheep farms.

Vertical integration combined with specialization, scale, and process innovation to help reduce the real costs of the Model T by three-quarters between 1909 and 1924, as illustrated in Exhibit 1.3. But it also helped triple asset-intensity, increased operating leverage, and—once heavier closed bodies began to replace the Model T's open-car design in the 1920s—proved very inflexible: Ford lost long-term leadership to General Motors (GM) as it changed over from the Model T to the Model A in 1927–1928.[40] Other vertically integrated auto operations also experienced pressure from independent suppliers' excess capacity and product innovation capabilities in the 1920s and 1930s. Furthermore, vertical integration did not so much solve coordination or incentive problems as transfer them from outside to inside the firm (e.g., the thorny issue of transfer pricing). In addition, vertical integration to avoid holdup by parts suppliers increased exposure to holdup by the industry's formidable labor union, the United Automobile Workers (UAW).

Increasing (and Using) Bargaining Power

After World War II, despite some deintegration at Ford, overall levels of integration remained high. GM, Ford, and, to a lesser extent, Chrysler manufactured at least some of their requirements of every basic component (and up to 100 percent in the case of such critical items as engines, transmissions, and axles), while outsourcing the rest to a number of suppliers with whom they played hardball.[41] The automakers fragmented their supplier base and further reduced suppliers' added values by maintaining large in-house R&D staffs, forcing innovators to part with their technologies, breaking down systems into parts, and making every part into a commodity through comprehensive specifications. Contracts focused on prices, rarely ran for more than one year, and often were not renewed. Other ways in which the domestic Big Three put pressure on prices included using inspection teams to estimate suppliers' costs, letting small, low-overhead suppliers make low bids that could be used in negotiations with other suppliers, linking price concessions on a particular part sourced from a large supplier to continued purchases of other parts, and even starting rumors about potential competition.

Most of these practices represented attempts to counter supplier power, as discussed in the context of the "five forces" framework, so that framework does have something useful to say about the threat of holdup. Note, however, that taking just this bargaining/hardball perspective raises the risk of going too far in marginalizing suppliers, to a point where the shrinkage in the size of the pie outweighs the increased share of the pie that such efforts might secure. The other approaches discussed in this section remind us that maximizing relative bargaining power is not the only way to address the holdup problem.

Building Mutual Dependence

Large-scale entry by Japanese automakers into the U.S. market in the 1970s and 1980s forced the domestic Big Three to rethink their hardball approach, especially as the role of supplier relationships in the success of the Japanese became clearer.[42] Despite less vertical integration than their U.S. counterparts, Japanese automakers worked with far fewer suppliers with whom they maintained long-term relationships, exchanged employees and information, and partnered in innovation as well as production. Specifically, most parts supplied were "black boxes," with the automaker providing only general specifications and the supplier preparing all of the detailed specifications and blueprints, which made it difficult to switch suppliers. The suppliers, in turn, invested in assets specific to individual automakers: the typical Japanese supplier-partner relied on a single automaker for 60 percent of its sales, versus a figure of 34 percent in the United States.[43] In other words, both sides built up their confidence in each other to the level where they were both willing to invest in a profit stream that would materialize only *if* they continued to work together. Such **interorganizational relationships** can be self-sustaining only if each player is allotted a sufficiently large share of the gains from cooperation. Opportunism may then be limited by the threat of disappearance of the large profit stream available from cooperation.[44] This is very different from the approaches discussed so far in this section, all of which emphasize the minimization of dependence on others.

During the 1990s, the domestic Big Three moved to cooperate more with their suppliers. GM and Ford spun off their large internal parts operations, Delphi and Visteon, helping address independent suppliers' fears that any improvements they proposed would be passed on to the internal parts operations and their value thereby held up. But Chrysler, the least integrated to begin with, moved farthest in reshaping its supplier relationships by investing in coordination, recognizing suppliers' needs to make a fair profit, soliciting feedback and sharing the savings, shifting toward longer-term contracts, and creating the expectation of business beyond the life of the contract if suppliers performed. GM and Ford never got as far and, in the grip of the industry downturn of the early 2000s, all of the Big Three began to revert to focusing mainly on prices.[45] Since then, the U.S. auto parts industry has experienced a wave of bankruptcies (including Delphi's), divestitures, and restructuring—and refocused on other automakers whose output is actually growing.

Developing Trust

The stability of cooperative relationships can also be enhanced by trust. The Japanese business environment, for example, seems to deal with opportunism by placing more emphasis on social institutions (norms, etc.) and less on legal institutions than in the United States. It is possible that Japanese automakers have benefited from this general social context in establishing cooperative relationships with their suppliers. However, researchers continue to disagree about whether the Japanese auto industry *really* exhibits trust in a sense that goes beyond self-interested calculations that recognize mutual dependence—especially given recent moves at Nissan and even Toyota toward "less Japanese" supplier relationships.[46]

It is also worth noting that the broader context in which a business operates can create a different type of holdup threat: one reflecting unilateral **expropriation** rather than bargaining based on resource dependence or cospecialization. Social norms about acceptable levels of profit and market power, in particular, can generate legal and other nonmarket challenges that threaten the appropriation of added value. Legal restrictions are worth understanding in some detail here and in the context of some of the discussions in the preceding chapters, because along a number of dimensions, the law can be more constricting than personal conceptions of what is fair or ethical. And governmental intervention is especially worth watching out for in certain types of industries. These include industries that already feature a high level of governmental involvement (through procurement, funding, regulation, public ownership, etc.), loom large in terms of size, investments, employment, votes, or general political salience (e.g., media ownership), are considered part of the national patrimony (e.g., natural resources), or supply mass consumption staples or "entitlement" goods (e.g., food or even pharmaceuticals). Of course, in such environments, companies often strive to be involved in rule-making. At a broader level, while the origins of nonmarket threats of holdup differ from those of the market-based threats on which this section focuses, some of the same remedies (with the obvious exception of vertical integration) can be employed to mitigate them.

To summarize, holdup is a systematic threat to the appropriability of added value that tends to be based on resource dependence or cospecialization. Strategic responses to holdup vary in the extent to which they emphasize competition versus cooperation. Given the traditional strategic bias toward taking the competitive approach and increasing one's slice of the pie, explicit attention should also be paid to the possibility of growing the pie. Or to repeat one of the messages from Chapter 2, strategists must think about relationships both cooperatively and competitively.

THE THREAT OF SLACK

Slack is an internal threat to the appropriation of added value that can be defined as the gap between the value actually appropriated over time and the amount potentially available given the other threats to sustainability discussed earlier (and the strategic responses to them). In dynamic terms, slack reflects persistent suboptimization by a business that dissipates appropriable added value or even reduces added value over time. In some contexts, it is more natural to discuss the inverse of slack, what might be referred to as **organizational effectiveness**.

Although slack is relatively easy to define, it can be hard to measure. Distinguishing between slack and poor choices about how to deal with other threats to sustainability, while desirable, is often difficult. There are, in addition, a host of other complications. Some "slack" may be needed to attract customers (e.g., law offices). Some may be essential for experimentation with new strategies and innovative projects, which might not be possible in a more resource-constrained environment. Some may reflect nonmonetary compensation to employees. And so on. The broader point is that some apparent slack may be of considerable value.

These complications notwithstanding, researchers have tried to measure slack anyway. Statistical estimates, while not very precise, suggest that various inefficiencies dissipate between 10 percent and 40 percent of revenues in U.S. manufacturing.[47] Large amounts of slack are also suggested by the capability differences among direct competitors that were cited in Exhibit 5.3. But while slack is of general significance, it is of particular interest here because of its relationship to sustained success. Without current or past success, a business is unlikely to have much room to suboptimize (although well-funded start-ups may be exceptions to this rule). Success in the form of appropriable added value expands the scope for suboptimization and can also—as a result of arrogance or other corporate sins—compromise the quality of choice. In plainer language, rich diets are relatively likely to lead to a hardening of corporate arteries. So it is unsurprising that the most stupendous contemporary case of slack involves a company that was, for decades, the world's largest industrial enterprise, General Motors.

GM's financial performance has been abysmal for some time now. Its manufacturing operations have lost money for the last few years and, at the end of 2007, its equity market value was $14 billion, barely up from $13 billion at the end of 1980—and down by more than one-half in real terms. By the end of 2008, that figure had dipped to $2 billion, and bankruptcy loomed.

But between 1980 and 2007, GM's strategic investments—net capital expenditures plus R&D—amounted to $346 billion if simply added up and $1,172 billion in terms of their present value in 2007 if carried forward at a 10 percent annual rate (see Exhibit 5.4)! Even if one assumes that the company's market value would have collapsed to zero in the absence of these strategic expenditures, and that it would have been unable to pay stockholders the $35 billion in dividends that it did, the amount of value destroyed at GM over this period ran into hundreds of billions of dollars.[48] In other words the benefit-to-cost ratio of GM's strategic investments between 1980 and 2007 was *much much* lower than one. As H. Ross Perot, briefly a GM director, pointed out, the company could have bought Toyota and Honda in the mid-1980s for *half* of the $80 billion it spent on a program to automate its factories.

GM's poor performance partly reflects industry effects: average profit margins in the auto assembly industry have declined from 20 percent in the 1930s to around 10 percent in the 1960s and zero to negative levels in the 2000s. But that is not the whole

EXHIBIT 5.4   Market Value versus Cumulated Strategic Investments at General Motors.

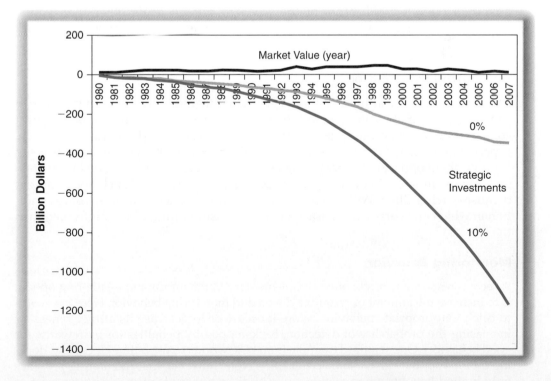

story: the Japanese Big Three, particularly Toyota, have performed well financially over the last two decades, and even the smaller of the U.S. Big Three did not destroy as much value as GM in proportionate terms. So one must also look at GM-specific explanations.

There are many such explanations, of which only a few can be cited here. GM failed to respond effectively to the surge in sales of light trucks, and many of its car designs continue to be boxy. Its factory automation program proved both very costly and ineffective. It maintains an oversized production infrastructure in the hope of reversing the erosion of its market share. It continues to receive worse marks for its supplier relationships than Chrysler and Ford. Its relationship with the UAW has arguably been worse as well and has involved greater direct exposure, given a history of more backward integration—although the decline of labor and related expenses, from one-third of revenues in the mid-1980s to one-ninth by 2003, cast some doubt on the company's tendency to emphasize labor holdup as *the* problem.

Whatever the "real" explanation for GM's poor performance, it seems clear that value destruction on this scale would have been impossible if GM had not previously accumulated a pool of resources that afforded it large **free cash flows**. Its ability to destroy several times its assessed market value at the beginning of the 1980s presumably reflects the fact that expectations of high, ongoing levels of slack were also built into the valuation of these cash flows. And GM's ongoing struggles with slack more than a quarter century after Japanese competition shook up the U.S. auto industry suggest that slack is often sustained by powerful inertial forces. As one might expect, GM scores high on most of the indicators of inertia flagged on the basis of organization theory in Exhibit 4.5—size, maturity, complexity, bureaucratization, thick culture, insularity, poor information, and continuity at the top—as well as on governance-related indicators of the scope to pursue goals other than value-maximization. Organization theory also suggests some remedies for sustained slack that will briefly be mentioned here.[49]

Generating Information

The difficulty of measuring slack increases, rather than decreases, the importance of generating information about it. **Benchmarking** against direct competitors or against companies that are best-in-class in certain activities is obviously useful. Simulation, experimentation, and direct investigation of the effects of changes are other ways of learning about opportunities for improvement. But an added emphasis on information gathering is unlikely to be an adequate basis for identifying all such opportunities because of what Oliver Williamson has referred to as **impacted information**: a condition in which one party to a transaction or relationship is much better informed than the other(s).[50]

Monitoring Behavior

A second response to slack, often complementary to the information-gathering option, is to increase the amount of resources devoted to monitoring behavior. Here the goal is to catch inappropriate behavior before it occurs or to decrease its attractiveness by increasing the probability of detection, backstopped by penalties (or by rewards for good behavior). One standard example is making workers punch time clocks and docking their pay if they arrive late or quit early. Note, however, that monitoring provides only limited benefits when a wide range of discretionary legitimate choices exist or when resources are what are referred to as plastic. Is a software developer sitting beside a brook with her eyes closed slacking off or having a commercially valuable vision?

Offering Performance Incentives

Even when monitoring behavior is impractical or uneconomical, it may be possible to reward good behavior indirectly by rewarding good performance. Such an approach works best when an individual's (or group's) behavior is tightly connected to the performance outcomes that are actually observed. This condition is often violated, though, when there are significant coordination requirements or other reasons why performance can be measured only in highly aggregated terms. In addition, a high degree of emphasis on financial incentives can upset norms (especially about equity), exacerbate attempts to game the system, and divert creativity from real to paper entrepreneurialism.

Shaping Norms

A fourth approach to dealing with slack involves supplementing economic rewards or punishments with appeals to norms, values, a sense of mission, and so forth. Underlying this approach is the idea that people in organizations are motivated by more than just sticks or carrots. Of course, **moral suasion** alone is unlikely to be totally effective. Given the heated debate between economists and other social scientists about the relative efficacy of economic versus "intrinsic" motivation, the safest conclusion is that a manager intent on reducing slack should consider both types of levers as opposed to fixating on only one of them.

Bonding Resources

Bonding resources is a top-down approach to containing slack. It is derived from Michael C. Jensen's theory of the agency costs of free cash flow.[51] According to Jensen, managers are imperfectly policed by shareholders, have incentives to grow the resources under their control, and are most able to take such steps when free cash flow is large—leading to investments that destroy shareholder value. One obvious remedy is to pile up debt so as to reduce free cash flow (by creating contractual obligations to pay fixed interest expenses). The risk is that the company may become overloaded with debt (i.e., end up with negative free cash flow).

Changing Governance

Bonding resources is just one of several top-down ways of dealing with slack. Others include creating small but well-informed and powerful boards of directors, restricting the ability of CEOs and other insiders to dominate those boards, requiring board members and top managers to own substantial amounts of a firm's equity (in relation to their personal wealth), encouraging (other) large, active investors, and unwinding cross-subsidies.[52]

Mobilizing for Change

Forcing change at the top may often be necessary to reverse slack-related problems, but it is rarely sufficient by itself. Research on change management suggests a number of complementary tactics that address inertial barriers: creating dissatisfaction with the status quo, communicating a powerful vision of what can be accomplished with change, and changing people and processes as well as organizational structure.[53]

In summary, slack is an internal rather than external threat to the appropriation of added value. This does not imply, however, that slack is easier to control than the other threats to sustainability discussed in this chapter. The scope for slack is highest in companies that have enjoyed, or are enjoying, considerable economic success. It is amplified by the difficulties of gathering information, offering high-powered incentives, or otherwise directing the organization toward value creation and capture instead of value dissipation.

AN INTEGRATIVE EXAMPLE: WAL-MART

Exhibit 5.5 summarizes the four threats to sustainability as well as responses to them. Note, however, that these threats have so far been discussed in isolation. An integrated perspective on them is of interest, since companies typically face more than one threat at a time. For an integrative example that also illustrates the value of systematically thinking through threats to sustainability even in a situation where the scope for sustainability might seem relatively limited, consider the case of Wal-Mart, which posted a net income of $11.3 billion on sales of $345 billion in 2007, and had a market value at the end of the year of $190 billion. These numbers made Wal-Mart the world's largest company and, with 1.9 million employees, the world's largest private employer as well.

To begin by linking back to Chapter 3, Wal-Mart's competitive strategy has been to outperform its competitors by achieving lower operating costs and higher asset turns/efficiency (i.e., lower fixed costs per unit). The emphasis on low costs—and the

EXHIBIT 5.5 **Responding to Threats to Sustainability.**

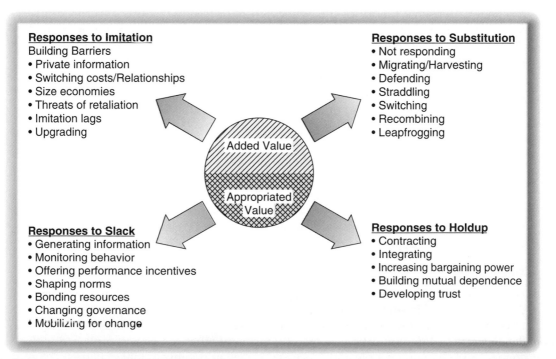

associated themes of buying in bulk, pricing low, focusing on metrics such as sales per square foot, and operating frugally, among others—have been in place at Wal-Mart for a long time now. In fact, these themes predate the startup of the first Wal-Mart store in 1962; they also characterized the Ben Franklin stores that Wal-Mart's founder, Sam Walton, operated as a franchisee in the 1940s and 1950s. So it seems to make sense to think of Wal-Mart as having been designed around a broad strategic target, low cost, with some continuity in terms of its definition and pursuit, but also some evolution in the context of an adaptive, analytical culture that searches out and spreads improvements across many physical locations.

Given Wal-Mart's focus on *discount* retailing, it is not very surprising that a low-cost/low-price position has proven to be the biggest engine of economic value creation within that industry. What *is* more surprising is Wal-Mart's ability to sustain superior performance with this apparently obvious strategy: it has posted a return on equity in excess of 20 percent in all but a handful of years since the early 1970s while growing revenues a thousand-fold. Why *hasn't* this successful strategy fallen prey to the four threats to sustainability: imitation, substitution, holdup, and slack?

To begin with imitation, Wal-Mart is protected by an array of barriers, some of which it has deliberately erected:

- *Scale Economies:* Wal-Mart initially tapped local scale economies by locating in towns large enough to accommodate one discounter but not two. It moved on to exploit regional scale economies by building up its hub-and-spoke distribution system, followed by the pursuit of national scale economies in dealing with suppliers and intermediaries.
- *Learning/Private Information:* Wal-Mart has gone to great lengths to analyze the myriad details of retailing: how to load trucks to minimize storage space, unpack boxes, schedule part-time labor, juggle fixture heights for maximum impact, and so on. In addition, it aggressively "borrows" ideas from all over and maintains the second-largest customer database in the world.
- *Switching Costs/Relationships:* Wal-Mart is often perceived as having the lowest prices even in markets where it doesn't. Lock-in is also increased by its ability to persuade suppliers to make major Wal-Mart-specific investments in systems such as Retail Link, which furnishes them with computerized access to real-time data on the sales and inventories of their products at the store level.
- *Threats of Retaliation:* Wal-Mart's policy of allowing store managers to match or beat the lowest competing price on an item in their trading area by as much as 5 percent has presumably had a chilling effect on competitors/ potential entrants in its local markets, as has its general reputation for fierceness.
- *Lags/Upgrading/Complexity:* Wal-Mart has kept competitors off balance by continuously upgrading its capabilities, particularly in information technology and logistics, and making discrete resource commitments to initiatives such as Retail Link. Imitating Wal-Mart's culture or its entire complex activity system would probably take a very long time even if it *were* feasible.

The principal substitution threats that Wal-Mart has faced have been related to the risk that its discount retailing operations might be replaced by a new format. This kind of format risk is highlighted by the theory of the "wheel of retailing," which predicts that operators of old formats will have trouble adjusting to the new ones. But Wal-Mart has actually been quite active in exploring potential substitutes for its traditional discount stores: it entered warehouse clubs in a big way, enjoyed enormous success with the hybrid food-nonfood format of Supercenters, and is exploring a smaller format with Neighborhood Markets. This kind of mobility across formats should not be too surprising, because Sam Walton started up Wal-Mart as a way of switching from one retailing format to another. Wal-Mart also tries to be a leader in figuring out how to deploy new technologies with transformational potential—such as RFID or wireless tags that can be used to track goods passively as they pass from suppliers to warehouses to stores.

As for holdup, it is useful to distinguish between suppliers of merchandise and employees. In regard to the former, Wal-Mart's extraordinary growth has allowed it to build up an unusual amount of bargaining power, even vis-à-vis very large suppliers. Thus, in 2007, Procter & Gamble derived 15 percent of its total revenues from sales to Wal-Mart, while the same dollar amount represented 3.3 percent of Wal-Mart's revenues.[54] Wal-Mart does bargain hard with its suppliers by, for example, focusing on a single pricing number; getting suppliers to pay for modular displays, promotions, and the like, on top of that; and developing private labels after learning the business from them. But it also seems to afford suppliers enough surplus—in terms of real-time information and shared expertise as well as volume and terms—to induce them, for example, to invest much more in the aggregate in its Retail Link platform than the $4 billion that Wal-Mart itself reportedly spent. And companies that supply Wal-Mart seem to perform better than those that focus on other retailers.[55]

Labor holdup is more of an issue. Wal-Mart has fiercely and so far successfully resisted unionization efforts. Holding the line on wages is critically important, since a $1 per hour across-the-board increase might reduce Wal-Mart's income by one-quarter. But there has been enormous negative fallout, ranging from employee demotivation and very high turnover rates to unflattering public portrayals—for example, of Wal-Mart employees living below the poverty line or lacking health-care coverage. Behind the public portrayals is heightened public scrutiny of Wal-Mart now that it has become the largest company in the world and a related shift in public perceptions of the company—in former CEO David Glass's words—from endearing underdog to overbearing top dog. Wal-Mart has moved to address these issues and there are indications of some recent success in this regard. That said, public perceptions of Wal-Mart's penny-pinching and power are likely to continue to be concerns—and possible catalysts of nonmarket holdup—for the foreseeable future.

Finally, Wal-Mart seems to have experienced limited slack so far, for a number of reasons. The scope for deliberate departures from value-maximization is limited by the Walton family, which owns a little over 40 percent of the company's stock and whose interests are represented by Sam Walton's eldest son, Rob Walton, who serves as chairman of Wal-Mart's board of directors. Employees are motivated through incentives; particularly at the store-manager level and above, tight performance monitoring that is facilitated by the pursuit of a cost-based strategy, and social control through deeply embedded norms about frugality, performance improvement, and so on. Nonetheless, slack may become a significant issue in the future: because of the challenges of communicating with two million employees well enough to preserve at least elements of Wal-Mart's traditional culture, doing so despite weakening bonds between store managers and employees because of larger stores and 24-hour operation, dealing with widening horizontal spans of control and increasing bureaucratic complexity (especially given the centralization of decision making at corporate headquarters), and similar factors.

EXHIBIT 5.6 Wal-Mart Revenue Growth, 1971–2007.

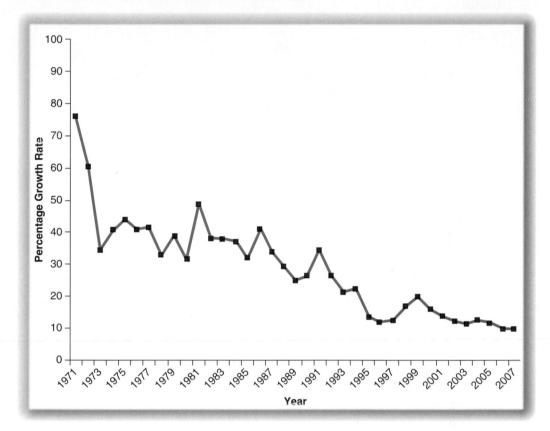

In addition to creating organizational challenges for Wal-Mart, growth has become a challenge in its own right (see Exhibit 5.6). Wal-Mart's declining growth rate reflects its increasingly large share of a retailing category, discounting, that has grown at only 2–3 percent per year recently. The reason Wal-Mart has done as well as it has in the last decade is because it has built up a major growth engine outside its traditional core with its Supercenter format. It now faces the challenge of developing another new growth engine or two by accelerating expansion into other businesses or geographies. Such decisions about horizontal and geographic scope are, respectively, the topics of Chapters 6 and 7.

Summary

Like Chapter 4, this chapter concentrated on dynamics. Unlike Chapter 4, it focused on situations in which players are more numerous or faceless and identified four evolutionary dynamics that threaten sustainability in such contexts. Two dynamics—imitation and substitution—threaten businesses' added value, and two others—holdup and slack—threaten their owners' ability to appropriate that added value for themselves. Understanding these dynamics and looking across all of them should afford managers extra insight into the evolution of the business landscapes on which they operate and the issue of how to counter threats—or even turn them into opportunities.

Glossary

appropriability
benchmarking
capability
causal ambiguity
complexity
commitment
contestable
cospecialization
cross-sectional fit
disruptive technologies

expropriation
free cash flow
holdup
imitation
impacted
information
interorganizational
relationships
learning
moral suasion

organizational
effectiveness
retaliation
scarcity value
slack
social complexity
sticky resources
substitution
sustainability
tetra-threat framework

Notes

1. These data were originally reported in Pankaj Ghemawat, *Commitment: The Dynamic of Strategy* (New York: Free Press, 1991).

2. Robert R. Wiggins and Timothy W. Ruefli, "Sustained Competitive Advantage: Temporal Dynamics and the Incidence and Persistence of Superior Economic Performance," *Organization Science* 13, no. 1 (January–February 2002): 82–105.

3. Anita M. McGahan and Michael E. Porter, "The Emergence and Sustainability of Abnormal Profits," *Strategic Organization* 1, no. 1 (February 2003): 79–108.

4. Ghemawat, *Commitment*, chap. 2.

5. The basic idea can be found in Kenneth R. Andrews, *The Concept of Corporate Strategy* (Homewood, Ill.: Richard D. Irwin, 1971), but was revived in 1984 in an article by Birger Wernerfelt, "A Resource-Based View of the Firm," *Strategic Management Journal* 5, no. 2 (April–June 1984): 171–180.

6. For example, Wernerfelt, "Resource-Based View," defined resources very broadly as "anything which could be thought of as a strength or weakness of a given firm" (p. 172).

7. Consider, for example, what seems to be the most popular resource-based framework for assessing sustained strengths and weaknesses, the VRIO framework proposed by Jay Barney, where V denotes value, R rarity, I inimitability, and O organizational effectiveness. V, R, and I seem to have a high degree of overlap, especially in a dynamic context, although this framework *does* provide some interesting ways of thinking about I and about complexity that are briefly discussed later in this chapter, in the section on the threat of imitation. See Jay B. Barney, *Gaining and Sustaining Competitive*

Advantage, 2nd ed. (Upper Saddle River, N.J.: Prentice Hall, 2002), chap. 5, pp. 149–192.

8. Steven A. Lippman and Richard P. Rumelt, "A Bargaining Perspective on Resource Advantage," *Strategic Management Journal* 24, no. 11 (November 2003): 1069–1086.

9. To make the connections with Chapter 4 precise, this is equivalent to replacing game-theoretic equilibrium in strategies with equilibrium defined in terms of observed outcomes and underpinned by the behavioral assumption of "one smart rival." The latter assumption embodies much weaker rationality requirements than Nash equilibrium, as explained in John Sutton, "One Smart Agent," *Rand Journal of Economics* 28, no. 4 (Winter 1997): 605–628.

10. Adam M. Brandenburger and Barry J. Nalebuff, *Co-Opetition* (New York: Doubleday, 1996), chaps. 5 and 6.

11. The evidence on imitation is discussed in more detail in Pankaj Ghemawat, "Sustainable Advantage," *Harvard Business Review* 64, no. 5 (September–October 1986): 53–58. The article provides specific citations.

12. Stephen P. Bradley, John R. Wells, and James Weber, "The Pharmaceutical Industry in 2003," (Harvard Business School Publishing Case no. 704-470, Boston, 2004).

13. Leila Abboud, "Raging Hormones: How Drug Giant Keeps a Monopoly on 60-Year-Old Pill," *Wall Street Journal,* September 9, 2004, p. A1.

14. The details in this paragraph are based on Marcia Angell, *The Truth About the Drug Companies: How They Deceive Us and What to Do About It* (New York: Random House, 2004).

15. It is also worth noting the related category of *network externalities,* which exist when the

attractions to buyers, suppliers, or comple-mentors of joining a network increase with its size.

16. For an example of the pressure that this has put on large generic manufacturers, see the discussion of Teva of Israel in Leila Abboud, "Clone Wars: An Israeli Giant in Generic Drugs Faces New Rivals," *Wall Street Journal*, October 28, 2004, p. A1.

17. Citations for most of these sources can be found in Ghemawat, *Commitment*, chap. 5. See also Richard Hall, "The Strategic Analysis of Intangible Resources," *Strategic Management Journal* 13, no. 2 (February 1992): 135–144.

18. *Public Citizen*, "Rx R&D Myths: The Case against The Drug Industry's R&D 'Scare Card'" (2001 [accessed November 2, 2004]); available from www.citizen.org/documents/ACFDC. PDF, cited in Angell, *Truth About the Drug Companies*, p. 269, fn. 7.

19. Jeffrey R. Williams, "How Sustainable Is Your Competitive Advantage?" *California Management Review* 34, no. 3 (Spring 1992): 29–51.

20. Steven A. Lippman and Richard P. Rumelt, "Uncertain Imitability: An Analysis of Interfirm Differences in Efficiency under Competition," *Bell Journal of Economics* 13, no. 2 (Autumn 1982): 418–438.

21. Jay Barney, "Firm Resources and Sustained Competitive Advantage," *Journal of Management* 17, no. 1 (March 1991): 99–120.

22. Michael E. Porter, "What Is Strategy?" *Harvard Business Review* 74, no. 6 (November–December 1996): 61–78.

23. W. Carl Kester, "Today's Options for Tomorrow's Growth," *Harvard Business Review* (March–April 1984): 153–160.

24. For a book-length treatment of commitment decisions that also discusses how uncertainty can be folded into the analysis—basically, through the concept of flexibility value—see Ghemawat, *Commitment: The Dynamic of Strategy* (New York: Free Press, 1991), esp. chap. 6.

25. For the original discussion that frames these and other issues concerning capabilities, see David J. Teece and Gary P. Pisano, "The Dynamic Capabilities of Firms: An Introduction," *Industrial and Corporate Change* (1994 No. 3), pp. 537–556.

26. See, for example David M. Upton, "Flexibility as Process Mobility: The Management of Plant Capabilities for Quick Response Manufacturing," *Journal of Operations Management* 12, nos. 3–4 (June 1995): 205–224; Rebecca Henderson and Iain Cockburn, "Scale, Scope, and Spillovers: The Determinants of Research Productivity in Drug

Discovery," *Rand Journal of Economics* 27, no. 1 (Spring 1996): 32–59, Kim B. Clark and Takahiro Fujimoto, *Product Development Performance: Strategy, Organization, and Management in the World Auto Industry* (Boston: Harvard Business School Press, 1991), and Gary P. Pisano, *The Development Factory: Unlocking the Potential of Process Innovation* (Boston: Harvard Business School Press, 1997).

27. For some tips on how to conduct a capability audit, see Dave Ulrich and Norm Smallwood, "Capitalizing on Capabilities," *Harvard Business Review* 82, no. 6 (June 2004): 119–126.

28. See Dorothy Leonard-Barton, "Core Capabilities and Core Rigidities: A Paradox in Managing New Product Development," *Strategic Management Journal* (1992): 111–125.

29. Joseph A. Schumpeter, *Capitalism, Socialism, and Democracy* (New York: Harper, 1942), p. 84. See also Ingemar Dierickx and Karel Cool, "Asset Stock Accumulation and Sustainability of Competitive Advantage," *Management Science* 35, no. 12 (December 1989): 1504–1511.

30. Clayton M. Christensen, *Innovation and the General Manager* (Boston: Irwin/McGraw-Hill, 1999), idem, *The Innovator's Dilemma: When New Technologies Cause Great Firms to Fail*, The Management of Innovation and Change Series (Boston: Harvard Business School Press, 1997).

31. Christensen, *Innovator's Dilemma*.

32. Ibid.

33. Richard N. Foster, *Innovation: The Attacker's Advantage* (New York: Summit Books, 1986).

34. W. Chan Kim and Renee Mauborgne, "Value Innovation: The Strategic Logic of High Growth," *Harvard Business Review* 75, no. 1 (January–February 1997): 102, reprinted in June 2004 issue.

35. This comparison and the preceding information on the Ambassador Bridge are based on John Lippert and Erik Schatzker's "Matty's Bridge," Bloomberg, March 2003.

36. "Michigan Gives Thumbs Up to Twin Ambassador Span," Today'sTrucking. com, March 16, 2007, at http://www.todaystrucking .com/news.cfm?intDocID=17626; "Ambassador Bridge Representatives Lash Out," June 13,2008, at http://liberalmedianot. blogspot.com/2008/ 06/ambassador-bridge-representatives-lash .html; "Ambassador Bridge To Expand," *Detroit News*, June 17, 2008, at http://www .clickondetroit.com/news/16631725/detail. html;

37. For the pioneering discussion of holdup, see Oliver E. Williamson, *Markets and Hierarchies, Analysis and Antitrust Implications: A Study in the Economics of Internal Organization* (New York: Free Press, 1975).

38. For a historical overview on which some of this discussion is based, see Susan Helper, "Strategy and Irreversibility in Supplier Relations: The Case of the U.S. Automobile Industry," *Business History Review* 65, no. 4 (1991): 781–824.

39. Reasons include bounded rationality, uncertainty about the future, and asymmetric information. See Williamson, *Markets and Hierarchies,* and the discussion in Chapter 6.

40. William J. Abernathy and Kenneth Wayne, "Limits of the Learning Curve," *Harvard Business Review* 52, no. 5 (September–October 1974): 109–119.

41. Michael E. Porter, "Note on Supplying the Automobile Industry (Condensed)" (Harvard Business School Publishing case no. 386-176, Boston, 1986).

42. Jeffrey H. Dyer, "Does Governance Matter? Keiretsu Alliances and Asset Specificity as Sources of Japanese Competitive Advantage," *Organization Science* 7, no. 6 (November–December 1996): 649–666.

43. Ibid.

44. For a general discussion of how interorganizational relationships can lead in this fashion to sustained competitive advantage, see Jeffrey H. Dyer and Harbir Singh, "The Relational View: Cooperative Strategy and Sources of Interorganizational Competitive Advantage," *Academy of Management Review* 23, no. 4 (October 1998): 660–679.

45. Michelene Maynard, "Auto Parts du Jour; Suppliers Are Forced to Learn Flexibility," *New York Times,* August 31, 2001; and Andreas Maurer, Frank Dietz, and Nikolaus S. Lang, "Beyond Cost Reduction: Reinventing the Automotive OEM-Supplier Interface" (Boston Consulting Group, 2004): 18.

46. See, for instance, Pankaj Ghemawat and Rajiv Shukla, "The Coevolution of Auto Supply Chains: The U.S. and Japan" (Harvard Business School Publishing case no. 700-062, Boston, 2000).

47. Consult, for example, Richard E. Caves and David R. Barton, *Efficiency in U.S. Manufacturing Industries* (Cambridge, Mass.: MIT Press, 1990).

48. For more details on this methodology and an application to General Motors between 1980 and 1990, see Michael C. Jensen, "The Modern Industrial Revolution, Exit, and the Failure of Internal Control Systems," *Journal of Finance* 48, no. 3 (1993): 831–880.

49. For a more extended discussion of some of the ideas touched on here, see Paul R. Milgrom and John Roberts, *Economics, Organization and Management* (Englewood Cliffs, N.J.: Prentice-Hall, 1992), chap. 6.

50. Williamson, *Markets and Hierarchies,* 14.

51. Michael C. Jensen, "Agency Costs of Free Cash Flow, Corporate Finance, and Takeovers," *American Economic Review* 76, no. 2 (1986): 323–329.

52. Jensen, "Modern Industrial Revolution, Exit, and the Failure of Internal Control Systems."

53. For a managerial discussion, see John P. Kotter, "Leading Change: Why Transformation Efforts Fail," *Harvard Business Review* 73, no. 2 (March–April 1995): 59–67.

54. Proctor & Gamble's acquisition of Gillette did not change their situation much: Wal-Mart accounted for 16-1 of P&G and Gillette's combined revenues in 2004, and their sales to it represented 14-1 of Wal-Mart's revenues.

55. Marco Iansiti and Roy Levien, *The Keystone Advantage: What the New Dynamics of Business Ecosystems Mean for Strategy, Innovation, and Sustainability.* (Boston: Harvard Business School Press, 2004).

Choosing Corporate Scope
Pankaj Ghemawat and Jan W. Rivkin

> *But we must now refer to one question about systems in general, and about organization systems in particular, the answer to which is of fundamental importance. I refer to the question as to whether the whole is more than the sum of the parts . . . whether there emerge from the system properties which are not inherent in the parts.*

—CHESTER BARNARD, *THE FUNCTIONS OF THE EXECUTIVE* (1938), P. 79

This book has focused, for the most part, on strategy for a free-standing business in one industry. Yet large companies tend to operate in multiple industries. Procter & Gamble, for instance, expanded from its 1837 roots in the soap and candle industries to enter the markets for vegetable shortening (1911), laundry detergent (1933), hair care (1934), toothpaste (1955), toilet paper and paper towels (1957), diapers (1961), coffee (1963), pharmaceuticals (1978), cosmetics (1989), pet food (1999), and shaving products (through the acquisition of Gillette in 2005) among others. Though founded in 1892 on the basis of a handful of electrical inventions, especially electric lighting, General Electric (GE) now operates in industries as diverse as media and entertainment, health care, aircraft engines, energy infrastructure, household appliances, commercial and consumer finance, and insurance. This chapter examines the logic that underlies such choices of corporate scope.

Scope itself has several dimensions: horizontal scope (in what industries should a company compete?), vertical scope (should a company make its own inputs?), and geographic scope (where should a company compete?). To keep the scope of this chapter manageable, it focuses on horizontal scope. (For a brief discussion of vertical scope, see the section on holdup in Chapter 5). And geographic scope is dealt with in Chapter 7, on global strategy.

Systematic research suggests that the effects of common corporate ownership on the operating performance of businesses, while statistically significant, tend to be smaller than within-industry differences in performance that operate at the business level (the topic of Chapter 3) and differences in average performance at the industry level (the topic of Chapter 2). That said, **corporate strategy** cannot be ignored, for several reasons. First, the estimated corporate-level effects on performance, while smaller than direct business-level effects, are far from negligible. Second, inferences to be drawn from such estimates remain somewhat controversial. Third, the focus on ongoing operating performance used to isolate corporate effects in such studies misses out on at least some potential mechanisms for corporate value addition; for example, through one-time moves into or out of an industry, as appropriate. Finally, current corporate effects on performance seem to represent lower bounds on the strategic headroom afforded by corporate strategy, given our sense that there is a wide gap between best practice and average practice in this area. It is hard to deny that the best practitioners of corporate strategy—companies like GE, Danaher, Disney, and Berkshire Hathaway—have historically boosted the performance of their business units enormously.

The next section of this chapter reviews the evolution of the practice of corporate strategy. The rest of the chapter focuses on two tests to be applied to (horizontal) corporate strategy: the **better-off test** and the **best-alternative test**. Note the parallels to the discussion, in a single-business context in Chapters 3 and 5, of the challenges of adding value and appropriating value.

THE PRACTICE OF CORPORATE STRATEGY OVER TIME

Chapter 1 described the diffusion of portfolio plannings for charting corporate strategy among large U.S. corporations during the 1970s. It also discussed some of the doubts that quickly set in about, among other things, the mechanical determination of resource-allocation patterns on the basis of historical performance data and, in many cases, an arbitrary assumption of self-financing that effectively ignored the existence of capital markets. The 1970s also saw the first systematic empirical analyses of the performance implications of different types of diversification strategies, which began to suggest that, in the United States at least, related diversifiers outperformed unrelated diversifiers.[1]

Despite these developments, portfolio planning techniques continued to hold sway through the 1980s: the decade's most celebrated corporate strategy was Jack Welch's insistence on "#1, #2 or out" at GE, which focused attention on the market-share axis of the growth-share matrix. Further development of corporate strategy as strategy for a portfolio of strategic business units (SBUs) was heavily influenced, however, by the revolution in U.S. financial markets in the 1980s. A rising stock market and financing innovations such as junk bonds, abetted in a number of sectors by domestic deregulation and intensified foreign competition, fueled a wave of hostile takeovers and company restructurings that forced many firms to reevaluate their strategic thinking. Specialist consulting firms began to promote "value-based management" that made heavy use of financial measures of performance. According to one such firm, Marakon,

At least one-third, and probably more, of all units generate rates of return on equity capital each non-recession year that are significantly less than the respective costs of equity capital. Further, most of these units . . . also consistently invest equity capital at these unprofitable rates!!! Thus, they impose capital confiscation—capital losses—on their owners, not once or twice, but over and over again.[2]

By the end of the 1990s, value-based management techniques had been refined to proprietary levels (e.g., EVA, a trademarked acronym for economic value added), and 43 percent of large-company survey respondents reported that they had implemented formal value-based management systems.[3] This number was comparable to the 45 percent that had reported using portfolio planning techniques in a survey (by one of the same authors) two decades earlier.[4] The stated reasons for implementing value-based management paralleled the ones identified in the 1980s by Marakon, and were headed by "We could not clearly determine where value is created or destroyed in our company" and "Our employees did not appreciate that capital has a cost."

But the biggest change in the practice of corporate strategy in the 1990s was associated with the popularization of the concept of core competence by C. K. Prahalad and Gary Hamel.[5] In an article that went on to become the best-selling reprint in the history of the *Harvard Business Review,* Prahalad and Hamel launched a full-fledged attack on the SBU-level foundations of portfolio planning. They argued that in an SBU-based architecture, no single SBU feels responsible for maintaining a viable position in core products or competencies that cross business boundaries, competencies developed within an SBU are not shared across SBUs, and opportunities for growth are missed. As an alternative, they recommended a corporate-wide strategic architecture for competence building and asserted that the successful organizations of the future would be the ones that shifted their focus from SBUs to core competencies, because these formed the foundations of future growth.

While the model of related diversification implicit in writings on core competence was not entirely new, the suggestion that organizations reorganize around "relatedness threads" sparked considerable strategic activity at the corporate level. As of 2007, core competences ranked fifth among 25 popular management tools in terms of usage in a global survey by Bain and Company, behind strategic planning, customer relationship management, customer segmentation and benchmarking, in that order.[6]

As in the case of portfolio planning, however, doubts about the doctrine of core competence began to emerge within a few years of large-scale diffusion. Two academic strategists dismissed it as "a 'feel good' exercise that no one fails." After all, "every company can identify one activity that it does relatively better than other activities and claim that as its core competence." For this reason, the definition of a firm's core competence should not be based on an "internal assessment of which activity, of all its activities, the company performs best. It should be a harsh external assessment of what it does better than competitors, for which the term distinctive competence is more appropriate."[7]

The empirical case for focusing on core competences also remains in doubt. The core competence argument implies that diversifying in related businesses will yield higher returns than unrelated diversification. Yet extensive unrelated diversification remains common, and apparently profitable, in many countries outside the United States. Even in the United States, one can find successful companies such as

Berkshire Hathaway that have ignored the stricture to focus on their core competences. One can also find companies that have expanded in directions suggested by alleged core competencies yet stumbled badly. Consider, for instance, the "socks and stocks" corporate strategy of Sears, Roebuck.[8] In 1981, Sears acquired Coldwell Banker, the largest real estate brokerage firm in the United States, and Dean Witter Reynolds, a major securities broker. The acquisitions, added to Sears's long-held insurance and consumer credit-card businesses, marked the company's full-scale diversification from general-merchandise retailing into financial services. Explaining the move in the mid-1980s, Sears's CFO explained how the acquisitions would leverage Sears's expertise in data processing, its credit-card relationships with tens of millions of consumers, and the trust it enjoyed in the eyes of many customers.[9] Cross-selling efforts stalled, however, hampered by such factors as the reluctance of business-unit executives to share customer lists. Apparently distracted by the company's foray into financial services, Sears executives failed to address the company's weakening position in the retail business—a fiercely competitive industry made more challenging by the rise of Wal-Mart. By 1988, Sears was struggling to hold off hostile bidders, and in 1992, the company announced that it would exit financial services and narrow its scope to retailing. Sears shareholders paid dearly for the scope maneuvers. A $100 investment in Sears stock on January 1, 1980, turned into $746 by the end of 1994, while the same investment over the same period in a set of narrow-scope companies that mimicked Sears's industry portfolio would have produced $1,256. As one set of researchers put it, "homemade diversification outperformed Sears' diversification strategy."[10]

Sears's troubles exemplify the concerns of consultants whom we contacted to size up the state of current practice related to scope choices. As one put it,

> In our experience, most firms have stopped even thinking through all the benefits, costs and risks [of scope choices], never mind actually trying to calculate them. Instead, they've adopted "relatedness religion" in which they believe that being able to name the ways in which their business units are related means they must, by definition, be achieving synergies.

TWO TESTS

Consideration of inadequate corporate strategies, such as the one at Sears, should, of course, be balanced with recognition that cross-business strategies can also create enormous economic value. One of the most successful scope expansions of the 1990s was Wal-Mart's diversification from discounting general, nonfood merchandise—its original line of business—into discounting food as well. Wal-Mart's Supercenter format offers food and general merchandise under one roof. Substituting Supercenters for nonfood discount stores was not obviously a winning idea: the razor-thin margins on food would cause the new format to have lower average operating margins than the old format. Wal-Mart realized, however, that supermarkets were saddled with expensive unionized workforces and had failed to invest enough in information technology, logistics, and the like. That stirred Wal-Mart's interest in offering lower food prices as a way of growing volumes, including those for nonfood items under the same roof, to an extent that might outweigh the decrease in operating margins.

Specifically, if one assumes that a mature Supercenter would have nearly double the sales of a discount store and would, because of shared infrastructure, experience lower average capital costs, then, the net present value (NPV) to Wal-Mart of a new Supercenter might be 15–20 percent higher than the NPV of a new discount store. But a much bigger payoff from building traffic stems from the fact that Wal-Mart needs a population of just 75,000 people to support one of its Supercenters in the United States, versus 150,000 people to support a (smaller) discount store. Opening two Supercenters rather than one discount store in a region with 150,000 people allows Wal-Mart to quadruple its revenue in the region and raise its NPV by 130–140 percent! Operating in two industries rather than one has proven to be extremely lucrative: Supercenters are estimated to account for the bulk of Wal-Mart's market value—over $100 billion—and to have a higher return on assets than traditional discount stores do.

How can managers distinguish good opportunities to expand and exploit horizontal scope, such as Wal-Mart's move from general-merchandise retailing into groceries, from poor opportunities such as Sears's move from the same base into financial services? The two examples seem to suggest that, in any discussion of corporate strategy, managers should focus intently on the corporate strategy's impact on *individual business units*. Competition occurs at the level of the individual business unit in a particular industry. Therefore, corporate strategy succeeds or fails to the extent that it aids or undermines business units as they strive to win in their specific markets. But how can we know whether membership in a particular corporate family is likely to help or hamper a specific business unit? We find two tests to be especially telling.[11]

1. *The "Better-Off" Test:* Do combining and coordinating the activities of multiple business units, as one can do in a corporation with broad scope, enable the units to create and capture more value than they could as independent, unassociated units? In other words, what is the corporate added value?
2. *The "Best-Alternative" Test:* Suppose the units pass the better-off test and coordinated action is valuable. Is common ownership by a single corporation the best way to reap the benefits of coordinated action—better than alternatives like joint ventures, strategic alliances, licensing deals, and arm's-length transactions? Conceptually, this test focuses on value appropriation instead of value addition.

The better-off test asks whether a particular set of business units should be working together. The best-alternative test asks whether the set must be jointly owned in order to maximize the amount of value created and captured.

We find these tests to be useful whether one is considering the addition of a business unit to broaden horizontal scope, thinking about divesting a unit to narrow scope, or deciding how to manage an existing portfolio of businesses. In the context of adding a business unit, managers will also want to analyze the financial implications, asking whether the benefits of the addition outweigh the cost—in terms of their consequences for total profits (not just profitability, which went down in the case of Wal-Mart's Supercenters). In an efficient market for corporate assets, the answer is likely to be yes only if the two tests are passed. Similarly, when considering divestiture, managers will want to examine financials. A divestiture is likely to unlock value by freeing business units of one another only if the corporation fails at least one of the tests.

Some observers of corporate strategy suggest a third test, even tougher than the better-off and best-alternative tests: the "best-parent" test: "The appropriate benchmark for value creation is not what would happen without a [corporate] parent, but what the best available parent would achieve."[12] Taken literally, this seems too stringent. It probably does not make sense for every company to dispose of all businesses that it cannot run as efficiently as, say, GE could (unless GE is willing to make a high bid for the business). Having said that, we are sympathetic to a milder formulation of the third test, the "Good Parent" test, in which, even if a proposed opportunity to expand scope apparently satisfies the first two tests, it is worth asking yourself whether your company is particularly well-placed to observe or act upon the opportunity identified before you actually move to capitalize on it. In an ambiguous world marked by the possibility of the winner's curse, to do less would be deficient on diligence. Such caution also recognizes strong forces that tend to push managers toward overexpansion. These forces include the following:[13]

- Human beings tend to be overly confident about their abilities. In surveys, for instance, 93 percent of Americans rate themselves as above-average drivers.[14] The bias toward overconfidence may be especially prominent among successful executives, and there is evidence that this is reflected in their investment choices. A recent study shows that companies whose CEOs display overconfidence in their personal financial portfolios are particularly likely to spend free cash flow on fresh investments instead of paying out dividends or reducing debt.[15]

- An unexamined belief that bigger is better, a focus on "stretch goals," a failure to recognize the reality that growth rates tend to drop as organizations age, an urge to mimic the expansion of competitors and, frankly, confusion as to whether market share is a symptom of success or a valid strategic goal in and of itself—all of these may encourage corporate managers to overexpand.

- Even without such encouragement, poorly governed top managers may act on a personal desire to build an "empire" and to increase the resources under their control. Moreover, managers may diversify in order to reduce the unsystematic risk that they face personally—even though shareholders may not value such reductions.

- Managers often get advice about mergers and acquisitions from investment bankers and other parties whose fees depend on deal-making.

Building on the rest of this book, especially the discussions in Chapters 3 and 5, we examine the two tests by looking at the activities of business units across their value chains. Others have approached corporate strategy very productively by focusing not on the activities of business units but on the resources that span business units.[16] Indeed, we touch on the nature of such resources when we discuss the best-alternative test later. But, consistent with the treatment in the other chapters, we emphasize analysis of costs and benefits in terms of activity flows even when we are ultimately interested in evaluating different resource stocks that underlie them.

Our hope is that hard-nosed examination of the costs and benefits of broad scope (the better-off test) and an objective look at alternatives to expansion (the best-alternative test) can help bring the discipline of business-level strategy to bear on issues of corporate strategy. Note that the aim is not to propose a radically new point of view on corporate strategy but to use conventional theory to improve practice—an area that seems to offer large opportunities.

THE BETTER-OFF TEST

To pass the better-off test, an expansion in horizontal scope must enable a corporation's business units to create and capture more value together than they could as separate, single-business entities unrelated to one another. Indeed, the incremental value must more than offset the costs of the corporate center. Where can such incremental value come from? Obviously, a scope expansion can increase the aggregate volume of business on which it is possible to earn positive (or negative) economic margins. In view of the pro-growth biases discussed earlier, however, as well as the frequent business-specificity of many key resources, we remain cautious about thinking of scope expansions in purely scalar terms.[17] The better-off test forces us to look, in addition, for other possible gains related to the concepts that have been discussed in earlier chapters. Sometimes, a scope expansion can improve the structure of the industries in which a company competes. More often, an expansion can increase the added value of business units within their industries—that is, widen the wedge between the willingness to pay that they generate and the costs they incur. Finally, an expansion can sometimes create value for a business by reducing the risk it bears.

Industry Attractiveness

There are two senses in which a scope expansion can improve the structure of the industries in which a company competes. First and simply, broad horizontal scope can improve structure directly by mitigating the five forces discussed in Chapter 2. Rivalry, for instance, may be muted among broad-scope firms that meet one another in multiple markets. Fearing that aggressive behavior in any one market will provoke fierce competition everywhere, they may refrain from aggression anywhere. The resulting "mutual forbearance" may lead to higher prices and profits in all of the markets.[18] In line with this argument, pairs of U.S. airlines that meet on numerous routes have been found to compete less fiercely with one another on overlapping routes than do pairs that rarely meet.[19] A similar pattern has been observed in the commercial banking industry.[20] Broad scope may also reduce another of the five forces, the threat of new entry, by denying new firms access to complementary inputs. The U.S. Department of Justice's case against Microsoft, for instance, centered on the claim that Microsoft's dominance in multiple lines of businesses (operating systems, word processing, spreadsheets, presentation software) made it difficult for new firms such as Netscape to establish themselves. A proposed remedy was to narrow Microsoft's scope, separating the company's operating-system business from its application-software operations.[21]

Second and more subtly, broad scope may give a firm an opportunity to migrate out of a structurally poor industry into a more attractive setting. Gradual experimentation over decades, accelerating in the 1990s, allowed Nokia to move from its traditional base in forest products, rubber, cables, and electricity generation to become a leading player in the fast-growing mobile handset industry. Through its diversifying merger with Time Warner, America Online (AOL) managed to take its shareholders' stake in the fast-deteriorating market for online services and trade it for assets in more stable industries like cable television, magazines, and film. Horizontal diversification can also bring efficient or creative new players into sleepy industries, sharpening skills and boosting industry performance. Cooper Industries, for example, earned high returns for decades by bringing world-class manufacturing skills and professional management to mature, low-tech manufacturing industries such as the market for hand tools.

One should be cautious, however, about industry-attractiveness rationales for broad scope. It is difficult for one company alone to change the structure of its entire industry by means of its scope choices (unless, perhaps, you are Microsoft, which dominates its industry). Broad scope may open up an opportunity to migrate to a more attractive setting, but decision-makers can use this as a management tool only if they have better foresight than other potential entrants about what industries will be attractive in the future. Maneuvers like AOL's presumably depend on the existence of counterparts with inferior insights into the future or internal constraints on acting on their insights.

Competitive Advantage

More common and often more compelling are efforts to use scope to improve a company's position *within* its industry. As discussed in Chapter 3, a firm's ability to create value within an industry depends crucially on its driving a wedge between the costs it incurs and the willingness to pay it generates among buyers. Competitive advantage requires that this wedge be wider than competitors'. Corporate-level scope choices often have the greatest impact by influencing the wedges that business units can attain within their individual industries. There are many ways that scope choices can widen the wedges. Some operate clearly on the cost side of the equation—reducing costs without sacrificing willingness to pay. Others almost always affect the willingness to pay side—raising willingness to pay without incurring extra costs. Yet others can widen the wedge by influencing either costs or willingness to pay. We will examine these three categories—and the various limitations and drawbacks to which they are subject—in turn (see Exhibit 6.1).

EXHIBIT 6.1   Effects of Horizontal Diversification on Competitive Advantage.

Component	Levers for Value Creation	Limits
Cost Effects	– Shared cost economies across businesses • Shared activities • Shared resources	– Diseconomies of scale or scope – Costs of • Conflict/politicking • Compromise • Coordination – Mixed motives – Cognitive conflicts – Reputational risk
Willingness-to Pay/Price Effects	– One-stop shop/one-vendor sales and support – Cross-promotion/cross-selling – Umbrella branding – Bundling, particularly of complements	
Dual Effects	– Superior internal resource markets/transfer mechanisms – Other superior skills and capabilities – Cross-business learning/innovation – Size-based political influence	– Availability of market/interfirm alternatives – Typical breadth versus depth trade-off – Internal/inside-the-box biases – Antitrust laws/political backlash

COST EFFECTS *Shared cost economies*, the first row of entries in the exhibit, feature prominently in most horizontal diversification and can be thought of as the multi-business version of economies of scale within a single business. Simply noting the existence of such economies is not enough, however: their significance must be assessed. This often involves analyzing the cost structures of individual businesses activity by activity, sizing up the fraction of total costs that can be shared across the businesses, and estimating how sensitive those shared cost elements are to total size. An example illustrates how one can make such estimates.

- The Scotts Company makes and markets a wide array of lawn and garden care products.[22] Specifically, its four business units sell grass seed and fertilizers, plant food for gardens, soil, and pesticides. In 1999, the units handled most of their procurement separately. The grass seed and fertilizer business unit purchased $30 million of pesticide inputs while the pesticide business unit bought $32 million of raw material. By combining their purchases, the unit managers felt that they could drive a harder bargain with raw material suppliers. Industry experts estimated that a doubling of purchase volume could reduce per-unit raw material costs by 5 percent. This would amount to annual savings of 5 percent × ($30 million + $32 million) = $3.1 million. Moreover, the four units paid unit-level procurement personnel a total of $2.9 million in annual salaries and benefits. Centralization of purchasing, it was estimated, might permit a headcount reduction that would reduce those salaries and benefits by $0.7 million per year.
- Scotts also spent $16 million per year on less-than-truckload transportation to get its products from factories to retail sites. These outbound logistics costs were spread across its four business units. By consolidating the shipments, managers felt that they could shift half the volume to full-truckload shipping, which they knew to be 75 percent cheaper per unit. This could lead to annual savings of $16 million × 1/2 × 75 percent = $6 million.
- Each Scotts business operated its own sales force, ranging in size from a few people for pesticides to 79 salespeople for the grass seed and fertilizer business. Each sales force, it was estimated, incurred fixed costs of roughly $3 million plus salary, benefit, and bonus costs per salesperson of $54,000. Consolidation of the sales forces would not allow much reduction in headcount, simply because the sales personnel called on different buyers and were already fully employed. Consolidation would, however, reduce redundant fixed costs associated with sales offices, sales management software, and so forth. The potential savings were estimated to be 3 × $3 million = $9 million per year.

Shared cost economies, like scale economies, can arise anywhere in the value chains of the business units. They typically occur when business units can coordinate activities for efficiency or spread the cost of some lumpy, underutilized resource over the volume of multiple business units. The resource involved might be tangible, like a piece of equipment, or intangible, like a brand, a reputation, a body of knowledge, or a capability.

It is crucial to recognize, however, that the savings from shared cost economies can be offset—to an extent that must also be examined—by *diseconomies of size or scope*. To see the possibility of such diseconomies, even for an outstanding management team, we can return to Wal-Mart. Especially with its diversification into food retailing, Wal-Mart has become massive. As the world's largest company, it now faces the challenge, given high turnover rates, of hiring about 1 million workers per year just to maintain the size of its workforce at 1.9 million—which exposes it to heightened public scrutiny as well as increased bureaucratic complexity, as elaborated toward the end of Chapter 5.

The savings from shared cost economies can also be offset by the extra *costs of conflict, compromise, and coordination* that reflect heterogeneity in requirements, goals, and beliefs across businesses (which is likely to be larger than within one business).[23] Often these costs are so large that managers opt not to exploit potential economies. Thus, even consolidation-minded Royal Bank of Scotland passed up opportunities to share costs when it acquired Coutts, a bank serving 70,000 individuals of very high net worth, including the Queen of England. It feared that such sharing would compromise Coutts's ability to delivery a customized service to highly discerning clients.

Wal-Mart also faced costs of conflict, compromise, and coordination between its food and nonfood businesses, but managed to overcome them in a variety of ways. It designed the Supercenter to optimize the relationship between the two businesses. (Fourteen different variants were reportedly tried out.) Moreover, Wal-Mart set up the Supercenter format as a profit center and grew it organically, but grouped it with the format that it was cannibalizing into one gargantuan division—with more than $208 billion in sales in 2006. This, along with the company's tradition of top-down strategic decision-making, aided the ongoing transfer of resources and the sharing of activities, systems, and the like.

But such conflicts et cetera *do* erect significant barriers to value creation in many cases, especially when companies are trying to redeploy existing resources or coordinate across businesses with traditions of decentralized decision-making. In the wake of the AOL Time Warner merger, for instance, the famously autonomous divisions of the old Time Warner resisted the cross-business coordination that was supposed to create much of the value of the company's expanded scope. So, in deciding whether to broaden scope by adding a business, or in choosing how to integrate a business that has already been added, managers must weigh carefully the benefits and costs of tapping potential economies.

WILLINGNESS-TO-PAY/PRICE EFFECTS   *Willingness-to-pay and price effects*, the second row of entries in Exhibit 6.1, are not quite as commonly cited in horizontal diversification as cost reductions, but they can be very important. When Spanish bank Santander acquired Abbey National in the United Kingdom, for instance, it planned to reduce costs by € 450 million over three years, but also targeted revenue enhancements of € 220 million.[24]

The revenue benefits of broad scope typically come from two sources: (1) increases in willingness to pay for a combined offering, and (2) improvements in a company's ability to price in a way that extracts willingness to pay. We consider each in turn. Willingness-to-pay effects include the following:

- Customers often value the convenience of *one-stop shopping* that comes with broad scope. In a consumer context, consider the convenience of Wal-Mart's Supercenters. In a business context, having one vendor or a single point of contact for sales, service, and other support can be a significant draw—especially when systems sales are important. When appointed CEO of a beleaguered IBM in 1993, for instance, Lou Gerstner resisted a plan to break the company into a dozen

"Baby Blues." Large corporate customers valued the ability to purchase entire solutions from one vendor, he argued, and IBM's uniquely extensive scope enabled it to deliver integrated packages better than the competition. Gerstner's decision to "go to market as one IBM" is often considered one of the strategic masterstrokes of the 1990s—and is, in a sense, being reemphasized by Sam Palmisano.

- Much of the rationale for media conglomerates seems to derive from significant and apparently cost-effective *cross-promotion* of their properties across lines of business as well as within businesses. A vivid example was provided by Rupert Murdoch's aggressive use of his British newspapers, particularly *The Sun*, to promote his British satellite TV start-up, SkyTV, against its rival, BSB (British Satellite Broadcasting). SkyTV's war of attrition with BSB culminated in a merger of their assets into BSkyB and Murdoch's effective assumption of control of what is now a fabulously valuable franchise. Similarly, Disney undertakes cross-promotion on a massive scale. When Disney releases a new animated feature film, for instance, the film's characters appear in Disney's theme parks, in its stores, in its Broadway theater, and on its ABC television network. From its film *The Lion King*, for instance, Disney took in $1 billion of revenue at the box office and $1 billion through other businesses.
- *Umbrella branding* enables multiple businesses to reap the willingness-to-pay benefits of a strong brand. Virgin, for instance, has used its umbrella brand to enter businesses ranging from airlines and record stores to mobile telephony, rail service, finance and money, and health and shopping.

Broad scope can also alter the pricing approach of a company. Microsoft, for example, benefits enormously from integrating into and offering an array of complementary products (e.g., its Windows operating system, Microsoft Office application software, Internet Explorer browser, etc.) The company's broad scope not only raises barriers to entry, as mentioned earlier, but it also affects pricing in two ways. As an integrated player, Microsoft can set prices in complementary markets in a coordinated manner, extracting more profits than could unintegrated players with similar market power in separate markets.

Once again, however, there are a number of limits to these levers for value creation.

- The issues of *conflict, compromise, and coordination* that were discussed earlier often also show up in the context of willingness to pay, although in the form of price penalties rather than extra costs. For example, attempts to bundle complements often lead to compromised offerings instead of ones as compelling as the Supercenter, or they founder because of more fundamental coordination problems. Bundling efforts can also open opportunities for narrow-scope competitors. In the wake of the AOL Time Warner merger, for instance, rivals such as Yahoo! made considerable progress in forming alliances with competing cable providers. After PepsiCo purchased fast-food restaurants Pizza Hut, Taco Bell, and Kentucky Fried Chicken, Coca-Cola persuaded Wendy's and Burger King to switch their soft-drink offerings from Pepsi to Coke.
- If the offerings of different businesses are substitutes instead of complements, it is even trickier to manage across them because of *mixed motives* due to fears of

self-cannibalization and similar concerns. For example, Clay Christensen's emphasis on disruptive technologies keys off the mixed motives that an incumbent using one technology faces in dealing with a new technology that underserves the needs of most of its current customers but is on a more rapid performance-improvement trajectory.[25] Or to take a somewhat different type of example, full-service airlines have failed to create a compelling "product" for the low-fare segment of the marketplace in part because they know that such an offering will draw traffic away from their existing higher-fare service.

- *Cognitive conflicts* in the minds of customers (or even employees) can also constrain horizontal scope if scope expansion threatens to blur a company's external (or internal) message. Thus, Disney has always been very careful about the products for which it licenses images of Mickey Mouse and the rest of its wholesome menagerie. This caution has proven to be well-placed. The 1994 release of the controversial film *Priest* by Disney's Miramax subsidiary, distant from Mickey, led the Catholic League to call for a boycott of the entire Disney corporation, not just the film. More broadly, Disney has found that actions in one domain can endanger prospects elsewhere. Disney's production of *Kundun,* a movie about the Dalai Lama, allegedly led Chinese officials to threaten in 1996 to reevaluate the full range of Disney's plans in China. And when Disney barred Miramax from distributing the controversial *Fahrenheit 9/11* in 2004, some analysts speculated that Disney feared a conservative backlash in other parts of its business. (Ironically, the action itself led to a backlash, causing some liberal groups to call for a boycott of all Disney products.)
- Finally, umbrella-branding efforts carry significant *reputational risk.* Think of what might have happened to Accenture if it had remained tightly coupled to Andersen Accounting, including continuing to call itself Andersen Consulting, when Andersen Accounting's dealings with Enron began to come to light.

In our experience, thoughtful managers who are considering an expansion of horizontal scope are relatively skeptical of willingness-to-pay/price effects and tend to rely more heavily on "hard" arguments about cost economies. As one management consultant told us, "If the move can't be justified on the basis of cost savings, that's a bright red flag." We are somewhat sympathetic to this point of view, given how much easier it is to dream up revenue "synergies" than to realize them. Cost synergies are subject to at least some of the same problems, however. This suggests a careful, critical analysis of both willingness to pay and costs rather than an approach that always emphasizes one over the other.

DUAL EFFECTS Sometimes it is hard to separate opportunities to create competitive advantage cleanly into cost effects and willingness-to-pay effects. Consider, for instance, an example from the Scotts Company, the lawn and garden care manufacturer mentioned earlier.[26] In 1999, Scotts experimented with deploying in-store counselors at major home-improvement retailers like Home Depot. These counselors helped customers select the Scotts product that matched their needs. Stores with experienced counselors typically saw a 20 percent increase in sales of Scotts products—a major boost. Simple calculations of margin per product line revealed that only one of the four Scotts business units, the grass seed and fertilizer unit, could justify the expense of the counselor on a standalone basis. As independent entities, none of the other three units had enough volume per store for a 20 percent boost in sales to support a counselor's wages. Because they were members of the Scotts corporation, however, the three small units were able to enjoy an important advantage over rivals with narrower product lines. This advantage can be classified as a willingness-to-pay advantage, reflected in the 20 percent increase in volume, or as a cost advantage, reflected in the lower cost of a counselor's wages spread over more volume.

Such inseparabilities should not prevent a careful analysis of the impact of scope on competitive advantage; after all, advantage depends not on one or the other, but on the gap between the two. In this regard, it is useful to acknowledge, as in the third row in Exhibit 6.1, various levers of corporate advantage that widen the wedge between costs and willingness to pay, but, depending on the circumstances, can do so by influencing the cost side of the equation, the willingness-to-pay side, or both. *Superior internal resource markets, transfer mechanisms,* and *skills and capabilities* are directly relevant to the best-alternative test and will therefore be discussed further in the next subsection. *Cross-business learning and innovation* have the potential to improve both costs and willingness to pay over time. For instance, 3M has created competitive advantages for decades by sharing deep knowledge of a handful of core technologies across tens of thousands of product lines. One such technology involves expertise in coating, where a set of more than 40 specific techniques support thousands of products ranging from Post-it memo stickers to medical items—products that account for roughly two-thirds of corporate revenue. However, cross-business learning and innovation can also entail an *internal bias* that deemphasizes external know-how or thinking outside the box of the current business portfolio. Finally, there is the possibility of *size-based political influence:* a political version of economies of size. However, *antitrust laws* often constrain some of the horizontal moves that might prove the most profitable (e.g., the challenges to Microsoft's bundling strategy in the United States and Europe) and, as noted earlier in the context of Wal-Mart, size can actually lead to somewhat of a *political backlash.*

Risk Considerations

When asked to explain their scope choices, many corporate executives make a risk-related argument: diversification reduces volatility in overall corporate performance by averaging returns across businesses subject to different shocks, cycles, and trends. Managers of Cendant offered an explanation of this kind as they pieced together the corporation's collection of real estate franchises, rental-car agencies, hotels, tax services, relocation services, travel-distribution systems, and financial services operations. The plan, as one observer put it, was "to buy up businesses to create a company with enough size and diversity that no one shock could pummel it."[27] If a weak economy hurt the travel-related business units, for example, the associated low interest rates would boost the real estate units.

For publicly traded companies participating in well-oiled capital markets, modern finance theory has seriously undermined this type of argument. Investors can diversify inexpensively on their own, constructing a portfolio with the balance of risk and return they desire. There is no reason for the corporation to do so on their behalf. Moreover, a corporation that spots a great investment opportunity but is short on funds can raise capital in the public markets.

The risk-reduction argument does, however, hold more water in other contexts. Firms with limited access to efficient capital markets may legitimately create value by diversifying to smooth performance and create internal capital markets. The business groups that dominate many emerging economies have recently been viewed through this lens.[28] Similarly, individual- or family-owned corporations whose owners wish to retain control and avoid public capital markets often diversify for risk-reduction reasons. But except when access to efficient capital markets is seriously constrained, firms must justify their scope choices and pass the better-off test on the other grounds we have mentioned.

THE BEST-ALTERNATIVE TEST

The essence of the better-off test is to ask whether the business units of a corporation can create more value under common ownership than they would as isolated entities, even after netting out the direct and indirect costs of corporate membership. This test compares commonly owned business units with standalone business units; thus it focuses on what we might call **corporate added value**. The best-alternative test, in contrast, realizes that common ownership is not the only possible basis for coordinating across business units. Business units might, instead, remain independently owned but partner with one another, form strategic alliances, sign long-term contracts, and so forth. The best-alternative test asks, Can a corporation that owns its business units outright accomplish its ends better than the same business units coordinated in some other way? Note that, conceptually, this test focuses on value appropriation and not just value addition. For instance, in assessing the wisdom of a strategic partnership as an alternative to joint ownership, managers must not only compare the total value created under each arrangement, but must also consider whether the partner might hold up the firm and appropriate the value that was created.

Applied to some of the examples we developed earlier, the best-alternative test raises questions like the following: Could Wal-Mart have reaped most of the benefits of its Supercenters by partnering with and co-locating with local supermarket chains? Could a set of small lawn-care manufacturers, even if they are not jointly owned, band together to place sales counselors in retail stores? Could Disney exploit its animated characters by licensing the characters to theme parks and retail stores owned by others, or must it own its own parks and stores? The careful comparison of corporate ownership to alternate arrangements sheds light on whether a set of businesses should be jointly owned. As we will see next, it also helps us understand how the set might be managed.

Transactions Costs and Ownership

As the many examples of broad horizontal scope make clear, there are often times when managers judge ownership to be better than alternate arrangements. Yet at other times, managers prefer alternate arrangements; for example, when a company decides to contract out excess manufacturing capacity instead of using it to expand horizontal scope, enters into a cross-marketing agreement with another company, or licenses its intellectual property instead of using it internally. Disney, for instance, licenses its characters to McDonald's rather than operating its own fast-food stores. (Disney experimented with fast-food operations, Mickey's Kitchens, during the 1980s but abandoned the concept.) Yahoo!, the Internet portal, partners with companies like SBC (now AT&T) and British

Telecom to provide high-speed Internet access, and it has resisted the notion that it needs to own distribution resources (or be owned by a company with such resources). To expand its scope into the printer industry, Dell resells printers made by Lexmark, in sharp contrast to Hewlett Packard, which produces its own printers.

The concept of *transaction costs* can help us understand which transactions tend to take place within a corporation instead of across firm boundaries.[29] The relationship between two business units—whether they are sister units within a corporation or alliance partners or arm's-length traders—can be thought of as a set of transactions. Governing a transaction involves certain costs, including the costs of finding a transaction partner, negotiating the terms of an agreement, and making sure the transaction is completed to the parties' satisfaction. Different governance arrangements involve different transaction costs. Transactions are generally expected to migrate toward the form of governance that permits them to be completed effectively and at low cost.

Many types of transaction costs are straightforward, and comparing these costs across forms of governance is easy. Take, for example, the costs of finding a trading partner. Internal ownership often makes it inexpensive to find a partner. When Disney's film division develops a new animated character in a film and wants to market the character in a theme park, it incurs no costs in finding a willing theme-park partner. It simply turns to Disney's theme-park division.

Other types of transaction costs, however, are more subtle. Studies of corporate scope have identified one particular type of cost that explains many differences in governance choices: the cost of preventing *opportunistic behavior.* When parties enter into a relationship, each might legitimately worry that the other will exploit opportunities to take unfair advantage of the relationship—the threat of holdup discussed in Chapter 5, but with a focus on vertical rather than horizontal integration. Thus, if Disney were to license its characters to the theme parks owned by Six Flags, for instance, it might worry that Six Flags would use the characters in ways not authorized by Disney.

A common way for companies to overcome concerns about opportunistic behavior is to write contracts that lay out clearly what each party can and must do under various circumstances. When contracts work relatively well, companies are more likely to find it cost-effective to complete transactions through arrangements that involve other parties: arm's-length purchases, licensing deals, alliances, joint ventures, and so forth. When they do not, companies are likely to prefer broad-scope and in-house deals. Researchers have identified several impediments to contracting efficiency.[30]

- *Contractual complexity and incompleteness.* It is very difficult to write contracts that comprehensively cover long-term business relationships in highly uncertain settings. Consider again the potential deal between Disney and Six Flags. The contract for such a deal has to cover a huge range of contingencies. What happens if the film and its characters are not as popular as anticipated? How will gains be divided if the film is more successful than expected? If there is an accident on the film-related park ride, who will be liable, and who will manage public relations? Will Six Flags be allowed to locate less-wholesome attractions near the Disney ride? Will Disney have recourse if the ride's staff is impolite or the lines for the ride get too long? And so forth. A contract for such a deal may run into hundreds of pages and still fail to cover many of the events that might arise. Because it is prohibitively costly to write a contract that covers every contingency, opportunities remain for Disney and Six Flags to take advantage of one another.

- *Unclear property rights.* One role of a contract is to specify who has rights to what property under various circumstances. This is a relatively straightforward task for tangible pieces of property—machines, vehicles, buildings, parcels of land, and so forth. For intangible resources—knowledge, ideas, skills, brands, innovations, and the like—property rights are much harder to define. As a result, contracting over intangibles is much more difficult, and markets for such resources are more prone to break down. Consequently, we often see intangible resources shared across business units within a corporation, while tangible resources are shared across corporations by means of other arrangements.

- *Poor enforcement of contracts and property rights.* A contract—even one that can easily and clearly be written down—will not allay parties' fears of opportunistic behavior unless they expect the contract to be enforced. In most developed economies, the baseline assumption is usually that courts and governments will enforce and uphold contracts and, more broadly, defend property rights. In many emerging economies, in contrast, contract enforcement and property rights seem more fragile. In such settings, trade across corporate borders can be risky. A buyer can realistically fear that a good it pays for will never be delivered. A seller can legitimately worry that it may never be paid after delivering a product or service. Where such concerns are prevalent, corporate scope might be especially broad. This appears to be another reason (in addition to risk-reduction) why highly diversified conglomerates dominate the private sectors of many emerging economies. Consider, for instance, the business houses of India, the *grupos* of Latin America, and the *chaebol* of South Korea.[31]

- *Relationship-specific or cospecialized resources.* The effects of the contracting hazards identified earlier are all amplified if, before transactions can take place, transactors have to make up-front investments whose value is specific to their relationship. Such relationship-specific or cospecialized resources were discussed in some detail in Chapter 5, in the section on holdup, but can be illustrated once again with the potential deal between Disney and Six Flags. To consummate it, Six Flags would have to build rides in its theme parks, and Disney would have to create and market its films. Making such relationship-specific investments is risky. Before Six Flags built the ride, for example, Disney might promise that it would charge Six Flags a low fee to license its characters. Once a hard-to-alter ride is built, however, what would prevent Disney from reneging on its promise and charging a higher fee, especially after expiry of the initial contract? And knowing that this might happen, Six Flags might build a ride that is less expensive, less appealing, and less durable than would be optimal. Because of such dangers, investments in relationship-specific resources tend to be made within corporate boundaries rather than across them—although it is worth recalling from the discussion of holdup in Chapter 5 that integration is just one of several possible responses to such problems. As a result, when the resources shared by two business units are highly specific in this sense, it is more likely that the units will be owned by one corporation.

Conversely, relationships that do not involve as much resource-specificity can often be managed well across corporate boundaries. Take, for example, Disney's arrangement to license its characters to McDonald's. To incorporate Disney characters into its

Happy Meals for kids, McDonald's undertakes some modest and short-lived specific investments: it buys some toys based on Disney characters, prints some bags with the characters on them, and does a little marketing. The scale of the investment it puts at risk is modest compared to the many millions of dollars of thoroughly sunk investment that might be required to design and build a theme park ride. (A ride recently added to Disney's California Adventure theme park, for instance, reportedly cost $75 million.)

More broadly, while all of these factors point to conditions in which the transaction costs of alternate arrangements might be especially high and common ownership might be especially attractive, it is important to remember that "internal" transactions among jointly owned business units are costly as well. Even within a corporation, managers must find parties to transact with, negotiate internal terms such as transfer prices, and maintain coordination after a deal is struck. They must allay concerns, often intense, that one business unit will take advantage of another. Moreover, the biggest cost of an internal transaction may often be an opportunity cost: the cost of forgoing access to attractive transacts with third parties. For example, in the wake of the AOL-Time Warner merger, AOL's rival Yahoo! felt that it would have a significant advantage over AOL in finding Internet content. AOL would feel obliged to obtain content from Time Warner divisions, whereas Yahoo! could shift freely among content providers, selecting the best of them and playing providers off against one another. In addition to enhancing cost-efficiency, independence can also be directly valuable to one's customers. For years, Andersen Consulting (now Accenture) won information technology integration contracts over IBM because it was viewed as independent while IBM integrators were thought to push the hardware and software of sister businesses.

To summarize, one can apply the best-alternative test by envisioning the transactions that two business should undertake to maximize the wedge between costs and willingness to pay and by comparing the various ways these transactions can be governed—within a single corporation or across corporate boundaries. To justify broad scope, one must argue that common ownership makes more sense in governing the relevant transactions than arm's-length deals, licensing arrangements, alliances, joint ventures, or other options. Broad scope is most likely to be justified when contractual complexity and incompleteness are high, property rights are intrinsically unclear, enforcement of contracts and property rights is poor, and large investments in relationship-specific resources are involved.

Models of Corporate Management

The best-alternative test helps us understand not only what sets of business should be jointly owned, but also how such a set of businesses can be managed. While diversified corporations are managed in many different ways, this diversity can usefully be simplified into the three models of corporate management along the continuum shown in Exhibit 6.2. Each management model tries to meet the best-alternative test in a distinct manner.

- *Dominant-business corporations* consist of relatively few business units—often one or two core businesses surrounded by a coterie of peripheral units. Wal-Mart, discussed earlier, is one example. Dominant-business corporations strive to meet the best-alternative test and beat alternatives to joint ownership by investing in a set of highly specialized resources that separately owned companies cannot match and, often, by achieving more extensive cross-unit coordination.

EXHIBIT 6.2 **Models of Corporate Management.**

Source: Based on David J. Collis and Cynthia A. Montgomery, *Corporate Strategy: Resources and the Scope of the Firm* (Chicago: Richard D. Irwin, 1997).

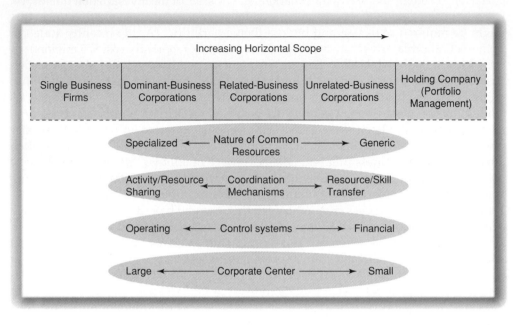

Thus, it is hard to imagine separate companies matching the co-location, shared logistics systems, and joint operational capabilities of Wal-Mart's general merchandise and food businesses. Because the corporate infrastructure required to develop specialized resources and to coordinate their use can be extensive, dominant-business corporations often have sizable corporate staffs.

• *Related-business corporations* typically have more business units than dominant-business corporations as well as a distinct bottom line for each business, but they maintain one or more common threads that link their businesses. A good example is Walt Disney, whose many businesses concentrate on entertainment and the management of creativity. Related-business corporations try to meet the best-alternative test either through one-time transfers of specialized resources or skills to new lines of business (or perhaps from them, if acquired) or, more ambitiously, through ongoing sharing of resources or activities. The collaboration across numerous units inevitably gives rise to conflicts and tradeoffs that would be difficult to govern through multilateral contracts. These, in turn, often engender a need for operating as well as financial controls, with corporate managers directly involved to achieve cross-business coordination. Consider, for instance, Walt Disney's sharing of cartoon characters, the Disney brand, and other resources across multiple businesses and its numerous mechanisms for coordination at the corporate level (e.g., a synergy committee, a corporate calendar, and so forth). If dominant-business corporations strive for deeper sharing and coordination than more loosely linked entities, related-business firms aim for broader sharing and coordination, across more businesses.

- *Unrelated-business corporations* often maintain sprawling business portfolios, with many units and sparse relations among them. They typically strive to satisfy the best-alternative test by building their corporate strategies around relatively unspecialized, or generic, resources. Thus, conglomerates in the United States generally emphasize tight financial controls as a way of optimizing cash management, increasing liquidity, and improving resource allocation relative to what external capital markets might be able to achieve. Given the usual limits to value creation through such approaches, they also tend to have relatively small corporate offices. A financial orientation also characterizes most other U.S. organizations involved in motley businesses, such as venture capitalists and private equity groups. As noted earlier, however, these conclusions seem to be very specific to country context. In emerging economies with poorly developed markets for capital and other resources and weak property rights, the best-alternative test has less bite, and highly diversified business groups can plausibly undertake a broader range of cross-business functions and sport correspondingly larger corporate offices.

Each of these models of corporate management should be thought of as a broad characterization within which there may be much specific variation. Both Disney and AOL Time Warner are related diversifiers, for example, but Disney has historically pursued far greater coordination and permitted far less autonomy across constituent businesses than AOL Time Warner. The variants within each model make the array of possibilities more a continuum than a limited set of discrete options. And companies that share the same broad model can differ not only in the variants that they implement but also in how effective they are in doing so. Among corporations with unrelated businesses, for instance, GE has managed its businesses more effectively over the long run than most other conglomerates in the United States.

Despite the variation in the implementation of these broad models, there has been extensive analysis of whether any one of them consistently delivers better corporate economic performance than the others. The prevailing wisdom, based largely on research in the United States, used to be that there was a conglomerate discount (with unrelated diversifiers underperforming other firms) and, more tentatively, an overall diversification discount (with single-business firms outperforming diversified firms in general). Specifically, such studies tended to report "diversification discounts" of 10–30 percent, with larger discounts, on average, for companies that operate in less-related arrays of businesses.[32] However, much of this work does not take on board the point that profit-maximizing firms should try to maximize total economic profits (profitability times volume) rather than just profitability per se. Moreover, even if one focuses on ratios rather than measures of total value creation, recent work has raised questions about whether the U.S. data actually indicate that diversification itself causes any such discount.[33] We have also learned that the conglomerate discount may not apply universally. In a number of emerging countries, for instance, affiliates of the sorts of diversified business groups cited earlier can systematically outperform standalone, less-diversified local firms.[34] So instead of trying to figure out which type of horizontal diversification model is best, it seems more sensible to recognize the pros and cons of the different—and internally consistent—models for corporate management described earlier and to focus on the model that makes the most sense for a given portfolio of businesses in a given context.

AN APPLICATION: MERRILL LYNCH'S ANALYSIS
OF THE AOL TIME WARNER MERGER

When companies announce moves that broaden horizontal scope, they inevitably publicize the "synergies" between sister units. It is important to find concrete benefits of broader scope, especially since acquisitions and mergers usually involve hefty premiums and internal expansion is often expensive. Unfortunately, many claims of synergy are logically flawed, in ways that are highlighted by the better-off test and the best-alternative test.

In order to illustrate the logic of the tests one more time, we examine one analysis of the potential gains from the 2000 merger of AOL and Time Warner. Exhibit 6.3 summarizes "You've Got Upside!" a research report published by the team of Henry Blodgett, a prominent analyst of Internet-related companies, at Merrill Lynch. (In fairness, note that the analysis was performed from the outside rather than the inside and was completed near the height of Internet euphoria.) The Merrill Lynch report claims that, by bringing together the Internet content and access resources of AOL and the traditional media and cable properties of Time Warner, the merger could increase earnings before interest, taxes, depreciation, and amortization (EBITDA) by $1 billion. Quotations from the report, in Exhibit 6.4, explain the reasoning behind some of the items in Exhibit 6.3. The quotations illustrate several of the logical flaws we most commonly see in discussions of corporate strategy.

- *Mutually beneficial arrangements that the companies could achieve via contracts, without common ownership, are touted as benefits of the merger.* Take, for instance, the argument that AOL can cut $200 million out of its $1 billion sales and marketing budget by marketing its online services through existing Time Warner channels (item 1 in Exhibit 6.4): "AOL discs can be included in Time Warner magazines and are already displayed in Warner's Studio Stores." If this is indeed an effective or low-cost way for AOL to market itself, little prevents the two companies from completing such transactions without common ownership. The fact that AOL discs are already displayed in Warner's stores makes this especially clear. The same argument can be applied to many of the other claimed benefits, including AOL's ability to purchase content from Time Warner (item 3), the sale of Time Warner advertising through AOL sales reps (item 4), the use of cross-promotions to drive incremental subscriptions (item 5), and the use of AOL programmers to move Time Warner's magazine subscription renewals online (item 5). The best-alternative test makes clear that, in assessing broad scope, only those benefits that cannot be achieved via other arrangements should be taken as valid arguments for common ownership.
- *It is assumed that additional business units can tap already-heavily-utilized resources with little or no additional investment.* The shared cost economies discussed earlier typically depend on some multipurpose resource that is underutilized. If the resource is too busy to be shared, however, then there is little opportunity to make two business units better off by bringing them together. Consider, for instance, the AOL customer support representatives who are underutilized early in the day (item 2). Their spare capacity seems to create an opportunity to ask the AOL reps, during their idle hours, to take on the tasks currently performed by Time Warner support reps. But what are the

EXHIBIT 6.3 **Potential Synergies (in millions of U.S. dollars) from the AOL Time Warner Merger.**
Source: Stephen P. Bradley and Erin E. Sullivan, "AOL Time Warner, Inc." Harvard Business School Case no. 702-421, Boston, MA 2002, p. 23.

Revenue Enhancement	Revenues	EBITDA
Ad Sales Upside	$200.0	$160.0
$200 of $600 million in estimated revenue upside at TW Online properties (CNN, CNNfn, CNNSI, *Time*, *People*, *InStyle*, *Entertainment Weekly*)		
More deals on AOL, ICQ through TW relationships	120.0	120.0
Higher Broadband Penetration	120.0	72.0
1 million more broadband subscriptions for TW relationships from AOL upgrades 500K average for year paying $20 more per month		
Incremental Subscriptions	25.0	12.5
New subscriptions to AOL and magazines (through cross-promotion)		
New AOL Premium Services	60.0	30.0
2mm AOL subscriptions sign up for $5 increase fee by year-end 2001 (for AOL TV, real-time stock quotes, etc.)		
Music	25.0	6.3
Downloads on early-generation music devices		
Increased Warner Music sales using AOL platform	10.0	2.5
Total Revenue Upside	**$590.0**	**$403.3**
Cost Savings: Reduced Operating Expenses	**Revenues**	**EBITDA**
Sales & Marketing, AOL (distribution of AOL software)	$200.0	$200.0
Sales & Marketing, Time Warner (movies and music)	100.0	100.0
Reduced spending on TW online initiatives (Entertaindom)	125.0	125.0
Overhead (finance, legal, HR)	50.0	50.0
Reduced customer support cost (in COGS)	50.0	50.0
Reduced cost of content purchased by AOL ($600 million over 4 years)	25.0	25.0
Reduced cost of member subscription and renewal	25.0	25.0
Reduced telecom/technology costs across AOL-Time Warner	25.0	25.0
Total Cost Savings	**$600.0**	**$600.0**

Time Warner support reps doing? They likely support Time Warner's cable systems, fielding telephone calls from customers whose television cables are malfunctioning. Demand for this kind of support probably peaks in the evenings . . . precisely when AOL support reps are fully utilized! (Some Time Warner support personnel visit customers' homes and repair cables, but AOL telephone support reps will surely not be able to replace those employees.)

Similarly, consider the argument that Time Warner "editorial and creative resources . . . can develop ad hoc proprietary content" for AOL (item 3). This helps the merged company pass the better-off test only if the editorial and creative

EXHIBIT 6.4 Rationales for Certain AOL Time Warner Synergies.
Source: Stephen P. Bradley and Erin E. Sullivan, "AOL Time Warner, Inc." Harvard Business School Case no. 702-421, Boston, MA 2002, p. 23.

---

1. Sales & Marketing AOL (distribution of AOL software)
$200 million in reduced operating expenses ($200 million EBITDA impact)
"AOL estimates that it can shave at least $200 million off of its nearly $1 billion marketing spend through a variety of cross-marketing programs and the use of remnant Time Warner advertising inventory. AOL software, for example, will likely be included on Warner Music CDs and movie DVDs. AOL discs can be included in Time Warner magazines and are already displayed in Warner's Studio Stores."

2. Reduced Customer Support Cost
$50 million reduction in operating expenses ($50 million EBITDA impact)
"We expect the combined company to achieve savings in customer support areas. AOL's 6,000 customer service representatives tend to be very busy for three to four hours late in the day, and underutilized at other times. Five percent of AOL's revenues, or $400 million this calendar year, goes toward customer support.....We do not know how much Time Warner spends in support, but think the combined company can achieve at least $50 million in savings here."

3. Reduced Cost of Content Purchased by AOL
$25 million reduction in operating expenses ($25 million EBITDA impact)
"We have also assumed that AOL can save about $25 million from reduced spending on content (AOL currently expects to spend about $600 million on third-party content royalties over the next four years). Through Time Warner, AOL will have access to all varieties of content already being produced, as well as to editorial and creative resources that can develop ad hoc proprietary content."

4. Advertising Sales Upside (Time Warner)
$200 million in revenues ($160 million EBITDA impact)
"AOL management points out that Time Warner's online properties altogether generate only $100 million out of an estimated $600 million in inventory value. . . . The Time Warner Online sites should be generating more revenue than they are. . . . We do think some of that under-performance relates to the fact the sales efforts for those web sites come second to those of the parent business (the cable network, the magazine). Therefore, we have estimated in 2001 AOL Time Warner will capture an additional $200 million of this $500 million ad sales upside."

5. Incremental Subscriptions
$25 million in new revenues ($12.5 EBITDA impact) + $25 million in reduced operating expenses ($25 million EBITDA impact)
"The company plans to drive new subscriptions through cross-promotion of everything from AOL membership to magazine and cable subscriptions. For example, a Time Warner magazine might bundle a discounted two-year subscription with the AOL service, or AOL's sports channel might promote *Sports Illustrated*. Second, the company plans to move as much of the Time Warner cable and subscription renewal process online as possible, thereby reducing churn and reselling costs. . . . Finally, the company envisions converting weekly subscribers of the Time Warner magazines to perennial subscribers—providing weekly print copies of the magazines but also providing those subscribers with magazine content online . . . We are estimating that AOL Time Warner can achieve $25 million in new subscription revenues. . . . We are also estimating that the company can save $25 million from reducing the cost of subscription management and renewal."

resources were underutilized before the merger. Otherwise, those resources must be distracted from other tasks in order to produce content for AOL, and the resulting content can hardly be considered "free." Likewise, the argument that AOL sales reps can sell Time Warner's left-over advertising inventory (item 4) is valid only if those sales reps are not already spending all of their time productively selling AOL ads. These objections are closely related to the next flaw.

- *The opportunity costs of common ownership are ignored.* For instance, when AOL promotes its new sibling *Sports Illustrated* on its sports channel (item 5), it may lose the opportunity to promote *Sports Illustrated*'s competitors. The Merrill Lynch analysis accounts for the benefit associated with the former, but it ignores the cost of the latter.

- *Benefits that are supposed to make the jointly owned units better off are counted twice, often once in each unit.* For example, the reduction in AOL marketing expense that comes from cross-promotion (item 1) appears to overlap with the incremental subscriptions to AOL's online services that also come from cross-promotion (item 5).

- *The costs and difficulty of cross-unit coordination are ignored; that is, cross-unit coordination is assumed to be free.* The Merrill Lynch analysts envision an enormous degree of cross-promotion and complex sharing of resources, which will require costly coordination efforts. Do the inevitable costs of coordination outweigh the benefits? If so, the merger fails the better-off test. And are such transactions better coordinated by contracts between independent firms than by managers within a firm? If so, the merger fails the best-alternative test.

The best antidote to logical flaws like these is a careful and dispassionate analysis of the costs as well as benefits of broad scope, weighed against a range of alternate arrangements. It seems that analysis of this sort could have identified the limited synergies from the merger of AOL and Time Warner ahead of time, and perhaps even helped predict that it would, as a result, be unstable even if it were consummated—as has turned out to be the case.

Summary

Both the stakes and the level of difficulty are high when a management team chooses the range of businesses in which a corporation will compete. Perspectives on such choices have evolved over time, and we see progression toward a view in which corporate-level scope choices are best seen as an overlay on business-unit strategies: corporate choices of scope are treated as effective or ineffective to the extent that they contribute to the success or failure of individual business units in their specific industries.

Broad scope that contributes to success passes two tests. First, the breadth must bring together business units that are made better off by their union. More specifically, it must increase the ability of units to add value, net of any incremental costs. Increased added value might derive from an increase in volume, improvements in industry structure, a widened wedge between willingness to pay and costs, or—occasionally—a reduction in risk.

A choice of broad scope that passes this first test must also clear a second one. Joint ownership must capture the benefits of breadth better than alternate arrangements such as arms'-length trade, licensing, strategic alliances, and joint ventures. We discussed circumstances that are likely to favor joint ownership over the alternatives, including contractual hazards and major investments in relationship-specific resources. We also considered how various models of corporate management address this best-alternative test in distinct ways.

The examples in this chapter illustrate the enormous power of corporate strategy both to create and to destroy value. We are likely to continue to see examples of both given the complexities of scope choices. Yet managers can improve the odds of value creation and capture by rigorously asking whether, and if so, why, business units might be better off under the same corporate umbrella than they would be if separated . . . or coordinated by some alternative to outright ownership.

Glossary

best-alternative test

better-off test

corporate added value

corporate strategy

good-parent test

Notes

1. See, for instance, Leonard Wrigley, "Divisional Autonomy and Diversification" (D.B.A. thesis, Harvard Business School, 1970), and Richard P. Rumelt, *Strategy, Structure, and Economic Performance* (Cambridge, Mass.: Harvard University Press, 1974).

2. Marakon Associates, *Commentary* 11 (June 1983).

3. Philippe C. Haspeslagh, Tomo Noda, and Fares Boulos, "Managing for Value: It's Not Just About the Numbers," *Harvard Business Review* 79, no. 7 (July–August 2001): 64–73.

4. Philippe C. Haspeslagh, "Portfolio Planning: Uses and Limits," *Harvard Business Review* 60, no. 1 (January–February 1982): 58–73.

5. C. K. Prahalad and Gary Hamel, "The Core Competence of the Corporation," *Harvard Business Review* 68, no. 3 (May–June 1990): 79–91.

6. Daryl Rigby, "Management Tools 2007: An Executive's Guide," Bain and Company, available at http://www.bain.com/management_tools/home.asp.

7. David J. Collis and Cynthia A. Montgomery, "Competing on Resources: Strategy in the 1990s," *Harvard Business Review* 73, no. 4 (July–August 1995): 118–128.

8. Pankaj Ghemawat, "Sears, Roebuck and Co.: The Merchandise Group" (Harvard Business School case no. 794-039, 1993).

9. Videotape of Richard M. Jones, President and Chief Financial Officer of Sears, Roebuck, addressing an Advanced Management Program class at Harvard Business School, November 11, 1985.

10. Stuart L. Gillan, John W. Kensinger, and John D. Martin, "Value Creation and Corporate Diversification: The Case of Sears, Roebuck & Co.," *Journal of Financial Economics* 55, no. 1 (January 2000): 103–137.

11. For others who employ similar and related tests, see Michael E. Porter, "From Competitive Advantage to Corporate Strategy," *Harvard Business Review* 65, no. 3 (May–June 1987): 43–59; Michael Goold, Andrew Campbell, and Marcus Alexander, *Corporate-Level Strategy: Creating Value in the Multibusiness Company* (New York: John Wiley, 1994); and David J. Teece, "Economies of Scope and the Scope of the Enterprise," *Journal of Economic Behavior & Organization* 1 (1980): 223–247.

12. Goold, Campbell, and Alexander, *Corporate-Level Strategy*, p. 14.

13. For further discussion of some of these points, see Pankaj Ghemawat, "The Growth Boosters," *Harvard Business Review* (July–August 2004): 35.

14. Ola Svenson, "Are We All Less Risky and More Skillful Than Our Fellow Drivers?" *Acta Psychologica* 47, no. 2 (February 1981): 143–148.

15. Ulrike Malmendier and Geoffrey Tate, "CEO Overconfidence and Corporate Investment," (NBER working paper no. w10807, 2004), available at www.nber.org/papers/w10807. For related theoretical work, see Simon Gervais, J. B. Heaton III, and Terrance Odean, "Overconfidence, Investment Policy, and Executive Stock Options" (Rodney L. White Center for Financial Research working paper no. 15-02, 2003), available at http://ssrn.com/abstract=361200.

16. David J. Collis and Cynthia A. Montgomery, *Corporate Strategy: Resources and the Scope of the Firm* (Chicago: Richard D. Irwin, 1997).

17. Having said that, we reiterate—here and elsewhere—that performance has to be looked at in terms of total economic profits rather than just profitability or margins.

18. B. Douglas Bernheim and Michael D. Whinston, "Multimarket Contact and Collusive Behavior," *Rand Journal of Economics* 21, no. 1 (Spring 1990): 1–26.

19. Joel A. C. Baum and Helaine J. Korn, "Competitive Dynamics of Interfirm Rivalry," *Academy of Management Journal* 39, no. 2 (April 1996): 255–291.

20. Arnold A. Heggestad and Stephen A. Rhoades, "Multi-Market Interdependence and Local Market Competition in Banking," *Review of Economics and Statistics* 60, no. 4 (1978): 523–532.

21. Robert M. Grant, *Contemporary Strategy Analysis: Concepts, Techniques, Applications*, 4th ed. (Malden, Mass.: Blackwell, 2002), p. 457.

22. Brian S. Silverman and Michael E. Porter, "Scotts Company: North American Corporate Strategy" (Harvard Business School case no. 701-002, Boston, 2000).

23. This typology was first proposed by Michael E. Porter; see Porter, "From Competitive Advantage to Corporate Strategy."

24. Pankaj Ghemawat, Eduardo Ballarin and Jose Manuel Campa, "Santander's Acquisition of Abbey: Banking Across Borders," (Harvard Business School Publishing case no. 707-485, Boston, 2006).

25. Clayton M. Christensen, *The Innovator's Dilemma: When New Technologies Cause Great Firms to Fail, The Management of Innovation and Change Series* (Boston: Harvard Business School Press, 1997).

26. Silverman and Porter, "Scotts Company."

27. Ryan Chittum, "Cendant Hopes Simpler Model Will Lift Stock," *Wall Street Journal*, May 20, 2004, p. C1.

28. Tarun Khanna and Krishna Palepu, "Why Focused Strategies May Be Wrong for Emerging Markets," *Harvard Business Review* 75, no. 4 (July–August 1997): 41–51.

29. Ideas concerning transaction costs were pioneered by Ronald H. Coase and Oliver E. Williamson. See especially Ronald H. Coase, "The Nature of the Firm," *Economica* 4, no. 16 (November 1937): 386–405; Oliver E. Williamson, *The Economic Institutions of Capitalism: Firms, Markets, Relational Contracting* (New York: Free Press, 1985); Oliver E. Williamson, *Markets and Hierarchies, Analysis and Antitrust Implications: A Study in the Economics of Internal Organization* (New York: Free Press, 1975).

30. The description of these circumstances draws in part from Bharat Anand, Tarun Khanna, and Jan W. Rivkin, "Market Failures" (Harvard Business School case no. 700-127, Boston, 2000).

31. Khanna and Palepu, "Why Focused Strategies May Be Wrong . . .," op cit.

32. Larry H. P. Lang and Rene M. Stulz, "Tobin's Q, Corporate Diversification, and Firm Performance," *Journal of Political Economy* 102, no. 6 (December 1994): 1248–1280; and Philip G. Berger and Eli Ofek, "Diversification's Effect on Firm Value," *Journal of Financial Economics* 37, no. 1 (January 1995): 39–65.

33. See also Jose Manuel Campa and Simi Kedia, "Explaining the Diversification Discount," *Journal of Finance* 57, no. 4 (2002): 1731–1762; and Belén Villalonga, "Does Diversification Cause the 'Diversification Discount'?" *Financial Management* 33, no. 2 (Summer 2004): 5–27 (who address self-selection biases in the previous literature).

34. On India, see Tarun Khanna and Krishna Palepu, "Is Group Affiliation Profitable in Emerging Markets? An Analysis of Diversified Indian Business Groups," *Journal of Finance* 55, no. 2 (2000): 867–891, and also Pankaj Ghemawat and Tarun Khanna, "The Nature of Diversified Business Groups: A Research Design and Two Case Studies," *Journal of Industrial Economics* 46, no. 1 (1998): 35–61. Tarun Khanna and Jan W. Rivkin, "Estimating the Performance Effects of Business Groups in Emerging Markets," *Strategic Management Journal* 22, no. 1 (January 2001): 45–74, provide a much broader perspective on the performance consequences of group affiliation in a broad range of emerging markets. And on highly industrialized countries other than the United States, see Eric R. Gedajlovic and Daniel M. Shapiro, "Management and Ownership Effects: Evidence from Five Countries," *Strategic Management Journal* 19, no. 6 (1998): 533–554 and Karl Lins and Henri Servaes, "International Evidence on the Value of Corporate Diversification," *Journal of Finance* 54, no. 6 (1999): 2215–2239.

Developing a Global Strategy

*For one country is different from another; its earth is
different, as are its stones, wines, bread, meat, and
everything that grows and thrives in a specific region.*

—PARACELSUS

Chapter 6 moved beyond the earlier chapters' focus on strategy for a free-standing business in one industry by considering strategy for diversified firms that operate in multiple industries. Chapter 7 looks at **geographic scope** instead of horizontal scope by considering strategy for firms that operate in multiple countries[1].

This geographic extension is important because of the growing importance of cross-border activities for many firms. One indication is supplied by the sustained increases, since World War II, in macromeasures of internationalization such as the ratios of international trade and foreign direct investment (FDI) to gross domestic product (GDP), as discussed further in the next section. Micromeasures of internationalization provide even more direct evidence. Thus, the share of foreign operations in the profits of U.S. corporations increased from about 5 percent in 1950 to nearly 30 percent by 2007.[2] For most other (smaller) developed countries, such measures tend to be significantly higher. They also tend to be higher when one focuses on large firms. At the other end of the size spectrum, firms seem to be considering cross-border activities at smaller scales or earlier in their lifecycles than before. Even firms that do opt to stay at home are often increasingly exposed to cross-border competition. And they are substantially less productive than exporters and, perhaps by an even bigger margin, than **multinational companies** (MNCs)—firms that make direct investments overseas.[3]

The first section of this chapter discusses the practice of global strategy, particularly its proneness to sizeism. The next two sections suggest that such sizeism (partly) reflects a discounting of the cultural, administrative, geographic and economic (CAGE) distances or differences between countries—differences that still have large effects on cross-border flows of products, capital, people, and so on. The two sections that follow apply the better-off and best-alternative tests to cross-border moves in a way that recognizes the differences across countries. The final two sections discuss different global strategies—as in strategies for dealing with international differences—and summarize them.

THE PRACTICE OF GLOBAL STRATEGY

In discussing the practice of global strategy, it is useful to begin by comparing it with corporate strategy.[4] Chapter 6 cited some of the strong forces that tend to push managers toward **sizeism** or overexpansion in choosing horizontal (and vertical) scope. The same forces also manifest themselves when it comes to choosing geographic scope. One indication is provided by the rationales that managers offer for globalizing. Paul Verdin and Nick Van Heck have compiled a confection of some of the common slogans: see Exhibit 7.1.[5] Note the extent of sizeism, unqualified by the sense that whether bigger is better might depend on industry attributes or competitive position and possibilities.

More structured surveys of managers suggest sizeism as well. Thus, in an online survey that *Harvard Business Review* (*HBR*) ran for me, 78 percent of respondents agreed with the statement that "globalization offers virtually limitless growth opportunities."[6] In addition, 64 percent agreed that "the truly global company should aim to compete everywhere," and 58 percent agreed that "globalization tends to make industries more concentrated."

These beliefs imply the norm of enormity—but seem fairly far removed from reality. Ubiquity may not be a sensible target given the international differences highlighted in the next two sections. And even if it were, it would require enormous geographic broadening by all but a handful of global giants, restricting interest in it to the very long run. Consider, for instance, all U.S. companies with foreign operations in 2004—themselves less than 1 percent of all U.S. companies. The largest number operated in just one foreign country, the median number in two, and 95 percent in fewer than two dozen.[7] And none of these summary statistics has changed since the mid-1990s!

Increased concentration as a result of globalization commands believers in the anti-globalization movement as well as among managers—but lacks any empirical basis. Data on the concentration of production in the hands of the five largest competitors in 18 global/globalizing industries show no general increase between the 1980s and the 1990s: concentration increased in some but was offset by decreases in others.[8] And a number of the industries reported as experiencing increases in concentration over that period (e.g., automobiles and oil production) actually experienced much larger decreases in the prior decades!

Given such unwarranted sizeism, it is unsurprising that firms' performance in the countries where they do compete is uneven and often even unprofitable. Some indications of the extent of the problem are provided by data that Marakon

EXHIBIT 7.1   A Web of Internationalization Slogans.

Source: Slogans from Paul Verdin and Nick Van Heck, *From Local Champions to Global Masters: A Strategic Perspective on Managing Internationalization*, p. 222. © 2001 Palgrave. Reprinted by permission.

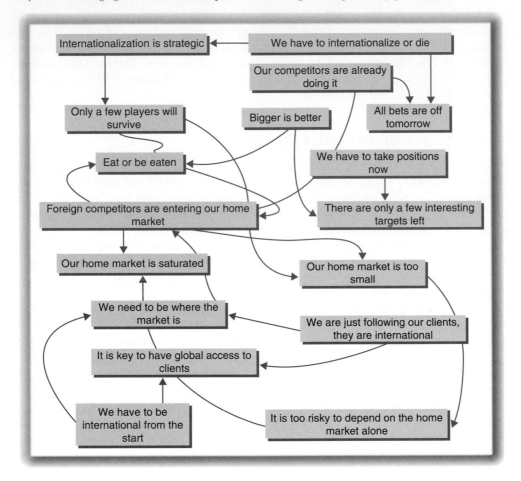

Associates (now Trinsum) analyzed at my request. They summarized their findings as follows:

> We found that half of the [large] companies we have looked at (8 out of 16) have significant geographic units that earn negative economic returns . . . [We] know from our clients' that their profitability by geography has stayed fairly stable over time unless they have specifically targeted action at specific countries/regions.

Exhibit 7.2 provides a fairly typical example of this type of problem. Note that in 2005, roughly one-fifth of this company's revenues destroyed economic value.

The broader point is that it is imprudent to simply focus on international revenues—like the many companies that still decree that international revenue will account for x percent of total revenues within y years. Or to just expand internationally

EXHIBIT 7.2   Economic Profits by Country for a Fast-Moving Consumer-Goods Company.
Source: Compustat. Value Line, Marakon Associates Analysis.

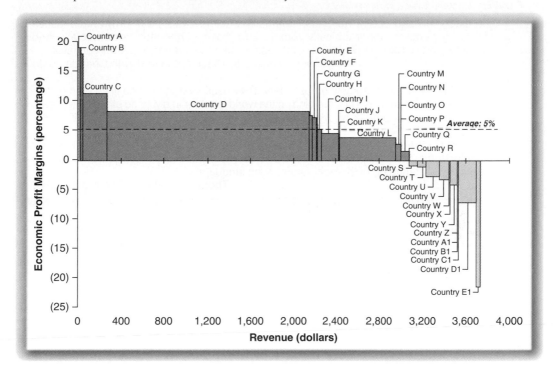

and hope that that will pay off—the approach apparently preferred by the 88 percent of the respondents to the *HBR* survey who agreed with the statement that "Global expansion is an imperative rather than an option to be evaluated"! What would be more helpful than pure boosterism is a value-focused perspective of the sort stressed throughout this book. The challenge is to tune it to the distinctive aspects of the international context, which are discussed next.

SEMIGLOBALIZATION: THE REAL STATE OF THE WORLD

Why is there so much sizeism in global strategy? As noted earlier, some of the forces parallel the ones discussed in Chapter 6 in the context of (horizontal) corporate strategy. But there is an extra source of bias in global strategy: the belief that borders between countries have disappeared or soon will. The quotes in Exhibit 7.3 suggest that such visions of a borderless world are not new and are often based on faith in the transformative powers of technology—although the specific technologies invoked have changed over time. The connection to sizeism, as pointed out by Bruce Kogut, is that without fundamental differences across countries, the answer to the question of "what is different when we move from a domestic to an international context . . . [is] simply that the world is a bigger place, and hence all economies related to the size of operations are, therefore, affected."[9]

In other words, if the world were indeed one, global strategy would just be domestic strategy applied to a bigger market. What makes global strategy interesting and challenging is that the world *cannot* be thought of as one giant country.

EXHIBIT 7.3 Visions of the Globalization Apocalypse.

> The extension and use of railroads, steamships, telegraphs, break down nationalities and bring peoples geographically remote into close connection commercially and politically. They make the world one, and capital, like water, tends to a common level.
> —David Livingstone, 1850s (cited in Nayan Chanda book)
>
> The airplane and wireless know no boundary. They pass over the dotted lines on the map without heed or hindrance. They are binding the world together in a way no other system can.
> —Henry Ford, *My Philosophy of Industry* (London: Harrap, 1929), p. 44.
>
> The world got flat . . . [creating] a global, Web-enabled playing field that allows for multiple forms of collaboration on research and work in real time, without regard to geography, distance or, in the near future, even language.
> —Thomas Friedman, *The World Is Flat*

Borders still seem to matter a great deal: most types of interactions that can occur either within or across borders are still very concentrated domestically, that is, exhibit substantial **home bias**. Consider some data:[10]

- *Products.* **Trade** accounts for about 27 percent of global GDP, but that percentage recedes most of the way back toward 20 percent if we strip out double counting.[11] And it approaches 10 percent if we focus in on cross-regional trade, because most trade occurs within regions (e.g., the European Union or North America).
- *Capital.* **Foreign direct investment** (FDI) has averaged about 10 percent of global fixed capital formation in recent years. Since acquisitions account for much of FDI, its real weight in new investment is smaller than that percentage would indicate. And again, more than one-half of FDI occurs within regions.
- *People.* First-generation immigrants, foreign students, and international tourists each represent less than 10 percent of the corresponding (domestic plus cross-border) totals. Cross-border flows of people also tend to be disproportionately regional.
- *Information.* **Offshoring** accounts for only 10–14 percent of currently offshore-able information technology (IT) services, themselves a small fraction of total IT services. Probably less than 20 percent (and declining) of the bits transmitted on the Internet cross national borders. Cross-border use of other media such as telephones is much lower still.

These data illustrate the continued importance of borders rather than their alleged demise, since actual cross-border movements are much lower than the levels implied by complete cross-border integration. To take just one example, the predicted trade-to-GDP ratio for the world if national borders did not matter at all would be, given the distribution of GDP across countries, about 90 percent.[12] Whether one adjusts the actual trade-to-GDP ratio for double counting or not, it falls far short of this ceiling.

The data also help address the contention that even if borders still matter, they soon will not. Look at some trends. Start with the trade-to-GDP ratio, which reached the 20 percent level for the first time in 1979, and, over the next 25 years, went up to

EXHIBIT 7.4   Globalization Indicators Versus Intuitions.

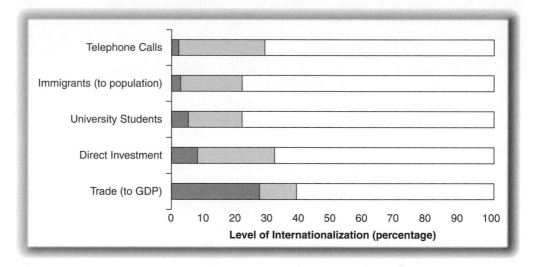

27 percent. Extrapolation implies a trade-to-GDP ratio of 35 percent by 2030—without any adjustment for double counting. This *would* be a big increase, but nowhere near 90 percent. And linear extrapolation seems overoptimistic: given the global economic downturn, the trade-to-GDP ratio is actually expected to decline in 2009.

Other globalization indicators have actually decreased or are decreasing: immigrant intensity and total capital flows in relation to GDP are lower than before World War I, and interregional Internet traffic is decreasing relative to the local/intraregional traffic.

Business people as well as business writers seem to have inflated intuitions about levels of cross-border integration. Thus, Exhibit 7.4 compares the average responses from the *HBR* online survey with the actual values for some of the cross-border percentages cited earlier. Note that all the indicators except trade are overestimated by a factor of three or more.

To summarize, the data indicate that the real state of the world is one of **semiglobalization** rather than either zero or complete cross-border integration. This suggests that neither strategies of local customization (tuned to zero integration) nor total standardization (tuned to complete integration) will do. What are needed, instead, are strategies that pay attention to the distinctively large differences that arise at national borders as well as to the bridges across them. To develop such strategies, it is necessary to drill down and understand exactly what the differences are that underlie the very big drop-offs in economic interactions that occur at national borders.

THE DIFFERENCES ACROSS COUNTRIES AND THE CAGE DISTANCE FRAMEWORK

The border whose influence on cross-border interactions has been studied the most is the U.S.–Canadian border. The United States and Canada have the largest bilateral trading relationship in the world. Does the border between them still impede trade?

Disaggregated data on Canadian provinces' trade with each other as well as with the United States have let trade economists estimate home-bias multiples, for example, the ratio of trade between the Canadian provinces of Ontario and British Columbia to trade between Ontario and the U.S. state of Oregon, which is about as far away from Ontario and has roughly the same economic mass as British Columbia. Note that if the border did not matter at all, the expected ratio would be one.[13]

As of 1988, before the North American Free Trade Agreement (NAFTA), the home-bias multiple on merchandise trade was actually estimated to exceed 20! NAFTA helped bring this multiple closer to ten by the mid-1990s, and it may have shrunk further since then, although it still clearly exceeds five. Furthermore, these estimates are just for merchandise; for services, the multiple is still several times larger.[14] As in the previous section, these numbers are substantially larger than the flat-world prediction of zero home bias, which would translate into a multiple of one.

What makes these large home-bias multiples even more remarkable is that compared to a randomly selected pair of countries, the United States and Canada are very similar to rather than different from each other. *Culturally*, the two share the same dominant language (English), religion (Protestant Christianity), race (white), and traditional elites (Anglo-Saxon as in WASP). They also embody similar cultural values: based on the most widely used schema of this sort, the United States ranks second out of 68 countries/regions in terms of cultural proximity to Canada, behind Australia, and Canada is third closest to the United States, behind Australia and the United Kingdom.[15] *Administratively*, Canada and the United States are united not only by NAFTA, but were (mostly) British colonies, which has led to commonalities in respects such as legal systems as well as the cultural dimensions mentioned earlier. *Geographically*, the two countries are not just close to each other but share the world's longest land border. In addition, while both are very large countries, more than 90 percent of all Candians live within 250 kilometers of the U.S. border. And *economically*, the two countries have similar levels of per capita income compared to a randomly selected country pair.

A large body of research on **gravity models**—which link economic interactions between countries to the product of their economic masses divided by some composite measure of differences along the kinds of dimensions that Canada and the United States resemble each other—explain not only why the United States–Canada trading relationship is the largest in the world, but also one-half to two-thirds of all bilateral trade flows between *all* possible pairs of countries. As a result, gravity models have been described as providing "some of the clearest and most robust empirical findings in economics."[16] Many of the same factors also help explain FDI or companies' foreign presence. Thus, for U.S companies that operate in just one foreign country, that country is Canada 60 percent of the time (and 10 percent of the time it is the United Kingdom).[17] Gravity models have also been adapted to explain cross-border equity trades, e-commerce transactions, patent citations, immigrant flows, international air traffic, phone calls, and even the incidence of wars.

At least in the context of trade, it is possible to offer relatively comprehensive gravity-based assessments of the average extent to the various types of differences across countries affect cross-border economic activity. See Exhibit 7.5 for the summary results of one such analysis.[18]

The signs on most of the estimates in the exhibit probably accord with your intuitions (although they *cannot* be reconciled with a flat world). The magnitudes of

EXHIBIT 7.5 Estimated Effects: A Gravity Model of Bilateral Trade.

Source: Pankaj Ghemawat and Rajiv Mallick, "The Industry-Level Structure of International Trade Networks: A Gravity-Based Approach." Harvard Business School working paper, February 2003.

Dimensions of Distance/Proximity	Determinant	Change in Trade
Cultural	Common Language	+42%
Administrative	Common Regional Trading Bloc	+47%
	Colony/Colonizer Links	+188%
	Common Currency	+114%
	Differences in Corruption	−11%
Geographic	Physical Distance: 1% increase	1.1%
	Physical Size: 1% increase	−0.2%
	Landlockedness	−48%
	Common Land Border	+125%
Economic	Economic Size: GDP (1% increase)	+0.8%
	Income Level: GDP per capita (1% increase)	+0.7%

some of the effects are more surprising. For example, countries with colonial ties are apt to trade almost three times as much as countries without such ties (or more, if one also takes into account the role of colonial ties in engendering cultural similarities)! The persistence of such large effects decades and, in some instances, centuries after the original colonial relationships were dissolved reinforces the conclusion drawn in the last section: complete globalization—as in the disappearance of the effects of such international differences versus similarities—is extremely unlikely any time soon. So do other coercive facts such as stubbornly high (perhaps even increasing) estimated effects of physical distance over the course of the twentieth century.[19]

The categories in the Canada–United States example as well as the variables in Exhibit 7.5 suggest a general framework—broader and more integrative than models that look at differences between countries piecemeal—for thinking about the differences between countries. The framework will be referred to as the **CAGE distance framework** since it is organized in terms of **C**ultural, **A**dministrative/political/institutional, **G**eographic, and **E**conomic distances between countries as summarized in Exhibit 7.5 and presented in more detail in Exhibit 7.6:

- *Cultural distance.* "Culture" as used here refers to the attributes of a society that are sustained mainly by interactions among people, rather than by the state (as lawgiver or enforcer). Cultural distance encompasses differences in religious beliefs, race/ethnicity, language, and social norms and values.
- *Administrative (or political) distance.* Historical and political associations (colonial linkages, free trade agreements, the current tenor of relationships) between countries greatly affect economic exchange between them. Of course, countries can also isolate themselves from others with unilateral measures that shrivel their international economic ties across the board.
- *Geographic distance.* The geographic dimension of distance involves more than just how far two countries are from each other: other attributes to be

EXHIBIT 7.6 The CAGE Distance Framework: Country-Level Analysis.

Source: Pankaj Ghemawat, "Distance Still Matters: The Hard Reality of Global Expansion," Harvard Business Review 79, no. 8 (2001): 137–47. © 2001 by the president and fellows of Harvard College. Reprinted by permission of Harvard Business School.

	Cultural Distance	Administrative Distance	Geographic Distance	Economic Distance
Bilateral (or multilateral) Attributes	–Different languages –Different ethnicities/ lack of connective ethnic or social networks –Different religions –Differences in national work systems –Different values, norms and dispositions	–Lack of colonial ties –Lack of shared regional trading bloc –Lack of common currency –Different legal system –Political hostility	–Physical distance –Lack of land border –Differences in climates (and disease environments) –Differences in time-zones	–Differences in consumer incomes –Differences in availability of • Human resources • Financial resources • Natural resources • Intermediate inputs • Infrastructure • Supplier/ distribution struct • Complements • Organizational Capability
Unilateral Attributes	–Traditionalism –Insularity –Spiritualism –Inscrutability	–Nonmarket/ closed economy (home bias versus foreign bias) –Lack of membership in international orgs. –Weak legal institutions/ corruption –Lack of govt. checks and balances –Societal conflict –Political/ expropriation risk	–Landlockedness –Geographic size –Geographic remoteness	–Economic size –Low per capita income –Low level of monetization –Limited resources, inputs, infrastructure, complements, capability

considered include contiguity, a country's physical size, within-country distances to borders, access to the ocean, topography, and, even, time zones.

• *Economic distance.* Consumer wealth and income and the cost of labor are the most obvious (and related) determinants of economic distance between countries. Others include differences in availability (or lack) of resources, inputs, infrastructure and complements, and organizational capabilities.

The most distinctive feature of the CAGE distance framework is that it highlights the bilateral attributes of country pairs (or multilateral attributes of groups of countries) as well as the unilateral attributes of individual countries. This is in stark contrast to most of the other frameworks that have been proposed for thinking about the differences across countries (or locations), which focus on just unilateral attributes by assuming that countries can be assessed one-by-one against common yardsticks to yield meaningful rankings.[20] But consideration of bilateral differences is necessary to envision countries as existing in (and even occupying) space in relation to each other, that is, as nodes in a network instead of as an array along a common yardstick.[21] And the extension is of real importance given the very large effects that bilateral attributes can have, as indicated by Exhibit 7.5.

Having drawn that distinction, it is useful to add that unilateral influences *can* be bedded down with the bilateral influences that gravity models emphasize. A formal link is supplied by a unilateral measure of isolation (or integration), which captures unilateral country-specific attributes that generally decrease (or increase) a country's involvement in cross-border economic activities and which can be treated as a common component of that country's distances along various dimensions from other countries. For example, really isolated countries (characterized by unique, ingrown cultures, closed administrative policies, physical remoteness, or extremely high or low incomes) can be thought of as being relatively distant from everywhere else. That said, bilateral attributes need to be added in to capture the idea that a company's home base affects which countries are close and which ones farther away.

The other point worth emphasizing is that different types of distance matter to different extents in different industries. Because geographic distance, for instance, affects the costs of transportation and communication, it is of particular importance to companies dealing in heavy or bulky products. Cultural distance, on the other hand, should be a crucial consideration for a media company, but it is much less important for a cement or steel business. Exhibit 7.7 provides a summary of some of the characteristics that are likely to make an industry particularly sensitive to a particular dimension of distance.

Since virtually all industries are sensitive to *some* kind of distance, and since distance complicates global expansion, such expansion has to be evaluated rather than treated as an imperative. This point has been underscored in the wake of the global economic downturn by moves by financial services firms, among others, to shrink geographic scope. The two tests discussed in Chapter 6, the better-off test and the best-alternative test, can also be applied to cross-border moves, as elaborated in the next two sections with a particular focus on moves to broaden geographic scope.

THE BETTER-OFF TEST

Using the better-off test to determine whether to broaden geographic scope involves asking "Does combining and coordinating activities across multiple geographies enable more value to be created and claimed than with country-by-country operation?" Obviously, a scope expansion can increase the aggregate volume of business on which it is possible to earn positive (or negative) economic margins. But in view of the differences between countries and the managerial biases toward overexpansion of scope discussed in Chapter 6, it is generally better not to think about geographic scope expansions in purely scalar terms.[22] The better-off test forces identification of

EXHIBIT 7.7   The CAGE Distance Framework: Industry-Level Analysis.

Source: Pankaj Ghemawat, "Distance Still Matters: The Hard Reality of Global Expansion," *Harvard Business Review* 79, no. 8 (2001): 137–147.

	Cultural Sensitivity	Administrative Sensitivity	Geographic Sensitivity	Economic Sensitivity
Industry Characteristics	–High linguistic content (TV programming) –Local tradition/identity (ego-expressive prod.) –Significant diff. in preferences (hor. Diff.) • idiosyncr. tastes (fish sausage, boxer shorts) • design diff. (autos) • diff. in standards (electrical appliances) • diff. in sizes/packages (processed foods) • diff. in target segments (boom boxes–U.S. vs. Japan) –Entrenched tastes –Home bias ("local" preferences) –Strong country-of-origin effects or vertical differentiation (luxury categories)	–High govt. involvement • procurement/funding (mass transportation products) • regulation (healthcare) • state ownership (telecoms) –Strategic industry status • size (autos) • votes/organization (agriculture, textiles) • public opinion (media) • national security concerns (telecommunications) • anointed national champions (aerospace) –National patrimony effects (natural resources) –Mass consumption/staple products (food, fuel/energy) –Asset specificity and the scope for holdup (infrastructure) –Specific restrictions on/preferences for foreign competitors	–Low value to weight/bulk (cement) –Hazards/diff. in transport. –Perishability (fruit) –Importance of connectivity (fin. Services) –Intense local supervision requirements (restaurants) –Other local perform. req. for value activities (many services) **NOTE**: Many of these conditions tend to favor FDI relative to trade	–Diff. in willingness to pay –Income-related differences in demand (automobiles) –Need for variety/agility/responsiveness (home appliances) –High intensity of labor, other factors prone to abs. cost or efficiency diff. (garments) –Potential intl. Scale/scope economies (pharma) –Different cycles (cement) –Infrastructural/capability requirements (adv. mfg.) –Differences in suppliers/channels (insurance) –Differences in complements (gas prices and cars, U.S. v. Europe)

other possible gains related to the concepts that have been discussed in earlier chapters. Geographic expansion can sometimes improve the industry structure(s) facing a company. More often, it can increase added value by widening the wedge between costs and willingness to pay. And such expansion can sometimes also create value by reducing risk.

The better-off test will be illustrated with two cases involving cross-border mergers: the string of acquisitions by Mexico-based Cemex that led to its becoming the third-largest competitor in the cement industry while maintaining the highest profitability level of any of the majors, and the combination, recently dissolved, of automakers Daimler-Benz and Chrysler.[23] Note that in the case of mergers and acquisitions, the better-off test is critical to value creation; if it is not satisfied, the only way to create value by buying out another company is if the seller underprices it.

Industry Attractiveness

Industry attractiveness is often ignored in analyzing global strategy but was historically the single biggest driver of Cemex's superior profitability. Some of this reflected Cemex's care in market selection, which led to a capacity footprint concentrated in countries with high cement prices. But Cemex did more than simply select structurally attractive markets: when analyzing a possible acquisition target, it also looked at the potential to restructure the market as a whole by reducing domestic rivalry and imports.

Cemex managed domestic rivalry by pursuing controlling stakes in targets that were local leaders or held least 25 percent of the local market and therefore presumably possessed price-setting power. In addition, there is clear evidence of "mutual forbearance" between Cemex and its leading global competitors, Holcim and Lafarge: local market downturns were less likely to lead them to cut prices locally because they recognized that aggressive behavior in any one market might provoke fierce competition everywhere, and therefore refrained from aggression anywhere. In fact, such considerations served as the initial spur to Cemex's globalization. Specifically, Holcim's investments in Mexico in 1989 prompted Cemex to begin investing heavily in Spain in 1992, where Holcim already had significant investments in place. The implication, spelled out by CEO Lorenzo Zambrano, was that if a price war erupted in Mexico, another might well erupt in Spain. As it turned out, *no* price wars erupted. The caveat is that such dominance and recognition of mutual dependence with other global competitors in particular has led to ongoing antitrust challenges as well as significant penalties in the past.

Of course, the management of rivalry locally wouldn't have helped profitability much if imports could flood in whenever domestic prices rose above a certain level. But Cemex also controlled what military strategists would call "strategic narrows" that allow it to influence the levels of imports into its key markets. Particularly important was its network of 60 marine terminals worldwide, which sheltered key markets such as Mexico from low-priced imports. This control was complemented by Cemex's role as the world's largest cement trader—with much of that cement produced by third parties. This is not a very lucrative business in and of itself. But trading other people's products is a good way to divert low-priced imports away from your own key markets, as well as to gain experience in other markets before you decide whether to acquire local capacity.

Improving industry structure was also one of the rationales for the Daimler-Benz and Chrysler merger but it failed to have much of an impact in this regard. The merger did increase the five biggest automakers' share of global production from 52 percent to 54 percent, but that increase paled against the backdrop of prior decreases in auto industry concentration, which had fallen substantially since Ford's Model T accounted for about one-half of the world's total stock of cars in the 1920s. The global auto industry's problem is not one of fewer and fewer players surmounting escalating scale thresholds but, instead, of more and more fragmentation and, relatedly, chronic excess capacity—and has been greatly exacerbated by the global economic downturn.

These two examples suggest some broader guidelines for thinking about the links between cross-border moves and industry attractiveness:

- *Account for international differences in industry profitability.* The simplest way to illustrate international differences in industry profitability is to note the very large variation in average profitability across countries. Thus, while data on more than 4,000 firms from 42 countries indicate an average pretax return on assets of 5 percent over 1993–2003, the average profitability for the top quartile of countries was 12 percent, and for the bottom quartile −2 percent.[24]
- *Understand the structural dynamics of your industry.* The determinants of industry profitability can change in a way that should be accounted for— particularly for moves with long payoff periods. Cement has seen significant increases in effective concentration in the last few decades but the auto industry has registered significant declines—even though many executives in the industry believe otherwise!
- *Think through whether moves will de-escalate/escalate the degree of rivalry.* Analysis at the industry level is necessary but not sufficient: detailed competitor analysis, including analysis of competitors' beliefs and perceptions (see Chapter 4), is needed to explain why multimarket contact may have raised prices in some industries, such as cement and light bulbs, but has led—as competitors "invaded each other's turf"—to price wars in other industries, such as tires.

Cost Effects

Cost effects are, along with volume effects, the focus of many strategies of expanding geographic scope but need to be analyzed rather than assumed. Thus, given cement's commodity status, most published accounts of Cemex ascribe its success as a global competitor to the achievement of lower production costs than its competitors. But the differential between Cemex and its leading global competitors in this regard turns out to be quite modest.

Globalization has actually had a much bigger impact on the company's capital costs, which decreased from 13 percent in 1992 to 8 percent in 2002. This reflected, in part, pooling across product markets, as discussed later, under risk. In addition, product market globalization was accompanied by (and at least partly enabled) capital market globalization. When it was still a local company, Cemex relied on local sources of finance. But after two big Spanish acquisitions, it financed new acquisitions through its operations there to exploit the tax-deductibility of interest in Spain as well as the collateral value of assets in a developed country exempt from "Mexico risk." (Remember that in a semiglobalized world, capital markets should not be thought of as completely integrated.) While this gambit did *not* help create an advantage vis-à-vis Cemex's major rivals, all of whom are headquartered in Europe, it did help mitigate what would have been a major disadvantage.

The Daimler-Benz and Chrysler merger also focused on cost reductions: the key rationale offered for it was that the combined company would be able to achieve significant scale economies as the fifth largest automaker in the world. But the initial cost savings targeted by the merger amounted to just $1.4 billion, or 1 percent of the two companies' combined revenues, and were mostly confined to procurement and back-end activities such as finance, control, IT, and logistics. The potential for further cost reductions in other areas was limited by the close-to-zero product overlap between Daimler and Chrysler. And on the other side of the coin, there were increased expenses, including transaction costs of hundreds of millions of dollars, more than $400 million a year in recurring expenditures to bring the pay of the merged company's German managers up to par with their American counterparts' and, from the perspective of Daimler's shareholders, the takeover premium of nearly $10 billion paid to Chrysler's shareholders.

Some of the (additional) lessons about cost analysis in a cross-border context include the following:

- *Understand the level at which economies of scale/scope really matter.* While it is often assumed in global strategy that global scale is what counts, there are many other possibilities: national scale, plant scale, share of customer wallet, and so on. In cement, national or regional scale is key. And the poor performance of General Motors, for decades the world's largest automaker (see Chapter 5), dramatizes the lack of a causal relationship between global scale and profitability in autos.
- *Look at cost drivers other than scale/scope.* While the earlier discussion focused on scale/scope, there are, as noted in Chapter 3, many other potential drivers of costs. Ones that stand out in a cross-border context include location, institutional factors (e.g., unionization) and governmental regulations (e.g., tariffs).
- *Consider cost increases as well as decreases.* The large differences between countries highlighted in the previous section can sometimes lead to cost decreases (see the discussion of arbitrage strategies that follows) but, as indicated by the payroll problems at Daimler-Benz and Chrysler, cost increases are a possible outcome as well.

Differentiation Effects

Differentiation effects seem even more prone to being assumed instead of analyzed. Thus, the observation that Cemex commands much higher average prices than its leading global competitors can elicit very creative explanations of how it might be increasing willingness to pay. There has been some product innovation such as the development of white rather than gray cement. Cemex may also be helped, particularly on bagged cement sold to small buyers, by its international "CEMEX" brand, which it has begun attaching to the local brands that it has acquired. And on bulk sales to larger buyers, the company's delivery time guarantee, inspired by Domino's Pizza, has contributed to buyer value by reducing expensive downtime.

Common sense suggests, however, that such possibilities go only part of the way toward explaining prices that are, on average, 20 percent higher than Holcim's. Cement ranks within or close to the bottom decile of manufacturing industries in terms of both advertising-intensity and R&D-intensity, restricting the potential for product differentiation. Cemex's retention of local brands presumably further limits the power of global branding. And the delivery guarantee was, until recently, confined to a small percentage of sales in Cemex's home base in Mexico. As discussed earlier, industry attractiveness (i.e., better bargaining power rather than enhanced willingness to pay) is what mostly seems to account for the higher prices.

The auto industry offers more potential for differentiation but as the Daimler-Benz and Chrysler merger illustrates, achievement of this potential cannot be taken for granted. The vision of Mercedes' cachet somehow rubbing off on Chrysler and make the latter's products more attractive—"mass with class," as one periodical put it—ran into worries about spillovers of the opposite kind: Chrysler's mass-market image dragging down Mercedes. As a result, a "Brand Bible" issued after the merger decreed that the two divisions' marques would be kept completely separate, as would their European dealerships.

Implications for the cross-border analysis of differentiation effects include the following:

- *Relate the potential for differentiation to R&D/sales and advertising/sales ratios* for your company or industry. These ratios are the most robust markers of multinational presence, which is why product differentiation is considered key to strategies that seek to tap scale economies by expanding across borders.
- *Think through how globality affects willingness to pay.* There are some cases of globality boosting willingness to pay—for example, for individual customers who travel a lot or want to belong to a global community, or for companies that are themselves global. But especially in consumer businesses, cross-border appeal is often rooted in specific country-of-origin advantages (e.g., French wine).
- *Analyze how cross-country (CAGE) heterogeneity affects willingness to pay.* While the differences between countries sometimes underpin country-of-origin advantages, they more often reduce the willingness to pay for foreign products or services. Even subtle differences can render a product that works well in one country inferior or entirely unsaleable in another.

Dual Effects

As noted in Chapter 6, it is sometimes hard to parse the effects of a scope change into cost effects and differentiation effects. But once again, such inseparabilities should not prevent a careful analysis of the impact of scope on competitive advantage since advantage depends not on one or the other, but on the wedge between the two.

One (potentially) dual effect that has attracted great attention in international business is *cross-border learning and innovation.* Given international differences that are typically several times as large as intranational differences, exploiting variation is of particular interest in an international as opposed to domestic context. Thus, as Cemex moved outside Mexico, it was exposed to a range of practices that it implemented as "best practices" worldwide (see Exhibit 7.8). Some of this cross-border learning was serendipitous, but some resulted from a deliberate quest to develop and deploy information around the world.[25] Underlying all this was a range of organizational mechanisms referred to as "The Cemex Way": the adoption of a common language (English rather than Spanish); the rotation of managers globally; the use of international consultants; and sustained investments in technology, including information technology, to realize the potential unlocked by learning.

EXHIBIT 7.8 **Cross-Border Learning and Innovation at Cemex.**
Source: CEMEX Annual Report 2002. Reprinted by permission.

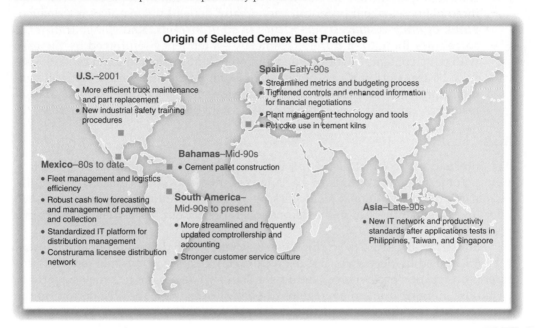

The Daimler-Benz and Chrysler merger also created opportunities for information exchange, but it appears that few were pursued. This is unsurprising given very limited attempts at integration. To cite just one indicator, CEO Juergen Schrempp, from Daimler, didn't speak at Chrysler's headquarters in Michigan until seven months after the merger had officially been finalized. In fact, subsequent developments direct attention to the dark side of too much variation given managerial bandwidth constraints. Chrysler turned out to be a far shakier company than Daimler-Benz's due diligence had suggested. Its aging product line and significant overcapacity contributed to losses of $4.7 billion in 2001 alone. This necessitated an intensive focus on rehabilitating Chrysler—distracting management's attention—as well as compromises at Daimler to keep reported profits up. BMW ended up overtaking Mercedes as the number one luxury car brand in the world in 2004.

Several additional points should be made about cross-border learning as well as other dual effects:

- *Assess how location-specific versus mobile knowledge is.* Knowledge transfer at Cemex was aided by industry characteristics: cement is cement, so ideas generated in one part of the world can be applied relatively easily (i.e., without much translation) elsewhere. Multidimensional distance between countries presents more of a challenge in other industries, requiring explicit attention to knowledge decontextualization and recontextualization if it is to work well.
- *Consider multiple alternatives for acquiring and deploying knowledge.* Discussions of knowledge transfer often focus on formal internal transfers of knowledge within MNCs to the exclusion of alternatives: personal interactions;

work with buyers, suppliers, or consultants; open innovation; imitation; contracting for the use of knowledge; and so on.[26] And even the effectiveness of internal knowledge transfer can vary greatly, depending on how it is managed.

- *Think of other resources/capabilities in similar terms.* Knowledge transfer is sometimes thought of purely technically—a tendency reinforced by the ease with which patents can be counted. But other kinds of information can also usefully be transferred across borders, for example, business model or management innovations such as franchising. More generally, other organizational resources/capabilities with broad effects might be analyzed in similar ways.

Risk Considerations

The international context also adds various risks and uncertainties relative to a purely domestic context (think of exchange rate fluctuations, for instance), flagging risk as an area for additional focus. Risk pooling across multiple geographies is the effect most frequently cited in the international context, but risk actually matters in a number of different ways.

To start with Cemex, the construction business, which drives the cement industry, is characterized by deep local and regional cycles. Pooling across markets with different construction cycles helped reduce the standard deviation in Cemex's quarterly cash flow margins from an average of 22 percent over the 1978–1992 period (in the run-up to its first foreign acquisitions in Spain) to 12 percent over the 1992–1997 period, contributing to lower capital costs, as discussed earlier. It also helped the company weather Mexico's currency crisis of the mid-1990s—the so-called "Tequila shock"—that might otherwise have forced it to sell out to a global competitor. And having globalized, Cemex, like other global competitors, was able to buy capacity at a fraction of its replacement cost when local competitors come under pressure in Asia in wake of the Asian currency crisis of the late 1990s. Also note that a significant fraction of the wealth of the controlling Zambrano family is locked up in the company, in a country with poorly developed capital markets, appropriately tilting it toward internalized risk reduction rather than a reliance on widely diversified shareholders.

The Daimler-Benz and Chrysler merger was apparently also partly motivated by the reduction of risks/capital costs: the hope seemed to be that broader global shareholding would lead to reduced capital costs for the merged company. In fact, the large "backflow" of shares from the United States to Europe in the wake of the merger triggered the company's ejection from the S&P 500, and it has been suggested that this may have led to more volatility, which may in turn have increased capital costs. It *is* clear that the market-value plunge of the combined company soured the traditionally cozy relationship between Daimler and Deutsche Bank, exposing Daimler to more capital market pressure in that respect. And more broadly, finance theory suggests that the risk-pooling argument makes little sense for a public firm with access to reasonably efficient capital markets .

Some of the (additional) lessons about risk analysis in a cross-border context include the following:

- *Characterize the extent and key sources of risk.* In your business (capital-intensity, demand volatility, etc.). While the global economic downturn makes cyclicality loom large in discussions of risk, other kinds of risks (e.g., related to shocks of various sorts) also need to be remembered. The relevant risks vary by strategy as well: a company reliant on cross-border supply chains faces very different risks from a competitor with more localized production.

- *Assess how much cross-border moves reduce risk—or increase it.* While geographic expansion historically reduced cashflow volatility at Cemex, it has fared less well in the global economic downturn of the late 2000s because of a large acquisition—of Rinker—at what turned out to be close to the top of the industry cycle, forcing it to consider significant asset sales. This serves as a reminder that cross-border expansion can increase as well as decrease risk, depending on the particular strategy option pursued, and that those particulars must therefore be analyzed.

- *Recognize any benefits that might accrue from increasing risk.* Risk can, given optionality, be valuable for the same reason that financial options are more valuable in the presence of greater (price) volatility. Thus, after the Asian crisis, Cemex swapped one million tons of capacity in Spain for four million tons of capacity in Southeast Asia with higher risks, but also growth potential. This exemplifies a perspective shared by many MNCs: think of emerging markets as strategic options rather than just as risk traps.

- *Consider multiple alternatives for managing exposure to risk or exploitation of optionality.* Thus, a company might enter a foreign market with a fully-owned greenfield operation, make an acquisition, work with a joint venture partner, or simply export there. Each alternative has different implications for the amount of risk incurred and how it is managed—and for returns.

That last point could be elaborated. It seems better, however, to take a broader, more systematic perspective on these alternatives since they embody the second of the two evaluative tests to be discussed in this chapter: the best-alternative test.

THE BEST-ALTERNATIVE TEST

Using the better-off test to determine whether to broaden geographic scope involves asking "Can common ownership of operations or activities in different countries enable more value to be created and claimed than if they were independent entities?" The best-alternative test, in contrast asks, "Are there any alternatives for coordinating cross-border activities that are superior to common ownership?" Or in other words, what advantages do firms or other organizational forms have at dealing with the difficulties of cross-border coordination through markets and the price mechanism?

This question was discussed toward the end of the previous section, in the context of decisions about how to enter foreign markets. But the alternatives listed in the first row of Exhibit 7.9, ranging from arm's-length dealings to ownership, apply to

EXHIBIT 7.9 Ownership and Alternatives: The Case of De Beers.

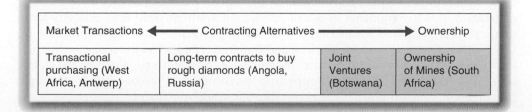

Market Transactions ◄———— Contracting Alternatives ————► Ownership			
Transactional purchasing (West Africa, Antwerp)	Long-term contracts to buy rough diamonds (Angola, Russia)	Joint Ventures (Botswana)	Ownership of Mines (South Africa)

other kinds of decision situations as well. For an example, revisit Chapter 2's discussion of De Beers' recent strategic shift: after more than 100 years of supporting the whole industry by mopping up as much of the world's rough diamond production as possible and stockpiling it if necessary, De Beers desisted and switched to a strategy of driving up demand by pumping up advertising and focusing it on its own brand.

While De Beers' new strategy is obviously more focused on demand, the big supply-side shift that it entails can usefully be framed in terms of Exhibit 7.9. De Beers had historically relied on all four modes of supply assurance depicted in the exhibit, but it recently disengaged from the first two, which involved assuming ownership of others' rough diamond output (the unshaded boxes in the second row of the exhibit). At the same time, it has increased its commitment to the other two modes of supply assurance (the two shaded boxes in the second row of the exhibit) by engaging in joint exploration/development and acquiring deposits/mines from others to supplement its historical reliance on internal development. And the ownership of De Beers itself has shifted, with the controlling Oppenheimer family leading a consortium that took the company private. The connection with the demand-side is that all these moves seem to be geared to maximizing De Beers' (or the Oppenheimers') ability to appropriate the value that would be created if the new strategy *did* increase willingness to pay for De Beers' own rough diamonds.

More broadly, of the alternatives identified in Exhibit 7.9, research on MNCs has placed particular emphasis on the choice between joint ventures and wholly-owned subsidiaries as modes of horizontal expansion. Proponents of ownership stress its advantages over joint ventures in terms of financial security and the control and protection of intellectual property, and emphasize that although the volume and value of cross-border mergers and acquisitions have surged since the mid-1990s, the number of cross-border joint ventures has fallen to a fraction of the highs recorded back then.[27]

Meanwhile, proponents of joint ventures highlight their advantages in tapping into local knowledge that would be hard to purchase, links in the local value chain that would otherwise be inaccessible, or local connections, including political ones. This makes joint ventures comparatively more attractive in new markets that are very different from a company's home base—especially if a company lacks much international experience. (In terms of the strategies introduced in the next section, joint ventures ease adaptation.)

Proponents of joint ventures also point out that venture dissolution is not the same as failure, note that joint ventures do reduce several kinds of risks, and point out that while the number of new international joint ventures may have declined, the incidence of cross-border contractual arrangements—involving defined relationships but not the set-up of a new legal entity—seems to have increased. They also argue that the lure of ownership through mergers reflects managerial inclinations toward control and empire-building more than real benefits to their shareholders. In addition, despite liberalization in many countries in recent years, joint ventures or at least majority local ownership are required for foreign companies to participate in sectors as diverse as U.S. airlines, Chinese financial services, and Indian retailing. And the scope and significance of such restrictions might increase again because of shifts triggered by the global economic downturn such as stepped-up governmental involvement—through procurement, regulation and even ownership—in company affairs.

Such broad-gauge arguments notwithstanding, common sense suggests that the choice between ownership and joint ventures is likely to be very sensitive to the specifics of a situation, limiting the usefulness of general principles regarding that broad choice in making specific decisions. Instead, consideration of those specifics in terms of the value components discussed in the previous section, and of the sustainability of that added value, as discussed in Chapter 5, is likely to prove a better basis for selecting the best alternative.

Some other, broader lessons about the development of better alternatives are also worth emphasizing here:

- *Articulate and analyze a broad range of alternatives.* While the choice between ownership and joint ventures *is* important, the De Beers case provides some perspective on this debate by reminding us that the range of alternatives is far broader. In fact, one can go well beyond the four boxes in the exhibit to include alternatives such as strategic alliances that stop short of joint-venture formation, licenses, franchising, and so on.
- *Broaden the bases for generating alternatives.* The transaction-to-ownership continuum in Exhibit 7.9 is only one basis for generating alternatives. Other ideas mentioned in Chapter 5 include stretching thinking about competitive variables and timing, explicitly considering asymmetries and informational imperfections, broadening and shifting the scope of strategic scanning, attempting radical shifts in perspective, and building organizational creativity.
- *Focus on differences as ways of generating global strategy alternatives.* Since the scope for distinctive content in global strategy stems from the large differences between countries, it suggests that a particularly useful way of generating global strategy alternatives is in terms of varied approaches for dealing with those differences. Such approaches, which can serve as cues for generating specific strategy alternatives, are the topic of the next section.

AAA STRATEGIES FOR DEALING WITH DIFFERENCES

Discussions of global strategy started with Fayerweather's (1969) identification of the basic tension between pressures for unification within companies and toward fragmentation from differences in national environments.[28] Prahalad and Doz (1987) elaborated this tension into the trade-off between what they called global integration and national responsiveness—and what I refer to as **aggregation** (to *overcome* cross-country differences and achieve scale/scope economies that extend across national borders, e.g., through regionalization) versus **adaptation** (to *adjust* to cross-country differences and achieve focus advantages or mitigate disadvantages, e.g., through variation or better ways of creating variety).

A useful direction in which to expand this basic global strategy set is suggested by the economic theory of MNCs, which distinguishes between **horizontal MNCs** (e.g., Coca-Cola, which sets up more or less complete business systems in the countries in which it competes) that seek primarily to exploit the similarities across countries and **vertical MNCs** (e.g., the oil companies) that seek primarily to exploit differences along some selected dimensions (in this case, primarily in the availability and cost of oil and, to a lesser extent, in terms of willingness to pay for end products).[29]

EXHIBIT 7.10 A The Horizontal Dimension: Adaptation Versus Aggregation, **B** The Vertical and Horizontal Dimensions: The AAA Triangle.

This suggests the vertical generalization summarized in Exhibit 7.10: adding **arbitrage** to *exploit* differences to the basic strategy set of adaptation to adjust to them and aggregation to overcome them. Note that the addition of arbitrage/verticalization fits well with what seems to have been a shift in interest, over the last decade or two, from the globalization of markets toward the globalization of production. The globalization of markets is easy to assimilate into horizontal models, but the globalization of production is intrinsically (mostly) a vertical phenomenon.

The strategies of adaptation, aggregation, and arbitrage will henceforth be referred to as the **AAA strategies**. Satisfactory global performance often requires a minimum amount of attention to each of them. Thus, even before its strategy shift, De Beers used all three AAA strategies to engage with cross-country differences, as summarized in Exhibit 7.11. The new strategy has shifted the focus of aggregation from the entire industry's output to own output, with firm-specific marketing and revamping of an already strong distribution system expected to help increase willingness to pay. (Advantages complying with the "conflict diamond" ban because of De Beers' end-to-end operations and steady internal throughput from nonconflict countries may also have helped in this regard.) The multiple points under each of the AAA strategies in the exhibit not only serve to illustrate them but hint at the many substrategies they subsume—which merit more detailed discussion.

Adaptation: Adjusting to Differences

Adaptation is perhaps the most obvious strategy for dealing with differences. If local markets have different preferences, offer them different products or services—and even think of tailoring policies, positioning, metrics, et cetera to them. But such

EXHIBIT 7.11   De Beers' Traditional AAA Strategies.

Adaptation to Adjust to Differences	Aggregation to Overcome Differences	Arbitrage to Exploit Differences
• **Focus** on owning mines in "weak governance countries"?	• **Infrastructure/activities** subject to large scale economies (e.g., sorting, storage)	• **Willingness to pay/volumes**: United States, Western Europe, Japan highest
• **Variation** in –terms to contract suppliers –rough releases over time –in advertising/marketing (but country of origin obscured)	• **Demand creation** –advertising –stockpiling→preservation of prestige	• **Raw material costs**: Sources in Africa, Russia, Australia, Canada), so >90% output traded
	• **Innovation** of various sorts (but, like demand creation, benefits mostly nonexcludable)	• **Labor costs**: India essential to absorption of smallest stones
• **Innovation** –market development/driving –directed product innovation	• **Leverage**: Build up of bargaining power of single channel, particularly vs. downstream trade	• **Financing costs**: Attractive terms to often constrained countries with CSO supply contracts
• **Mindset**: cosmopolitan –history of taking a global perspective –Central Selling Organization (CSO) location in the United Kingdom		• **Taxes?** Certainly arbitraged by some in the trade
		• **Information**: Superior information on differences possessed by De Beers/the CSO

variation is costly and in the extreme results in operations that are so different across countries that there is no value gained by keeping them together in a single company, that is, the better-off test is not satisfied.

Smart adaptation therefore typically involves not only appropriate decisions about the amount of variation but adroit application of one or more complementary substrategies that help reduce the costs of variation:

- *Focus.* Reduce the need for variation by focusing on a limited, particularly suitable subset of products, geographies, verticals, segments, and so on.[30]
- *Externalization.* Reduce the burden of variation by externalizing it via joint ventures, strategic alliances, franchising, user adaptation, networking, and so on.
- *Design.* Reduce the cost of variation by designing in flexibility, partitioning elements that will be varied, creating platforms or modular designs, and so on.
- *Innovation.* Improve the effectiveness of variation via innovations such as transferring ideas across geographies, explicit localization, recombination of elements of the home country business model, or even transformation of the local environment itself.

Aggregation: Overcoming Differences

Aggregation is all about using grouping devices—and intragroup coordination mechanisms—to create greater economies of scale/scope than country-by-country adaptation can provide. Thus, while countries differ, they are not equally different, which serves as the basis for a variety of country-based aggregation schemes.

Regional strategies, which aggregate based on *geography*, are worthy of special attention. As noted at the beginning of the chapter, more than one-half of all international trade and FDI takes place within regions. This degree of regionalization should come as no surprise because regions also tend to share commonalities along the *cultural*, *administrative*, and *economic* dimensions of the CAGE distance framework. And regional strategies themselves come in a number of different varieties: regional focus, regional portfolio, regional hubs, regional platforms, regional mandates, and regional networks.

Of course, companies can also aggregate along explicitly nongeographic dimensions of the CAGE distance framework. Tata Consultancy Services, India's largest IT services firm, aggregated on the basis of language (a *cultural* element), in setting up operations in Uruguay to serve Spanish-speaking markets, in Hungary to serve German speakers, and in Morocco to serve Francophones. Raytheon created a "Commonwealth marketing group" to take advantage of *administrative* similarities among countries in the British Commonwealth. And Cemex focused its international expansion in the 1990s on emerging markets (an *economic* base) before shifting to *geographic* aggregation. And then there are noncountry bases of aggregation: by global business unit (a frequent expedient for companies that operate in many businesses as well as countries), by global function, by global account, et cetera.

Arbitrage: Exploiting Differences

Arbitrage involves the exploitation of differences between national or regional markets, most obviously, by locating different parts of the supply chain in different places. Arbitrage is about seeking *absolute* economies rather than scale economies gained through standardization.

Arbitrage is the oldest strategy in international business: the Spice Road, for example, developed because spices could (initially) be sold in Europe for several hundred times what they cost in Asia. And arbitrage is still alive and well today. Wal-Mart, for example, generates several times as much value from procuring goods cheaply in China and selling them at a profit in the United States than from sales at its international stores. But despite arbitrage's long and storied history, many managers question whether arbitrage-based strategies can really be sustainable given the ability of other competitors to access low-cost inputs and the pressure on spreads that might be presumed to result.

Such critiques are based on analogies with financial arbitrage, where opportunities tend to be small and short-lived. They are also misguided in several respects. First, many arbitrage spreads such as cross-country differences in labor costs are much longer-lasting. Second, while cheap inputs are theoretically available to all, it often takes critical company-specific skills to employ them effectively. For example, any company can hire Brazilian engineers, but only Embraer has developed the capability to run a world-class aerospace operation amidst the turbulence and turmoil of contemporary Brazil. And finally, even arbitrage-based advantages that cannot be sustained indefinitely are often still worth undertaking, if only to avoid being stuck with a disadvantage relative to competitors that do engage in arbitrage.

The examples cited earlier focused on labor cost as a basis of arbitrage. However, the CAGE distance framework helps remind us of the broader range of arbitrage opportunities presented by a semiglobalized world. French luxury brands and U.S. fast-food chains engage in *cultural* arbitrage based on country-of-origin effects. More controversially from an ethical standpoint, examples abound of *administrative* arbitrage ranging from the use of offshore tax havens to locating factories in countries with more relaxed health, safety, and environmental regulations. *Geographic* arbitrage, arguably the oldest form of this strategy, continues to go on as well: think of international trade in fruits and flowers. Newer forms of geographic arbitrage in services take advantage of time zone differences to enable teams to work around the clock. And while labor cost differences are the most prominent base for *economic* arbitrage, one can also find examples of such arbitrage based on differences in capital costs, raw materials, the availability of knowledge, et cetera.

Integrating the AAA Strategies

While some level of awareness of and attention to each of the AAA strategies, adaptation, aggregation, and arbitrage, is generally necessary in global competition, their strategic implications extend well beyond the proposition that all three have to be kept in view. To see that, it is useful to note the deep differences between the imperatives of arbitrage as a cross-border function and those of adaptation and aggregation, which are traditionally stressed in the literature on horizontal MNCs. Exhibit 7.12 highlights the strategic differences across the three As. This way of looking at things does more than simply expand the range of possibilities by adding a third pure strategy (arbitrage) to the two that have traditionally occupied center stage (adaptation and aggregation). The AAA strategies are subject to significant trade-offs.[31] Most fundamentally, they involve the pursuit of different sources of value creation and, relatedly, are associated with different organizational types. If a company is emphasizing adaptation, a country-centered organization is often indicated. If aggregation is the primary objective, cross-border groupings of various sorts—global business units or product divisions, regional structures, global accounts, and so on—make sense. And an emphasis on arbitrage is often best pursued by a vertical, or functional, organization that tracks the flow of products or work orders through the organization. Clearly, not all three modes of organizing can take precedence in one organization at the same time. And although some approaches to corporate organization (such as the matrix) can combine elements of more than one pure mode, they carry costs in terms of managerial complexity.

The appropriate resolution of the AAA trade-offs depends, in part, on industry characteristics. Industries with high advertising-intensity typically offer more scope for adaptation (or sometimes aggregation) strategies, industries with high R&D-intensity ratios for aggregation strategies, and industries with high labor-intensity for arbitrage strategies. But that said, industry is not destiny: companies have the freedom to choose, and which of the AAA strategies is prioritized should depend on company as well as industry characteristics.

In my own experience, the implication that global strategy involves fundamental trade-offs nonetheless collides with the aspirations of energetic managers to

EXHIBIT 7.12 Comparing Adaptation, Aggregation, and Arbitrage.

AAA Strategy	Adaptation	Aggregation	Arbitrage
Competitive Advantage: Why globalize at all?	To achieve local relevance through national focus (while exploiting some scale)	To achieve scale and scope economies through international standardization	To achieve absolute (nonscalar) economies through international specialization
Configuration: Where to locate overseas?	To limit the effects of cultural-administrative-geographic-economic differences by concentrating on foreign countries that are similar to home		To exploit (selected) differences by operating in more diverse countries
Coordination: How should international operations be organized?	By country; emphasis on adjustments to achieve a local face within borders	By business; emphasis on horizontal relationships to achieve economies of scale across borders	By function; emphasis on vertical relationships, including across organizational boundaries
Checks: What to watch out for strategically?	Excessive variety or complexity	Excessive standardization	Narrowing spreads
Corporate Diplomacy: Which public issues need to be addressed?	Potentially discreet and robust given emphasis on cultivation of a local face	Appearances of and backlash against homogenization or hegemonism (especially on part of U.S. companies)	The exploitation or displacement of suppliers, channels, or intermediaries; potentially most prone to political disruption

do everything well. To reconcile this tension, it is useful to stress four points. First, especially given the headroom that most companies seem to have in making progress along each of the AAA dimensions, it is indeed useful to set up and use a globalization scorecard—a checklist, if you will—that covers all three dimensions, rather than relying, as often seems to be the case, on just some crude measure of the internationalization of revenues to track progress (see Exhibit 7.13 for an example).

Second, the possibility of progress along all three As does not mean they are all of equal importance. The competitive, organizational and other constraints highlighted in Exhibit 7.12 typically do force some choices on companies. To highlight the importance of thinking through that point, it is useful to ask managers which A is being emphasized by their business as its primary basis for excelling at cross-border competition. Top management teams often lack a shared understanding of the answer to that question!

Third, while companies with an appetite for the added complexity might seek to manage one of three AA tensions particularly well rather than focusing on a single A, it is usually a bad idea to try to beat all competitors on all three As. Better odds can be had by betting on trifectas at racetracks.

Fourth, if focusing on a particular A (or AA tension) seems very restrictive, remember that it can still subsume a very wide range of approaches. Consider, for example, the

EXHIBIT 7.13   A Sample Globalization Scorecard.

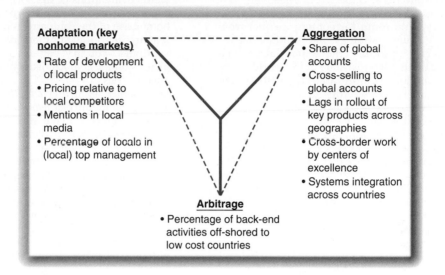

major home appliance industry, which demands a great amount of variety and therefore forces most of the major competitors to pay significant attention to adaptation—but in ways that range across the substrategies for adaptation discussed earlier. Electrolux of Sweden has traditionally emphasized more variation than its rivals. Arcelik, the most profitable of the top ten, is still largely focused on its home market of Turkey and, more broadly, Europe. GE Appliances traditionally relied on externalization through strategic alliances. Indesit of Italy has placed particular emphasis on modular design and production. And Whirlpool has pinned its hopes on innovation.

As a concluding note, the global strategy concepts explained in this chapter are also useful for strategy analysis within a single country when there are significant internal differences.[32] Such differences are apparent, for example, in the **BRICs**—Brazil, Russia, India, and China—which are large countries with poor infrastructure and other significant intranational CAGE distances. But they also crop up in advanced economies. Thus, early work on U.S. manufacturing estimated that 24 percent of value added was accounted for by industries in which competition was geographically localized or regionalized.[33] Casual empiricism suggests that while such fragmentation has probably decreased since then, it remains significant—and looms even larger in the (larger) service sector.

Summary

Global strategy has been a topic of great interest in recent years: much is made of globalization in many large companies' and many leading business schools' vision/mission statements. Yet the practice of global strategy is dominated by a crude sort of sizeism that fell out of fashion in single-country strategy decades ago.

Such sizeism seems related to exaggerated beliefs about cross-border integration that are strongly held despite the awkward implication that if the world effectively *were* one giant country, that would leave global strategy no room for content distinct from single-country strategy. One antidote to such beliefs is to look at the actual data, which indicate that the real state of the world is one of semiglobalization rather than either zero or complete cross-border integration.

Once one accepts that the real state of the world is one of semiglobalization, there are clear implications for global strategy, starting with the observation that what are needed are strategies that pay attention to the distinctively large differences that arise at national borders as well as to the bridges across them. The rest of this chapter can be summarized in terms of a three-step process for developing a global strategy:[34]

1. *Distance Analysis: CAGE Distance Framework.* Understand the dimensions of distance—cultural, administrative, geographic, and economic—that matter the most in your competitive situation, usually by drilling down to the industry level, and then adding in, as necessary, considerations specific to either a company's experience level or intended strategy. This step in the analysis yields evaluations of distance between countries (one of which is typically the home base of the company in question) that are important supplements to conventional country analysis, which focuses on the characteristics of individual countries.

2. *Development of Strategic Options: AAA Strategies.* Identify at least two serious strategy options, make sure that they cover the entire business enterprise, and ideally prespecify them at a level of detail that can facilitate implementation. General guidelines for developing better strategic options were discussed in Chapter 4. In addition, the AAA strategies provide useful cues by highlighting distinct approaches to dealing with differences (and a rich menu of substrategies) as well as typical trade-offs.

3. *Evaluation of Strategic Options: The Better-Off Test and the Best-Alternative Test.* The same two broad tests that were discussed in Chapter 6 in the context of corporate strategy can also be applied to the evaluation of global strategy options although the details of the applications do differ across these strategy domains.

Glossary

AAA strategies
adaptation
aggregation
arbitrage
BRIC (Brazil, Russia, India, and china)
CAGE distance framework

distance
Foreign direct investment (FDI)
geographic scope
gravity models
home bias
horizontal MNCs

multinational companies (MNCs)
offshoring
regional strategies
semiglobalization
sizeism
trade
vertical MNCs

Notes

1. The terrain covered in this chapter is discussed at substantially greater length in Pankaj Ghemawat, *Redefining Global Strategy* (Boston: Harvard Business School Press, 2007) and the other references listed therein.

2. Ratio of "receipts from the rest of the world" to "corporate profits" from the NIPA tables available at www.bea.gov. For an updated summary, see Floyd Norris, "Bulging Profits in U.S. Often Originate Overseas," *New York Times*, August 4, 2007.

3. On exporters versus nonexporters, there are many studies covering multiple countries: for data from the United States, for example, see Andrew B. Bernard and J. Bradford Jensen, "Exporting and Productivity in the USA," *Oxford Review of Economic Policy* 20, no. 3 (2004): 343–357. For a survey that also tries to bring FDI into the picture, see David Greenaway and Richard Kneller, "Firm Heterogeneity, Exporting and Foreign Direct Investment: A Survey," research paper no. 2005/32, Leverhulme Centre, University of Nottingham. Of course, the correlation of exports/multinationalization with productivity does not settle the direction of causality: does internationalization make firms more productive or are the firms that are already more productive the ones that internationalize first? I read the evidence as somewhat supportive, overall, of the idea that internationalization does act as a spur to productivity, not just reflect it. But there are also striking pieces of evidence that point in the opposite direction, e.g., a recent study by Alla Lileeva and Daniel Trefler, "Improved Access to Foreign Markets Raises Plant-Level Productivity . . . for Some Plants" (unpublished working paper, July 2007) that indicates that low-productivity Canadian plants are the ones that benefit the most from improved access to the U.S. market. While waiting for academics to settle whether cross-border activities primarily constitute a staging ground for developing new strengths or a proving ground for existing ones, note that that should not affect firms' (expanded) interest in making the most of their global opportunities.

4. This section is largely based on my impressions from a decade-long focus on global strategy in my work.

5. Paul Verdin and Nick Van Heck, *From Local Champions to Global Masters* (London: Palgrave, 2001).

6. This survey was designed by me and run by *Harvard Business Review*, to which I am very grateful for doing so. I have also surveyed many groups with these questions, with results broadly similar to those reported here.

7. Computations based on Bureau of Economic Analysis data kindly carried out at my request by Raymond J. Mataloni, fall 2007.

8. Pankaj Ghemawat and Fariborz Ghadar, "Global Integration ? Global Concentration," *Industrial and Corporate Change* (August 2006): 597–603.

9. Bruce Kogut, "A Note on Global Strategies," *Strategic Management Journal* 10, no. 389 (1989): 383–389.

10. For more extended discussions of the empirical underpinnings, or rather, lack thereof, of belief in a borderless world, see Chapter 1 of Pankaj Ghemawat, *Redefining Global Strategy* (Boston: Harvard Business School Press, 2007) or, for more academic treatments, Pankaj Ghemawat, "Semiglobalization and International Business Strategy," *Journal of International Business Studies* 34, no. 2 (March 2003): 138–152 and Edward E. Leamer, "A Flat World, a Level Playing Field, a Small World After All, or None of the Above? A Review of Thomas L. Friedman's The World is Flat," *Journal of Economic Literature* 45 (March 2007): 83–126.

11. Small entrepot economies such as Singapore, which reports a trade-to-GDP ratio over 200 percent, illustrate the seriousness of the problem of double counting.

12. This figure is equal to one minus the Herfindahl concentration index of GDP around the world: the sum of the squares of individual countries' shares of the world total. To interpret Herfindahl values, note that a world with n equally sized countries would have an Herfindahl index equal to $1/n$.

13. For a more detailed discussion of the differences between countries and the CAGE distance framework, see chapter 2 of Panka Ghemawat, *Redefining Global Strategy* (Harvard Business School Press, 2007).

14. John F. Helliwell, "Border Effects: Assessing Their Implications for Canadian Policy in a North-American Context," draft, September 2002.

15. This calculation is based on the four cultural dimensions originally identified by Geert Hofstede—power distance, individuality, masculinity, and uncertainty avoidance—and is based on squaring and summing the differences between the values reported on (http://www.geert-hofstede.com, accessed on July 25, 2008) for each possible pair of countries or regions.

16. Edward E. Leamer and James Levinsohn, "International Trade Theory: The Evidence," in Gene M. Grossman and Kenneth Rogoff, eds., *Handbook of International Economics*, (Amsterdam: Elsevier Science, 1995), pp. 1339–1394.

17. Susan E. Feinberg, "The Expansion and Location Patterns of U.S. Multinationals," unpublished working paper, Rutgers University, New Brunswick, NJ, 2005.

18. The estimates correct for unobserved thresholds for participation in trade and are all significant at the 1 percent level but are, in a number of cases, smaller than those reported in many other studies, apparently due to the correction.

19. Jean-Francois Brun, Céline Carrere, Patrick Guillaumont, and Jaime de Melo,"Has Distance Died? Evidence from a Panel Gravity Model," CEPR discussion paper no. 3500, August 2002; and Anne-Célia Disdier and Keith Head, "The Puzzling Persistence of the Distance Effect on Bilateral Trade," *Review of Economics and Statistics* 90, no. 1 (February 2008): 37–48.

20. Note that this characterization applies not only to cardinal indexes such as the World Economic Forum's Global Competitiveness Index or Transparency International's Corruption Perceptions Index, but also to ordinal ranking schemes such as Michael E. Porter's "diamond" framework for diagnosing the (relative) international competitiveness of different countries as home bases in specific industries.

21. For a more extended discussion of indexicality in a broader social science context, see Andrew Abbott, *Chaos of Disciplines*, (Chicago: University of Chicago Press, 2001).

22. Having said that, it is worth repeating that performance has to be looked at in terms of total economic profits rather than just profitability or margins.

23. For further discussion of Cemex, see Chapter 3 of Pankaj Ghemawat, *Redefining Global Strategy* (Harvard Business School Press, 2007) and Pankaj Ghemawat and Catherine Thomas, "Strategic Interaction across Countries and Multinational Agglomeration: An Application to the Cement Industry," *Management Science* Vol. 54, no. 12, December 2008, pp. 1980–1996.

24. Rogerio Victer and Anita McGahan, "The Effect of Industry and Location on Firm Profitability in the Global Market: Empirical Evidence that Firm Performance Depends on the Interaction between Industry Affiliation and Country Identity," unpublished working paper, Boston University School of Management, February 2006.

25. See, for instance, "An interview with Francisco Garza, CEMEX's President-North American Region & Trading," by Steven Prokopy, July 1, 2001, *Cement Americas*, http://cementamericas.com/mag/cement_cemex_interview_francisco/(accessed on September 2, 2005).

26. On this bias see, for example, Timothy G. Bunnell and Neil M. Coe, "Spaces and Scales of Innovation," *Progress in Human Geography* 25, no. 4 (2001) pp. 569–589

27. Securities Data Company.

28. John Fayerweather, *International Business Management: A Conceptual Framework*, New York: McGraw-Hill, 1969).

29. For an excellent textbook statement, see Richard E. Caves, *Multinational Enterprise and Economic Analysis* (Cambridge: Cambridge University Press, 2007).

30. The 'focus' substrategy is already familiar from the intranational context—think of Porter's generic strategies, for example—but the other elements of this list are not.

31. As noted earlier, the trade-offs between adaptation and aggregation are clear from the literature on international business in "integration versus responsiveness" and the additional trade-offs imposed by arbitrage are highlighted by the economic distinction between (and extensive discussion of) horizontal versus vertical MNCs.

32. Pankaj Ghemawat, "From Global to Local Strategy: Insights from Semiglobalization," unpublished working paper, IESE Business School (Spring 2008).

33. D. Schwartzman and J. Bodoff, "Concentration in Regional and Local Industries," *Southern Economic Journal* 37, no. 3 (1971): 343–348.

34. For a more articulated discussion of the process of developing a global strategy, see Chapter 8 of Pankaj Ghemawat, *Redefining Global Strategy* (Boston: Harvard Business School Press, 2007).

NAME INDEX

COMPANY INDEX

SUBJECT INDEX

Note: 'e' indicates an exhibit; 'n' indicates a note